MISSIONARIES, CHINESE,

AND DIPLOMATS

Missionaries, Chinese, and Diplomats

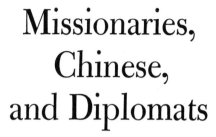

THE AMERICAN
PROTESTANT
MISSIONARY MOVEMENT
IN CHINA, 1890-1952

BY

PAUL A. VARG

PRINCETON, NEW JERSEY
PRINCETON UNIVERSITY PRESS
1958

L. C. Card 58-7134

Publication of this book has been aided by
the Ford Foundation program to support
publication, through university presses, of
works in the humanities and social sciences.

Paul A. Varg is associate professor of history
at the Ohio State University, whose particular field of interest is American diplomatic relations. He is also author of the
book, *Open Door Diplomat: The Life of
W. W. Rockhill.*

Printed in the United States of America

Second Printing 1960

TO MY FATHER

PREFACE

IF we are to understand the history of the American Protestant missionary enterprise in China, we must first recognize that the two cultures involved were basically different. Today this simple fact and its implications are infinitely more obvious to us than they were to the first missionaries, thanks to the rich contributions of Oriental studies and the modern anthropologists' study of culture. The concept of culture that they developed enables us to appreciate that each society has its own institutions and basic value patterns, that the mores of one society have a *raison d'etre* in that society, and that phases of one culture cannot be transmitted to another culture except when that which is transmitted becomes meaningful to the members of the other society in terms of their own experience.

In the same way it is necessary to take into account the change in religious point of view in the United States during the past century. Theology is no longer a popular vehicle for expressing the more profound impressions derived from human experience. Consequently the ideology of the early missionaries is likely to appear quaint or, even worse, irrelevant and obscurantist. The theological language of the early missionaries might be more meaningful to the lay person today if translated into the language of modern psychology.

Theological absolutes were a life-shaping force in themselves, but it would be a grievous error to explain the early missionaries wholly on the basis of their theology. The missionary spirit was not an isolated religious phenomenon; it was the religious aspect of the broader socio-economic and political movement that looked beyond the limits of national boundaries. Similarly, missionary candidates were not moved to their choice of a vocation wholly by religious motives. The young men and women who volunteered were seldom religious aesthetes, although the spiritual drive was central in their lives. They reflected the normal excitement over an unusual career in an unusual corner of the world, free from the more prosaic patterns of the ministry or a position in business at home.

This book is not a chronological history of the Protestant missionary movement in China. Rather, the author looks at the history of missions as a problem in the relationship between two basically different cultures, Western and Oriental. The central interest is in something broader than the missionary movement: namely, the difficulties involved in the attempt to export American ideology, whether it be Christianity, democracy, or capitalism. Today the American government is seeking to convince people all over the world of the advantages of Western institutions. It is not for the historian to make conjectures concerning the future, but the history of the missionary enterprise throws light on the problems to be met.

American Protestant missions were launched in China in the 1830's, came to full bloom during the years of secular overseas expansion after 1890, and were cut off by the Communist Revolution only sixty years later—scarcely a time span of sufficient length for them to achieve their ends. Whether another 200 years of activity and experiment would have led to the fulfillment of the missionary dream must remain an unanswered question. In the Roman period, the establishment of Christianity as the dominant religion took five centuries.

The author has chosen to concentrate on the period 1890 to 1952, because it was during these years that the missionaries made their major effort. The earlier years, 1830 to 1890, are examined, not with the aim of presenting a detailed study but rather to present the framework that had been developed and that governed the missionary movement after 1890. The treaty structure under which missionaries worked had been largely completed by that date. Likewise, a method for winning converts and a missionary ideology had taken form. These two developments are analyzed in the first two chapters. Because both the missionary and the convert became problems of American-Chinese diplomacy, and because the intervention of the American government in their behalf became one of the major factors influencing both the successes and the failures of the entire missionary effort, the author has chosen to deal rather fully with this aspect of the problem throughout the book.

Protestant Christianity, embodied in Western forms and represented in China by Westerners, had either to divest itself of Western institutionalism and adjust to Oriental molds or remain an esoteric foreign enterprise. It had to meet not what Westerners believed to be the needs, but what the Chinese themselves felt to be needs. However, missionary activity, although an exercise in both an intellectual and a practical philanthropy, was nonetheless subject to the usual egotistical elements and caught in the vortex of nationalistic crosscurrents. In the end American nationalism threatened to triumph over the religious. At the same time Chinese nationalism, expressing itself in a Marxist ideology, snuffed out Chinese humanism and Christian idealism. In the story of Christian missions in China is seen the tragic but overwhelming conflict of two cultures that never came to a full understanding of one another. An uncompromising power struggle has finally triumphed over the best of Confucianism and the more profound insights of Christianity.

The author approached the subject as an outsider to the enterprise, as one primarily interested in Sino-American diplomatic relations, and as a curious investigator anxious to know more about what happens when representatives of one society seek to solve the problems of another society. The study has been an exciting adventure through archives maintained by the missionary organizations and the archives of the Department of State, through hundreds of books and articles written by missionaries, and through the highly critical opinions of unfriendly observers, both western and Chinese. The subject is broad, encompassing data from all the fields of the Social Sciences, and the writer has also had to work in areas where there was but little previous scholarship of which to avail himself. Given these circumstances he is more hopeful of having opened up a new field than of having written a final and definitive study.

Preface

ACKNOWLEDGMENTS

I am indebted to all those who have in some way encouraged me to complete this study. Several of my friends have been kind enough to read parts of the manuscript: Foster Rhea Dulles, Robert Bremner, Harry Coles and David Spitz, all colleagues at the Ohio State University; Karl Olsson, of North Park College; Harald Jacobson, a former colleague now with the Department of State; and Richard Hopkins, one of my former students. Their criticisms have influenced the final product but they should not be held responsible for interpretations, the author's point of view, or errors he may have failed to note. In the course of my research I was privileged to make the acquaintance of two former missionaries, W. Plummer Mills and R. Pierce Beaver. Both of these men dispelled any lingering traces of the stereotyped picture of missionaries. Dr. Lucius Porter and the Rev. Hugh Hubbard, both of whom served under the American Board in China, have taken time to write informative letters full of thoughtful observations. Even though their view of the history of the movement may be quite different from that of the author, I shall always value their insights into missionary problems and their complete honesty in facing major issues.

The Ohio State University has been more than generous in encouraging the research. The Graduate School has given financial aid to cover the cost of a summer spent in Washington, D.C., and has helped meet the cost of typing the manuscript. In addition the University administration very kindly relieved me of teaching duties for an academic quarter.

The American Philosophical Society was generous in granting me sufficient funds so that I could spend two months doing research in the Missionary Research Library in New York, the Day Library of Missions at Yale, and in the Archives of the American Board of Commissioners for Foreign Missions at Harvard University.

My wife has paid the usual price of having to read the many drafts of the manuscript and of having to do much of the typing. The worn phrase "without her assistance this book would not have been completed" is wholly inadequate to describe her generous contribution.

CONTENTS

[xi]

Contents

MISSIONARIES, CHINESE,

AND DIPLOMATS

"Foreign Missions In Battle Array"
An endless line of splendor,
These troops with heaven for home,
With creeds they go from Scotland,
With incense go from Rome.
These, in the name of Jesus,
Against the dark gods stand,
They gird the earth with valor,
They heed their King's command.

Onward the line advances,
Shaking the hills with power,
Slaying the hidden demons,
The lions that devour.
No bloodshed in the wrestling,—
But souls new-born arise—
The nations growing kinder,
The child-hearts growing wise.

What is the final ending?
The issue, can we know?
Will Christ outlive Mohammed?
Will Kali's altar go?
This is our faith tremendous,—
Our wild hope, who shall scorn,—
That in the name of Jesus
The world shall be reborn!

Vachel Lindsay, *General William Booth Enters Into Heaven And Other Poems by Vachel Lindsay*, New York: The Macmillan Co., 1924.

CHAPTER I

"THE EVANGELIZATION OF THE WORLD
IN THIS GENERATION," 1830-1890

CHRIST'S command "Go ye into all the world, and preach the gospel to every creature," forgotten for long periods in the history of the church, has been brought forth again and again to justify the church undertaking missionary work in eras of expansionism. In the decades prior to the first world war, when the new imperialism gained ascendancy, the process was repeated. Again the churches elevated the scriptural passage into a primary article of faith, and this time the prevailing self-confidence of the West inspired the missionary movement with a vigor which it seldom, if ever, had achieved before. A measure of the new zeal was the goal which the intercollegiate Student Volunteers for Foreign Missions set for the whole of Protestantism: "The Evangelization of the World in this Generation."

In no other period did the young people fling themselves so recklessly into the Christian crusade as after 1890. Three of the student leaders at Yale, Horace Pitkin, Sherwood Eddy, and Henry Luce went to Union Theological Seminary to prepare for the China mission field. Eddy later recalled: "When I would box every afternoon with Pitkin and when we would run our daily mile in the gym or the open air, we would say, 'This will carry us another mile in China.'" John R. Mott, organizer of the Student Volunteers at Cornell, declared that his field would be "the world" but China was the focal point; Eddy noted: "China was the goal, the lodestar, the great magnet that drew us all in those days."[1]

Far beyond the horizon of material success Pitkin and his contemporaries saw a bright new world of Christian brotherhood. Bred in comfortable urban middle-class homes, or more

---

[1] Sherwood Eddy, *Pathfinders of the World Missionary Crusade* (New York: Abingdon-Cokesbury Press, 1945), p. 50.

often amid the happy circumstances of well-established families in small towns or on farms, this generation had no squeamish doubts about the superiority of American life. Its excellences they attributed to the influence of Protestant Christianity. Nor did they have any difficulty in accepting the then current picture of the dark practices of heathen lands so in contrast with the enlightened ways of the Christian world. To bring the former up to the level of the latter by infusing a Christian spirit among the heathen became their chosen task, a beguiling vision unmarred by any realization of the difficulties involved.

China in actuality provided no real basis for these extravagant hopes. Confucianism still enjoyed the prestige of more than two thousand years of history. In promoting "harmonious living," it could boast of a record unsurpassed by any other ethical system.

China was a civilization, not a nation. The structure of society was based on the teachings of Confucius and rooted in the dominance of family and guild. The central government at Peking was scarcely more than a symbol, especially after the decline of the armies of bannermen maintained by the Manchu dynasty. Consequently, it was powerless to contend with the intrusions of the powerful centralized nation-states of the West. This did not invalidate the native religions in the eyes of the Chinese even when they began to realize that the price for having a decentralized political system was loss of territory and impairment of sovereignty.

The great obstacle to Christianization as the early missionaries saw it was not the essential foreignness of Christianity to Chinese culture but the policy of exclusion of the Manchu dynasty. Missionaries were wholly barred from China, and the first to arrive had to conceal their identity by taking employment with foreign merchants. The latter carried on their activities under chafing restrictions; they could only gain entry in the one city of Canton, were subject to the duties local officials chose to levy at the moment, and could only deal with the Cohong, a small association of Chinese merchants. It was these restrictions on trade that led to the Opium War between Great Britain and China in 1840 and the Treaty of Nanking in 1842.

"Evangelization of the World"

In the early attempts to open up China to trade, the merchants found strong allies in the missionaries. In 1840 Dr. Peter Parker, an American medical missionary, left China for a visit at home. Convinced that the old restrictions were wholly unjust and unbearable, he devoted himself to convincing a number of high officials of the necessity of opening regular diplomatic relations and of gaining a greater measure of security for both merchants and missionaries. American merchants were already active in the same cause, and Parker did not have long to wait. In 1844 Caleb Cushing, former member of Congress and recently appointed Commissioner to China, concluded a treaty. Three missionaries helped Cushing in the negotiations, Peter Parker, Samuel Wells Williams, and Elijah C. Bridgman.[2]

The negotiations following the Opium War were turned to the advantage of missions by the French. Imperial edicts issued in 1844 and 1846, supplementary to the treaties, granted Christians the right to build churches and freedom of worship within the limits of the five ports opened by the Treaty of Nanking.

Thus the importunate West had wrested its first concessions from the Manchu-Chinese Empire by the use of force. That the war was unjust, the missionary S. Wells Williams admitted, but the results of injustice in this case led him to observe that "it is the prerogative of the Governor of nations to educe good out of evil, and make the wrath, the avarice, and the ambition of men to serve his purpose and advance his own designs, although their intentions may be far otherwise."[3]

Williams' optimism was premature. In the years after 1840 China proved to be stony ground. One of the early missionaries later recalled:

We were mobbed in the fu city, mobbed in the district cities, mobbed in the large towns. We got so used to being

[2] Frederick Wells Williams, *The Life and Letters of Samuel Wells Williams, LL.D.* (New York: G. P. Putnam's Sons, 1889), p. 127.

[3] S. Wells Williams, *The Middle Kingdom: A Survey of the Geography, Government, Literature, Social Life, Arts, and History of the Chinese Empire and Its Inhabitants* (New York: Charles Scribner's Sons, 1914), II, pp. 572-573.

pelted with mud and gravel and bits of broken pottery that things seemed strange if we escaped the regular dose. ... We went out from our homes bedewed with the tears and benedictions of dear ones, and we came back plastered over, metaphorically speaking, with curses and objurgations from top to bottom. It went badly with our chapels that we rented. They were often assailed; roofs were broken up, doors were battered in, and furniture was carried off.[4]

Conversions came slowly prior to 1860. The Methodists did not baptize their first convert until 1857, ten years after their arrival.[5] Their denominational brethren of the Methodist Episcopal Church, South, baptized a man and wife in 1852, four years after beginning their work in Shanghai.[6] Episcopalians had first worked in Batavia in 1835, but not until 1846 was the first convert won.[7]

Representatives of the American Board met even greater obstacles. Only at Amoy, where they made their first two converts in 1846, did they have any reasonable degree of success.[8] The Board sent missionaries to Foochow in 1847, and they wrote glowing reports of the opportunities in that city. People were friendly and the location was a healthy one. The city had 600,000 inhabitants, "all of whom are hurrying rapidly to a wretched eternity."[9] Yet, as late as June, 1854, a missionary at Foochow wrote: "But we dare not say that we have satisfactory evidence that God has renewed a single soul in connection

[4] Harlan P. Beach, *Dawn on the Hills of T'ang or Missions in China* (New York: Student Volunteer Movement for Foreign Missions, 1905), p. 104.

[5] Walter N. Lacy, *A Hundred Years of China Methodism* (New York: Abingdon-Cokesbury Press, 1948), p. 53.

[6] *Ibid.*, p. 49.

[7] Annette B. Richmond, *The American Episcopal Church in China* (New York: The Domestic and Foreign Missionary Society of the Protestant Episcopal Church, 1907), p. 17.

[8] William J. Pohlman to the American Board of Commissioners for Foreign Missions, May 1, 1846, quoted in *The Missionary Herald, Containing the Proceedings of the American Board of Commissioners for Foreign Missions*, Vol. XLII, September 1846, pp. 321-322.

[9] Seneca Cummings to the A.B.C.F.M., December 30, 1848, quoted in *The Missionary Herald*, Vol. XLV, July 1849, pp. 221-223.

with our labors, . . ."[10] Not until 1856, nine years after the arrival of the first missionary at Foochow, was there a convert. At Canton the discouragements were even greater. Dr. Peter Parker's hospital had more patients than the doctor could care for, but there was not a single convert until 1847, seventeen years after Elijah Bridgeman of the American Board had begun his preaching in that city.[11] Another convert was made two years later, and then there were no converts for many years. In its report for 1856, the Board understandably noted that the Canton mission was "one of peculiar trial to faith."[12]

Only that strange Christian movement known as the Taiping Rebellion, which burst forth in the 1840's, gave any promise of the Chinese welcoming a new religious faith.[13] It had its roots in unsatisfactory economic and political conditions. A series of crop failures added to the hardships of the peasants who were already heavily burdened with high rents and taxes. Banditry contributed to the unrest. Discontented with their economic lot, the peasants turned against their Manchu overlords who had been recently discredited by defeat in the Opium War with England.

The insurrection took the form of a Christian movement largely as a result of a series of fortuitous circumstances. The leader of the Taipings, Hung Siu-ch'üan, was a young scholar who had failed the provincial examinations. He suffered mental derangement for approximately a month after his third failure in 1837. It was while in this state that he had a series of visions in which he ascended into heaven and conversed with an old man seated upon a throne. The message he received placed before him the evil ways of men and their failure to worship Him who had created them.

Not until six years later did he discover what he believed to be the meaning of his visions. Persuaded by a cousin to read some Christian tracts which had been in his possession several

---

[10] *Missionary Herald*, December 1854, p. 386.

[11] *Ibid.*, October 1847, pp. 355-356.

[12] *Ibid.*, December 1856, p. 364.

[13] For a scholarly history of the Taiping Rebellion see William James Hail, *Tseng Kuo-Fan and the Taiping Rebellion With a Short Sketch of His Later Career* (New Haven: Yale University Press, 1927).

years, Hung began to relate what he read to his earlier visions. One of his first converts was a neighbor, Fêng Yun-shan, who soon became an effective preacher and organized his many converts into what were known as associations of God worshippers.

Hung went to Canton where he studied under the Rev. Issachar J. Roberts, a Baptist missionary from the southern part of the United States. He returned to the interior after only two months and joined with some of his earlier converts in leading the new religious movement. Issachar Roberts, who might have guided his newly won disciple, failed to give him further instructions.

Quite untutored in Christian theology, Hung interwove much that was Confucian and even more that was crude and primitive into his teachings. Most offensive to Westerners was Hung's claim that he was the younger brother of Jesus and that God himself had directly intervened to help the Taipings.

The Taiping army achieved a high degree of excellence largely as a result of the imposition of a stern discipline reminiscent of Oliver Cromwell's army. The Ten Commandments were strictly enforced, and baptism was administered to all followers. By January 1853 the Taipings had captured Nanking and were in a fair way to march on Peking and take control of the entire country. During the next eight years they controlled most of the Yangtze valley and the southern provinces. Eventually they were defeated, in part because of the aid the Manchus received from Western adventurers and the friendly policy of the Western nations toward the Peking government.

It was during the Taiping Rebellion that Western nations began to press the Peking government for a revision of the treaties negotiated at the close of the Opium War. The earlier treaties had proven wholly unsatisfactory largely because of Chinese recalcitrance, especially at Canton where the local authorities ignored some of the treaty provisions. In addition, China had yet to agree to regular diplomatic intercourse, and the West saw in this the only way to remedy some of its grievances. Peter Parker, who entered upon an important diplomatic career as Secretary of Legation after winning prestige as the first full-time medical missionary, advised Commissioner Robert McLane in 1854 that the United States must pursue a firm and bold policy.[14] He insisted that Peking must be opened to diplomatic representatives if the treaties were to be carried out.

In the summer of 1854, Parker and Walter Henry Medhurst, an English missionary, started for Peking for the purpose of preparing the way for the diplomatic representatives of England, France and the United States, who hoped to open negotiations for a revision of the treaties. At the mouth of the Peiho they were met by Chinese officials and long discussions followed. The Manchu-Chinese officials agreed to meet with Sir John Bowring, the English minister, and Commissioner McLane. When this meeting took place, the Chinese made it clear that they would not willingly liberalize the treaties.[15]

In January 1856 Peter Parker returned from a visit to the United States. The former medical missionary had been appointed Commissioner to China. Another missionary, S. Wells Williams, was Secretary of Legation. After years of experience with the Manchu-Chinese officials, these two knights-errant of the cross concluded that the Chinese were victims of false pride in their own assumed superiority and given to a policy of putting off the foreigner by perfidy. On his return to China, Parker told the American merchants in Canton: "My course with this government will be *friendly*, but *firm*. The time for nonsense is past, and trifling will be endured no longer."[16] He was convinced that China could be brought to her senses only if American naval forces were increased and if negotiations could be conducted at Peking or as close to that city as possible. Parker further suggested to the Secretary of State that England, France, and the United States should present themselves at the Peiho and if China still refused access to Peking, they should threaten to hoist the French flag in Korea, the English flag at Chusan, and the United States should occupy

14 Peter Parker to Robert M. McLane, November 10, 1854, U.S. Congress, Senate, 2nd. Session, 35th Congress, Ex. Doc. No. 22, Vol. 7, p. 303.

15 For an extremely interesting firsthand account of the meeting see Peter Parker's report cited above.

16 *Ibid.*, p. 765.

Formosa.[17] These territories should be returned to China as soon as she had granted satisfaction for past errors and agreed to more satisfactory arrangements for the future. Within the next few months Parker went a step further and urged that the United States take Formosa permanently.[18] The missionary saw in the island some wonderful advantages, mineral and agricultural wealth, possibility of a coaling station for American steamships, and a great asset "as respects the great principle of balance of power."

In 1857 Peter Parker was recalled by the new Buchanan administration. His plan of American empire had been carefully repudiated. William B. Reed, the first American to bear the title of Minister to China, took Parker's place. His instructions called for him to seek a renegotiation of the treaties and the protection of trade, but he was to make clear that the United States had no territorial ambitions.[19]

Renegotiation of the treaties came as a result of the use of force by the European powers. The causes of hostilities were the desire on the part of Westerners to expand their trade and the intransigence of China in refusing to enter into a system of relations common among Western nations. The immediate cause in the case of the British was the *Arrow* affair. The *Arrow* was a Chinese vessel temporarily flying the British flag and registered as a British ship. While at anchor in Canton, she was boarded by Chinese who hauled down the British flag and arrested fourteen of the Chinese crew on charges of piracy. The prisoners were released when the British Consul protested, but as the released prisoners were not accompanied by a Chinese official and the requested apology was not forthcoming, the British, in December 1857, promptly resorted to arms. The British were soon joined by Louis Napoleon of France who saw an opportunity to strengthen his position with Catholics in France. The failure of the Chinese government to punish

---

[17] *Ibid.*, pp. 1082-1083.

[18] *Ibid.*, p. 1208.

[19] Tyler Dennett, *Americans in Eastern Asia: A Critical Study of the Policy of the United States with Reference to China, Japan and Korea in the 19th Century* (New York: The Macmillan Company, 1922), pp. 290-291.

provincial authorities for their execution of a French missionary provided the French with a pretext for war.

In the spring of 1858 the British and French naval forces
proceeded to the mouth of the Peiho and made ready to go to
Peking to seek a revision of the earlier treaties. When the
Chinese delayed, the Taku forts guarding the entrance to the
river were destroyed. The Westerners then moved on to
Tientsin, where the Chinese finally consented to negotiations.

Neither the United States nor Russia had participated in
the hostilities but both countries were represented in the negotiations at Tientsin. William B. Reed was the American
envoy. Assisting him were two missionaries, S. Wells Williams
and W. A. P. Martin, a representative of the Presbyterian
Board. In his post as secretary and interpreter for the American
legation, Williams' piety found vent in the gaining of important concessions for missionary interests while in no way
obstructing his use of the methods of practical diplomacy.

At Tientsin in May 1858 the representatives of the Peking
government were as obdurate as ever, and early in the negotiations Williams observed: "I am afraid that nothing short of the
Society for the Diffusion of Cannon Balls will give them the
useful knowledge they now require to realize their own help-
lessness."[20] In June, when violence once again seemed imminent, Williams, while somewhat regretful, expressed the opinion:

> . . . however, they are almost necessary, for we shall get
> nothing important out of the Chinese unless we stand in
> a menacing attitude before them. They would grant noth-
> ing unless fear stimulated their sense of justice, for they
> are among the most craven of people, cruel and selfish as
> heathenism can make men, so we must be backed by force
> if we wish them to listen to reason.[21]

The Manchu-Chinese government had already been duly over-
awed by the force exhibited by the Westerners, and Williams
and the other negotiators concluded a new set of treaties in

[20] Frederick Wells Williams, *op. cit.*, p. 257.
[21] *Ibid.*, p. 268.

June 1858. The ratifications of the British and French treaties did not take place until another show of force in 1860.

Missionary questions had played no part in bringing on the hostilities of 1858 and 1860, but the treaty revisions were scarcely less beneficial to the missionary interests than to the merchants. Of inestimable importance to the missionaries was the opening of new cities to foreign residence, the right to travel in the interior, and the opening of the Yangtze River to foreign ships. Although the treaties did not grant foreigners the right to acquire property outside the treaty ports, the Chinese soon came to permit this too, thus making possible mission stations far in the interior.

The incorporation of religious toleration clauses in the treaties, first in the Russian treaty, then in the American treaty, and subsequently in others, greatly furthered the missionary cause. Williams, who was present at joint negotiations, was solely responsible for this insertion and had taken care to stipulate that Chinese converts as well as the Christian missionary should be protected. Once written into a treaty, the principle of religious toleration was no longer subject to unilateral action by the Chinese. This extraordinary intervention in the domestic affairs of China was fully recognized as such by Williams who wrote: "It must be said, moreover, that if the Chinese had at all comprehended what was involved in these four toleration articles, they would never have signed one of them."[22] Of course, the treaty provisions could only open the door to missionaries; they in no way compelled the native to accept the foreign teaching. Williams considered the toleration articles a great victory because they "proved to be a check upon the native officials, who have been taught therein not to destroy what they did not approve. I thank God that the Imperial Government was thereby bound not to become a persecuting government, as it has more than once since wished to be."

One effect of the treaties was to make Western treaty powers the guarantors of religious toleration in China. Thus missionary and convert alike appealed to representatives of the foreign powers for protection in their practice of Christianity. As cul-

[22] *Ibid.*, p. 271.

[12]

prits discovered they could on occasion escape from Chinese jurisdiction by joining the Christian church, a serious problem was created for the Chinese government as well as the missionary. The treaties had the effect of making the church a partner in Western imperialism.

With the ratification of the treaties in 1860, the missionary movement in China rapidly expanded its operations from the few treaty ports into most of the eighteen provinces. The number of Protestant missionaries rose from eighty-one in 1858 to 1296 in 1889;[23] of the latter approximately 500 were Americans. Likewise, the approximately 350 communicants in 1853 increased in number to 37,287 in 1889. Factors operating at home to stimulate missionary interest account for this growth in part, but it could never have taken place had not the Peking government been forced to open the doors to missionary enterprise in 1860.

All of the major denominations had begun mission work in China before 1890. The Presbyterian Church, North, had more missionaries than any other society excepting the China Inland Mission, which was largely English. The Methodist Episcopal Church, North, ranked next, followed closely by the boards of the Baptists and Congregationalists. Nineteen American denominations supported missionaries in China by 1890; the more important of these were the Protestant Episcopal Church; Methodist Church, South; the Southern Baptist Convention; the Presbyterian Church, South; and the Reformed Church of America. There were more English missionaries than American, the English numbering 724 and the Americans, 513.[24]

More significant than the growth of the missionary enterprise and the increase in the number of converts in the years 1860 to 1890 was the rapid enrichment of knowledge concerning China and the greater appreciation of Chinese culture. S. Wells Williams' seemingly supercilious pronouncements on

[23] *Records of the General Conference of the Protestant Missionaries of China Held at Shanghai, May 7-20, 1890* (Shanghai: American Presbyterian Mission Press, 1890), p. 732.

[24] Harlan P. Beach, *op. cit.*, Appendix E, "Statistics of Missions in China for 1904," opposite p. 202.

the character of Chinese diplomacy appear less so if measured against the now generally accepted historical interpretations of Manchu mid-nineteenth-century diplomacy. Manchu official-dom, as pointed out by the eminent John Fairbanks, author of *Trade and Diplomacy on the China Coast*, was inept and weak but strikingly arrogant. The same S. Wells Williams completed his sympathetic and monumental *The Middle Kingdom* in 1848. To this day Williams' volumes are universally acclaimed as an accurate and objective description of nineteenth-century Chinese society. Many other missionaries were similarly engaged in seeking to understand China, and the volumes of the Royal Asiatic Society during these years testify to their able scholarship.

CHAPTER II

A MISSION OF FAITH, 1830-1900

THERE must be no toning down of the doctrine of an arbitrary God, warned Stephen Baldwin, a missionary of the old school. He reduced the problem to a single purpose:

> In this field the work to be done is to "preach the gospel." Men are rebels to be brought into allegiance; sinners to be saved. There is only one authority competent to settle the terms, and this authority has settled them. The business of his ambassadors is to proclaim those terms.[1]

Prior to the turn of the century, and to a considerable degree up to the outbreak of World War I, this was the dominant attitude.

Missionaries spoke in terms of conquest but never of an easy victory. "The Conquest of China will not simply be taking advantage of an opportunity, but a bitter war with an adversary of greater power and more strongly entrenched, than the Church found in her conflict with the Roman Empire," wrote a Methodist missionary at Foochow.[2] It would, they acknowledged, take generations. One hundred years after the arrival of Robert Morrison, the well-known missionary of the American Board, Arthur H. Smith warned the impatient leaders at home, who were always stressing the number of converts, that Christianization of China must pass through at least eight stages. The first of these had now been completed, wrote Smith; every Chinese now finally knew that Christianity was a religion.[3] These missionaries of the old school were so conscious

[1] Stephen L. Baldwin, *Foreign Missions of the Protestant Churches* (New York: Missionary Campaign Library, 1900), p. 13.

[2] D. L. Anderson to Commission I, World Missionary Conference, 1910. The letters cited in this chapter are in the files of the Missionary Research Library at Union Theological Seminary.

[3] A. H. Smith wrote: "Of the several stages through which Christianity must pass as related to the minds of the people, it has thus far passed but one viz: Recognition. Everyone now knows that a Western religion

of the powers of evil that they expected only an occasional faithful convert.

At the core of the nineteenth-century missionary's theology was the idea that man found himself in a miserably sinful world where he was in rebellion against God. As a sinful creature he neither wished nor was capable of a reunion with God. He had been endowed with reason but reason was the slave of evil desire, pride, and blind human passion. Freedom came when God sent his son in human form into the world to point the way and to die on the cross so that men might be free from the world and achieve salvation.

This theology was an integral part of Western institutions and its widespread and almost uniform acceptance in Western society can only be explained by the fact that it accorded with typical human experience. Western society was always to some degree individualistic, whether Greek, Roman, or European. The individual was more or less a self-contained entity loosely tied to his family, medieval manor, urban community, or nation state. But while relatively free to go his own way and with only a minimum number of customs or laws binding him to a particular pattern of behavior, he also inherited a set of ideals which demanded that he respect his fellowmen and even that he do unto them as he would that they do unto him. He consequently found himself torn between the ideal of love for his fellowmen and his own desires, which impelled him to give uppermost consideration to his own immediate self-interest or to gratify his own emotional drives. Saint Paul had expressed the resulting tension in the passage, "For the good that I would I do not, but the evil which I would not, that I do." Saint Augustine and the early Protestant leaders, Luther and Calvin, as well as numerous other church fathers, had rediscovered this inescapable struggle between self and ideal. Christian theology gained its relevance out of this tension and offered one escape from it. Missionaries employed the term "sin" to

---

has arrived, although what it is and why, is uncertain. It is evidently desirable not to let the natural curiosity now awakened die out. There is a peculiar opportunity to get access to the minds of those who are influential in the New China. . . ." A. H. Smith to Commission I, World Missionary Conference, 1910.

describe man's incapacity to achieve his ideals, they spoke of the tension resulting from the gap between behavior and ideals as the "misery of sinners" and the release from this tension by constant reliance on God, they referred to as "regeneration." Only when viewed against this theological background can their language have any meaning.

The American Protestant missionary who went to China before World War I delivered in an authoritative manner a message cloaked in theological terms and ensconced in doctrines. Unconcerned with relating it to Chinese experience, he simply declared that the doctrines were true because they rested on the divinely inspired and infallible Bible. He had followed inherited prescriptions and they had worked for him. He was not given to analyzing the prescription or interpreting it in psychological terms or in terms of his own experience as a product of Western society. He was inclined to be literal, dogmatic, and more given to legalism than a broad tolerance. To many of his secular-minded fellow Americans who took their theology less seriously and who were primarily interested in the affairs of everyday business, he appeared a fool, a busybody, and an utterly strange creature. Only the missionary's educational and medical work were appreciated by the practical minded. While the missionary viewed these as important, the main goal was to convert the Chinese. That this would be difficult, he knew better than his most severe critic at home. But no matter how difficult, the missionary accepted it as his divinely ordained task.

Consistent with their general outlook, the missionaries saw the difficulties through theological eyes. Having read Saint Paul they believed that the Christian spirit was foreign to all human societies. Christ represented God's intrusion into history. The Christian message, as they saw it, was always difficult to convey because evil forces were everywhere opposed to it. Nevertheless Christianity in the eyes of the missionary had universal validity and was as well suited to Chinese as to Americans. As a human enterprise the conversion of the Chinese could only fail, but because it was the work of the Holy Spirit it must succeed in spite of all obstacles.

The Reverend J. E. Walker, for thirty-seven years a missionary of the Congregationalists at Foochow, said the truth was
that:

> The heathen are heathen, prone toward covetousness,
> lust and deceit. They habitually practice what they know
> to be wrong; and even those who are disposed to do better,
> show little *love* for the right or for their fellow men, but
> only hate the getting hurt and the getting dirty them-
> selves.[4]

He denounced the "misleading and harmful" teaching at home
of comparative religion whereby Christianity was depreciated
and pagan religions were whitewashed "in order to get them
near enough on a level to show a possibility of the latter having been evolved from the former." In Walker's eyes this was
futile, for Christianity was unique in its divine origin. It alone
had the power of regeneration and this was what the heathen
needed.

Christianity, then, must be imparted to the Chinese. It was
the only force that could save a degenerate, rebellious world.
Jesus "had made a matchless manifestation of the Fatherhood
of God and His infinite love and pity." He had "ascended to
the Father, and sent the Holy Spirit to be an omnipresent
resident force for righteousness and redemption." Only through
belief in the gospel could the disobedient gain light and renewal of his heart. There was no other way unto salvation.[5]

The Reverend R. E. Chambers also warned against the
study of comparative religion, maintaining that compromise
was a threat to convictions. "The effective evangelist," wrote
Chambers, "must needs be an uncompromising warrior." There
must be a positive and authoritative evangelistic message. He
said:

> Our Lord and his apostles speak in the indicative mood.
> They make unqualified assertions as to sin, salvation, hell,

[4] J. E. Walker to Commission I, World Missionary Conference, 1910,
August 9, 1909.
[5] *Ibid.*

[18]

heaven, faith and repentance. . . . If we have doubts as to fundamentals we cannot hope to win men to our Lord.[6]

This concept of the fundamental purpose of missions found expression in a policy of close observation and continued supervision of converts. For all their anxiety to win converts, the missionaries demanded that the Chinese provide evidence of having made a sincere and complete surrender. The Rev. W. O. Elterich in Shantung, a missionary of the Presbyterian Church, outlined the tests employed:

> The giving up of idolatry, superstitious practices and vice, the keeping of the Sabbath, attendance at worship, and other evidences of a changed life are made the tests for church membership. Repentance from sin, belief in the Trinity, a living faith in Christ as a Saviour, belief in the Scriptures as God's infallible guide for faith and practice and a sincere desire to live a Christian life, are the conditions for baptism.[7]

All denominations were extremely cautious in admitting converts to church membership. First, the convert was classified as an inquirer, a stage which lasted until the prospective Christian gave evidence of faith. During this time he was given instruction and examinations and other tests. In addition, one missionary advised:

> teach them the gospel and all you can of both Old Testament and New Testament. Set them a hymn singing. Hold prayer meetings where every one may pray. Let God the Holy Ghost lead in these prayer meetings. The Holy Ghost must have room and liberty.[8]

After a period as an inquirer, the convert was classified as a probationer or candidate for baptism. From nine months to a year later he was admitted to communion and membership

---

[6] R. E. Chambers' address on evangelization before the National Conference at Shanghai, March 11 to 14, 1913. This address is among the papers of the China Continuation Committee in the Missionary Research Library.

[7] W. O. Elterich to Commission II, World Missionary Conference, 1910.

[8] J. R. Adam to Commission II, World Missionary Conference, 1910.

if he met the tests of the missionary. Thus every effort was made to winnow the wheat from the chaff.

To assure further that the convert was truly regenerate and faithful to the teachings of the church, each denomination provided for church trials. Evidence of a minor departure might be dealt with by gentle expostulation, but repeated departures from what was considered the Christian life or a serious falling by the wayside resulted in a trial before the pastor and a committee of members. If found guilty, the erring one was suspended or excommunicated.

The objective was the planting of a church adhering to the tenets of evangelical Protestantism. There was no compromising, no satisfaction in merely extending the humanitarian and educational benefits of the West. All considerations of material well-being were as nothing compared to winning the Chinese over to an understanding of Christian faith and an acceptance of that faith. This remained true to a very large extent up to World War I, although some few missionaries had a broader conception of their function.

The logical result of this overwhelming concern with the spiritual condition of the heathen was a program of evangelization that adhered to Paul's charge to Timothy—"preach the word, be instant in season, out of season; reprove, rebuke, exhort with all long-suffering and doctrines." All missionary activities, the preparation of literature, the conducting of schools, the practice of the healing arts, were evangelical in purpose. But even then a prominent Southern Presbyterian felt compelled to warn that the main emphasis must be on preaching. Writers in preparing literature, he said, performed a useful function in the same way as generals in an army, "but the rank and file of the missionary corps must go into the enemy's camp, and wield the sword of the Spirit."[9]

In moving into a city or village the first problem of the missionary was getting a house, a difficulty that inevitably taxed both his ingenuity and patience, for the Chinese almost invariably exerted every conceivable form of pressure to prevent

[9] Hampden C. DuBose, *Preaching in Sinim* or *The Gospel to the Gentiles* (Richmond, Virginia: Presbyterian Committee of Publication, 1893), pp. 41-42.

anyone from selling or renting to a foreign devil. Once the house was obtained services were held there. The missionary very often made attendance by his house servants compulsory. Elijah Bridgman, one of the very first China missionaries of the American Board, in the early days at Canton, had encountered difficulty on this score. When the Chinese servants declined the first invitation, Bridgman posted a set of rules notifying them that they must either comply or leave the premises. In a letter to the American Board, he noted: "Some packed up, and some left the house, and all threatened to do so. No pains were spared in endeavoring to show and convince them that all our requirements were proper, and such as would promote their good."[10]

Once the missionary had secured a house, his next step was to rent quarters for a street chapel in some busy part of town. Hampton C. DuBose, a missionary whose book served as a guide for volunteers for the China field, wrote:

> The street chapel is the missionary's fort, where he throws hot shot and shell into the enemy's camp; the citadel, where he defends the truth; the school, where he teaches the A.B.C. of heaven; the home, where he loves to dwell; the altar, upon which he is laid a living sacrifice; the church, in which he worships; the throne, on which he rules the minds and hearts of the heathen; the happy land, where he enjoys communion with his Maker; the hill of Zion, where he sings sweet songs; the gate of heaven, where the angels ascend and descend.[11]

DuBose had battled for the Lord against the hosts of heathenism for twenty-one years, and it is not strange that he should have viewed the unpretentious street chapel as the beachhead from which he was launching the assault. The street chapel was the center of evangelistic activity—"Good News Hall" was its common name—with meetings extending throughout the day. Meetings were highly informal with alternate preaching

---

[10] Elijah C. Bridgman at Canton to the A.B.C.F.M., October 23, 1845, quoted in *The Missionary Herald*, Vol. XLII, March 1846, pp. 94-95.

[11] Dubose, *op. cit.*, p. 55.

and singing. Here the message of the evangelist was made as simple as possible in the hope of reaching those who had no previous knowledge of Christianity. Chinese would stop and listen to the foreigner out of curiosity. Occasionally one of them would ask the preacher a question. They would come and go as the spirit moved them, and neither their exits nor their entrances were quiet or unobtrusive. Only a man whose theology was like a rock could have long withstood the ceaseless washing of that vast sea of indifference.

The aim was immediate conversions. DuBose advised the newcomers to seek out the "hopeful cases," who should be persuaded to confess their sins, believe in Christ, and receive baptism. At home, this veteran missionary observed, a town might be moved by a revival service of three or four weeks, "but here these great cities need a protracted meeting of three or four centuries."

Much time was given to the street chapel, but the missionary was not content to limit his sowing of gospel seed to the immediate vicinity of the head station. Throughout the nineteenth century it was the practice to make frequent trips into the surrounding countryside and not infrequently to remote places. These evangelistic tours might last as long as three or four months. The missionary preached in the streets of the towns, distributed tracts, and held services in the homes of converts. Eventually little centers of converts in the distant villages became outstations where he would seek to have a native evangelist take over the work. By 1910, this form of itineration had come to be viewed as ineffective, the feeling being that the making of converts took long and patient work and that little was to be achieved by casting the gospel seed broadside.

Preaching, either by native or missionary, was the method most heavily relied upon in evangelization. The distribution of Bibles and tracts was another. The American Bible Society had a number of agents in China and also a great many native colporteurs, but the larger number of Bibles were distributed by missionaries. Each year the number of copies of the Bible, New Testament, and portions of the Gospels distributed reached a new peak. In 1914, 1,973,453 copies were put into the hands of the Chinese, and since 1876 the American Bible Society had sold or given away almost 17,000,000 copies of sacred literature in China.[12]

This deluging of the heathen with the Scriptures left a warm feeling of benevolence on the part of all American donors to the society. The chief effect on the Chinese, once he discovered that he could neither understand the Bible nor unload it on someone else without loss of capital, was a feeling of resentment. The Bibles sold contained no explanatory notes because the American Bible Society was interdenominational in character and it was feared that notes would offend some donor who disagreed with a particular interpretation.

These difficulties in the campaign to evangelize China by means of Bible distribution were recognized by at least some of the missionaries at the Shanghai Conference of 1890.[13] The symbolism, terminology, and customs described were utterly meaningless to the Chinese. They had never heard of the prophets and had no knowledge of Biblical lands. The frequent allusion to shepherds left most Chinese completely puzzled for in large sections of the country the inhabitants had never seen a sheep. In the areas where there were sheep, they were regarded as the lowest of animals, and the term shepherd did not have a pleasant connotation. The Biblical references to wine presses had no meaning because the Chinese did not make wine out of grapes. Biblical customs such as the washing of feet and the holy kiss were equally strange. Worse yet was the fact that Chinese customs were sometimes diametrically opposed to those of the West, e.g. "the well-known fact that the left hand is the seat of honor; white, mourning; also in contradistinction to us who associate the old serpent, the dragon, with Satan—the Chinese set forth as the symbol of intelligence, beneficence, and power and the dragon is their national

[12] *Ninety-Ninth Annual Report of the American Bible Society* (New York: American Bible Society, 1915), p. 368.

[13] Alexander Williamson, "On the Need of Concise Historical, Geographical, Ethnological and Philological Notes, etc.," Records of the General Conference of the Protestant Missionaries of China Held at Shanghai, May 7-20, 1890 (Shanghai: American Presbyterian Mission Press, 1890), p. 108.

banner, their royal coat-of-arms, and floats at the masthead of every ship." Most difficult of all obstacles was the fact that the concept of sin, which was at the very heart of the Biblical message, was utterly foreign to the Chinese. Indeed, the reader today can sympathize with the Chinese lack of comprehension of such terms as:

> the body of Christ, the bride of Christ, the bride of the Lamb's wife, the general assembly and Church of the first born, the city of the living God, the family in heaven and earth, the golden candlestick, the habitation of God, the temple of God, the heavenly Jerusalem, the pillar and ground of truth, and many others.[14]

The missionary who was concerned about this problem in 1890 thought all these terms could be made intelligible by the use of notes, whereas to a modern sociologist they would have suggested much more than a problem in semantics.

One Presbyterian missionary, the Rev. John L. Nevius, deplored the fact that people at home had not been told the truth. He said the impression had sometimes been produced in the West that there was actually a large demand for the Bible. He cited a report of the American Bible Society in which its supporters had been congratulated on the very large number of Bibles disposed of during the year. Particular satisfaction had been expressed because nearly all the copies disposed of had been sold rather than given away. Nevius thought a very different impression would have been produced at home if the further facts had been stated—that the books were sold at a nominal price and were bought only because the Chinese had been led to believe that the book would confer inestimable blessings on China and on any individual who followed its precepts. This the Bible could do only if made intelligible to the Chinese by means of explanatory notes.[15]

Nevius did not represent the typical point of view at the Shanghai Conference of 1890. To many his questioning seemed to throw suspicion on the adequacy of the Scriptures. One

[14] *Ibid.*, p. 111.
[15] *Records of the Shanghai Conference*, p. 129.

missionary dismissed all the objections which had been raised with a shrug of contempt. He had once been troubled by similar questions.

> But now I see that any Chinaman who can read John iii, 16, or any such plain statement of the Gospel, may be exercising the most simple kind of faith, become a child of God,—see John 1:12—and then may receive the Holy Spirit, who shall lead him into all truth, better than any Commentary or explanation that ever was written.[16]

This running away from the harsh facts was perhaps necessary. The missionary who began to examine either the justice of his cause or the soundness of orthodox strategy would have been in the position of the combat soldier who in the thick of battle took time to rethink his position. A large part of the missionary's effectiveness depended upon his unquestioning faith.

The first revival meetings in the American tradition were not held in China until the spring of 1900. Not until after the Boxer Revolt was there much reliance on special religious services where the aim was to bring the heathen to a quick decision to become a Christian.

Evangelization, it was always hoped, would also be carried on through native helpers. Chinese were given training in Bible study and preaching, and many of them became effective leaders within the church. The enlisting of Chinese in positions of leadership led to the problem of determining their sincerity and reliability. In a land of extreme poverty the smallest financial remuneration was a temptation, and there was no easy way to discover whether a person's motives were purely economic—whether he was a "rice Christian"—or not. An American Baptist missionary warned against the use of "saint seducing" silver and thought some scoffers might say of a few native preachers: "What makes all doctrines plain and clear? A hundred Mexicans a year!"

At the Shanghai Conference of 1890, John L. Nevius, a man

16 S. Dyer, "Bible Distribution in China—Its Methods and Results," *Records of the Shanghai Conference*, p. 117.

who had no hesitancy in citing unpleasant facts, reported that his station had employed fourteen Chinese. Of these, six had been excommunicated, four had been dismissed as unsatisfactory, one had died, and only three were still employed as agents. Nevius observed that two other stations of his denomination had an even less satisfactory record.[17] Another former missionary who has written an excellent account of a small denomination that was active in Hupeh found that forty per cent of the native evangelists and pastors left or were dismissed. In the records of his missionary board the most frequent grounds for dismissal were "un-Christian behavior," "unworthy," "fell into the snares of the devil," and "in need of repentance."[18]

The second great field of missionary activity was education. In aim and scope the schools established by missionaries were largely merely another agency for evangelization. The greatest number of schools were the primary schools established for the principal purpose of training the children of converts and shielding them from the influences of heathendom. Next in rank were the middle schools, which were likewise heavily evangelical in emphasis. They aimed at preparing young Chinese for college and for theological training. These two types of schools not only far outnumbered the Christian colleges but they also had a great many times more students. Most of the Christian colleges were founded later. By 1890 there were five Christian colleges. These originally placed greatest emphasis on training Chinese for the ministry. All Christian schools had required courses in Christianity and made attendance at Christian services compulsory. By 1890 there was a total of 16,836 students enrolled in the primary schools, the middle schools, and in the five Christian colleges.[19]

From the beginning these schools were Western islands in the sea of Chinese society. They invariably reflected the patterns of education in the country from which their founders

[17] John L. Nevius, "Historical Review of Missionary Methods—Past and Present—in China, and How Far Satisfactory," *Records of the Shanghai Conference,* p. 175.

[18] Earl Dahlstrom, *The Covenant Missionary Society,* Unpublished Ph.D. Dissertation at Hartford Theological Seminary, 1950, p. 93.

[19] *Records of the Shanghai Conference,* p. 732.

came and likewise mirrored the religious views of the missionaries and the churches at home. The Committee on Women's Work at the Shanghai Conference of 1890 urged that "the first place must always be reserved for religious instruction, the first object must ever be to bring the pupils to a knowledge of and belief in Christ as their Saviour."[20] No missionary in 1890 would have disagreed with that resolution.

Medical work constituted the third major area of missionary activity. The Chinese were not always willing to avail themselves of modern medicine, but it is also true that no foreign enterprise met as little opposition. During the first thirty years of the American Board mission in Canton, the number of converts averaged scarcely one in ten years, but Dr. Peter Parker's hospital and dispensary took care of thousands of Chinese and won the admiration of the highest officials. The healing of the sick seemed to the missionary a proper exercise of Christian benevolence and the example of Jesus was constantly cited as furnishing a scriptural basis for medical missions. Chinese needs were appallingly great, and the missionary who could look at the misery among the Chinese about him without wanting to help was not only rare but he was unknown. Yet, at least to the early missionaries, the spiritual shortcomings of the Chinese were even more alarming than physical illness. Consequently healing the sick was viewed as a means of gaining access to the heathen and winning them to Christianity.

Missionaries took particular delight in the opportunities offered by the hospital ward and the dispensary waiting room for conveying the gospel message. As late as 1913 Dr. J. Preston Maxwell of the Yungchun hospital cited the rules which should be followed in any Christian hospital. The walls of rooms should be decorated with texts from the Bible, tracts and hymn books should be distributed, and there should be morning and afternoon religious services for all well enough to attend. He recommended a special evangelistic service for Sunday afternoon. At these times the sermon should be directed to making conversions: "Christ and Him crucified, the need of sinners and

[20] Report of the Committee on Women's Work, *Records of the Shanghai Conference*, p. lv.

the hope of salvation. The writer [Dr. Maxwell] has little sympathy with abstract addresses on either God, or creation, or ethical subjects unless these lead directly and every time to the full presentation of the Saviour for sinners." The doctor also advocated that the missionaries engaged in evangelism should call on all who had been patients in a Christian hospital so that the good work might be continued. While there was no element of strength lacking in Doctor Maxwell's convictions, he admitted that it was not easy to sit down with a patient day after day and repeat the same things and teach the same hymns and texts. He observed that it was amazing "the way some patients are able to apparently absorb teaching, and pass it out without assimilating almost anything, and it is certainly discouraging, after 14 days work, to be told that the Name of the Son of God is 'Satan.' "[21]

Whatever objections the Chinese may have had to these gospel ministrations, the fact remains that in the nineteenth century the medical missionary and the missionary dispensary and hospital offered almost the only scientific medical treatment. The medical work begun by Dr. Peter Parker at Canton in 1834 had expanded by 1890 into thirty-two hospitals and eighteen dispensaries supported by American churches.[22]

The aim of the missionary was to impart to the Chinese what he would have called "knowledge unto the power of salvation." All else was secondary. That the missionary found China rocky ground for sowing he admitted. That he did is not strange.

As long as Chinese society was safely moored to its ancient institutions there was little reason to hope for success. The Chinese had no sense of sin for the simple reason that he actually lived up to the ideals set before him thanks to the social control exercised by the family, clan, and guild. His duties related to his family and clan; he recognized no responsibilities toward those beyond this limited circle.

To the Chinese evil was not a mysterious force driving him to unacceptable behavior. Evil was rather a question of spirits

[21] J. Preston Maxwell, "How Best to Obtain and Conserve Results in the Evangelistic Work amongst Hospital Patients," *The Chinese Recorder*, May 1913, p. 283.

[22] *Records of the Shanghai Conference*, p. 733.

who dwelled everywhere and who contrived to interfere with his good fortunes. These spirits had to be propitiated by magic rites but they were not considered to be angry with him because of any failure in his relations with his fellowmen. Nor did he grasp the Christian teaching of the sacredness of the individual for he had been conditioned to think of himself as the last link in a long chain of ancestors reaching back to antiquity. And the role of reason was, for him, largely reserved for very pressing matters of everyday existence, not as a guide to moral living. Moral precepts had been handed down from Confucius for his guidance in this realm and to question them was unthinkable.

Conversion required a sudden reorientation of the Chinese to an attitude toward life similar to that of the Christian missionary. This was manifestly next to impossible. Missionary correspondence offers ample testimony of the difficulties involved. The Chinese who heard the Christian message was usually of the lower class, extremely superstitious, and accustomed to propitiating spirits. He might find the message interesting, give outward acceptance, repeat the leading tenets in a more or less mechanical way, and observe the rules laid down by the missionary but he was scarcely able to grasp the spirit of Christian ethics. Consequently the practices which had always seemed proper and, indeed, bore the stamp of approval of his society, were still generally acceptable even after the missionary had warned against them. The result was, as one missionary wrote, much unconscious wrong doing.

The transgressions of converts listed by the missionaries were many. The Rev. W. O. Elterich observed that the most common failings were sabbath-breaking, gambling, intemperance, extortion, and adultery.[23] A Southern Presbyterian, the Rev. P. F. Price, stated the most frequent causes of difficulty in order named were "Sabbath breaking, covetousness, lying, adultery."[24] He confessed that among the converts there was much chaff and very little wheat. Another missionary cited the case of a member who had bought a slave girl for a small price in one locality and sold her for marriage in another locality "mak-

[23] W. O. Elterich to Commission II, World Missionary Conference, 1910.
[24] P. F. Price to Commission II, World Missionary Conference, 1910.

ing a handsome profit from the dowry received."[25] The Rev. James V. Latimer of the American Baptist Union expressed fear that not one of a hundred of the professing Christians had learned the secret of prayer and said that he had seen few manifest any great inward change or spiritual life although there were splendid exceptions.[26]

Sometimes acceptance of Christianity was followed by much stranger application of its teaching. The Rev. Louis Byrde told of how the London Missionary Society in the latter part of the nineteenth century had placed a brilliant Chinese, who had been a Yamen writer, in charge of the work in one area. He immediately assumed a high title, built chapels in scores of towns, and made membership such an honor that he was able to collect fees from two dollars up to eight dollars in one city. Local officials bowed to him and gave in to his commands so that it became necessary to join in order to receive any favors. His agents became the backers of numerous lawsuits. Triumphal processions, horses, banners and firecrackers became part of the festivities he sponsored. His fame spread and he became known as the "Generalissimo of the church of Christ in Hunan." This continued until he was relieved of his command of the mission stations. The missionary who related the story was certain that he had been sincere in the beginning.[27]

Usually Chinese misinterpretations were less bizarre but there was always present the danger that the convert who accepted the theological formulations of the missionary experienced no sudden reorientation of motives. He continued to act in conformity with the patterns of the society in which he lived even though he might abstain from idolatrous practices and other activities that the missionary had proscribed. The Christian in the United States undoubtedly had difficulty living according to the highest moral precepts of Christianity but to some extent the society in which he lived tended to make him conform to the teachings of the church.

[25] Henry V. Noyes to Commission II, World Missionary Conference, 1910.

[26] James V. Latimer to Commission II, World Missionary Conference, 1910.

[27] Louis Byrde to Commission I, World Missionary Conference, 1910, September 1909.

CHAPTER III

MISSIONARIES, DIPLOMATS,
AND BOXERS, 1890-1900

For all his proclaimed dependence on Jehovah, the missionary's fate depended upon the power represented in the foreign legation in Peking. So strong and so continuous was the antagonism toward the missionary that he could never have attempted to Christianize the country had not the Western nations with their superior force upheld his right to be there.

In turn, the reliance of the missionary on force led the Chinese to the conclusion that the missionary enterprise was part and parcel of Western imperialism and that the missionary was no different from the merchant, the diplomat, and the captain of the Western gunboat. Consequently the missionary had to bear the onus of everything that the West did, and of all features of the "unequal" treaties although only a few provisions of these treaties directly benefited the missionary. The treaties granted extraterritoriality to the foreigner, thereby freeing him from Chinese jurisdiction. Treaties determined the Chinese tariff. They likewise provided for foreign concessions in some of the cities setting off areas for the complete control of foreigners. In Shanghai there was the International Settlement, a section of the city immune from Chinese control. The fact that the West felt all aspects of these treaties were justified made no difference. The Chinese viewed them as insulting and they held the missionary just as responsible as they did any other westerner.

The Chinese hostility to the missionary was based first of all on the fact that Western Christianity was utterly strange and incomprehensible to the Chinese. After this came the opposition based on what they did understand, namely the missionary's revolutionary program.

The literati sensed from the very beginning that Christianization would deprive them of their power. So intense was their hostility that few missionaries considered it worth while to make any effort to win them over. In 1909 an American Presbyterian missionary in Shantung noted that in the entire history of her mission station no mandarin had ever been converted. The mandarins knew that the missionary not only disapproved of Confucius but that he wished to substitute for the Chinese classics a study of the Bible, scientific training, a knowledge of Western history, and an education which would fit the student for dealing with modern problems. The status of the mandarin rested on the ancient civil service examination system, which made mastery of the Confucian classics the test for office. All of his claims to preferment rested on his mastery of the classics. Quite naturally he resented the missionary who considered this ancient system of education quite useless. He also recognized, as few missionaries did, that to undermine the confidence of the Chinese people in the Confucian system was to undermine the basis of the whole Chinese social order.

When the mandarins observed missionaries working largely among the lower classes, the very group which presented the greatest danger of revolution, they became convinced that the missionaries posed a threat. This conviction was strengthened when they found the missionaries to be critical of political practices and institutions.

Of course, theoretically the preacher of the gospel was not anxious to interfere in politics, but what he found in China struck him as so objectionable and so contrary to his religious teaching that it was difficult for him not to protest. It soon became clear to the Chinese that the missionary was privately, and sometimes publicly, critical and that he was helping to undermine the confidence of his converts in the political *status quo.*

The desire of the Manchu government to maintain the *status quo* led it to evade its responsibility under the treaties to protect the missionary and to shield the Chinese converts from persecution because of their religious beliefs. The diplomatic representatives in Peking had to exercise eternal vigilance in order to have the Peking government take any action. Even then it preferred to tolerate slander that incited riots against the missionaries. Some of this lack of energetic action can be ascribed to a lack of power on the part of the central government but diplomats frequently observed that the government took strenuous action when the riots did not involve missionaries.

Secret societies promoted many of the riots against missionaries. Aside from their antagonism to all foreigners, they saw in such riots an opportunity to embarrass the central government with the foreign powers and thereby to weaken it and bring about its overthrow. In a majority of attacks on missionaries secret societies played a role.

The opposition was not limited to either the literati or members of secret societies. The ease with which the people could be aroused to attack the missionaries indicates a wide popular distrust. The difficulties put in the way of foreigners acquiring property also suggest that opposition was not limited to the literati. Any property owner who leased either land or buildings to a missionary faced strong censure from the community. In hundreds of cases, only representations from the home government enabled the missionary to acquire a base of operations.

The practice of Christian converts isolating themselves from community life provided another reason for resentment against the missionary. The convert refused to participate in ancestor ceremonies, an act tantamount to desecration of the sacred. He refused to contribute to village festivals because the missionary deemed these heathen rites. As a result his neighbors had to carry the convert's share of the cost.

Equally damaging to the missionary was his not infrequent involvement in litigation. Many a Chinese guilty of a serious or a lesser crime joined the Christians in the hope of getting the missionary to protect him. Converts were always subject to petty persecution, and the criminal who had been converted would claim that he was being punished for his religious beliefs. Missionaries had a natural concern for their followers and were anxious to protect them. They did not protect criminals knowingly, but it was not always possible for them to know all of the facts and consequently they sometimes were duped into intervening in behalf of the guilty. Protestant missionaries usually held that the Catholics were continuously doing this. The records indicate that the Protestants also intervened on occasion although missionary opinion generally looked with disfavor on the practice.

Indemnities to the missionary added to the hostility. In many cases when a missionary suffered injury or property damage, he appealed to his home government, which demanded reparations. The costs were assessed against the local population, adding to the heavy tax burden already borne by the poor.

The missionary's prestige at home stemmed in part from the public feeling that he was sincere and that he made a tremendous sacrifice in going to China. His comfortable compound and assurance of the necessities of life in China made quite a different impression upon the Chinese. To them it seemed that the missionary lived in luxury and quite apart from them.

Many an idealistic young missionary resented the wall this situation set up between himself and the poverty-stricken people he had come to help. A new missionary working in western China once bluntly charged his colleagues in the coastal areas with making the work difficult by living in fine residences which frequently had tennis courts. In many cases the young missionary, anxious to identify himself with his Chinese parishioners, adopted native dress and moved into a Chinese house. Almost always he gave it up.

From the earliest days until the closing years of missionary work the question of the isolated compound versus complete adoption of Chinese ways of living remained an issue. A vast majority of missionaries accepted the fact of their much higher standard of living with equanimity and justified it by stating that the Chinese felt there was something artificial about a Westerner who tried to live like a native. Considerations of health were also a major factor, for to leave the compound and live with the Chinese would have exposed the missionary to highly contagious diseases. This was a risk missionary boards were reluctant to have him take. Consequently the luxury of the compound as seen by the Chinese villager from his simple and dirty hovel remained a barrier shutting off the Western preacher of Christianity from those he was trying to win.

The relatively luxurious life of the missionary was not as significant a barrier to good missionary-convert relations as was the wall of different cultural values and mores that separated the American from the Oriental. The American evangelist was struck by the Chinese convert's lack of patriotism and concern for social welfare, his willingness to twist the truth in order to shield a member of his family, his different conception of marriage ties, and the fact that his sense of duty to family transcended his feeling of obligation to the church (a fact resulting in nepotism among Chinese workers). The missionary attributed these cultural differences to heathen influences and quite frankly made war on the whole Chinese value system. In this sense he assumed a position of superiority but one that was inherent in the very nature of foreign missions. This sense of cultural superiority could easily move over into a sense of racial superiority, and when it did, the Chinese resented it. At a meeting in Peking in 1913 before the Chinese Continuation Committee, a missionary asked how "can we ensure a wider and more fruitful effort to influence the people of this field to become Christians?" A Chinese, Pastor Fang, promptly replied: "Remove the barrier of racial prejudice existing between missionaries and Chinese Christian workers, and then see to it that the Christian workers are properly placed."

This is not to say that the missionary did not have loyal followers. He generally made friends and was well received on his tours through the villages. It would be wholly inaccurate to interpret the prevailing hostility as one where the missionary could not appear in public without being subjected to sneers or physical violence. From day to day he went his way meeting at least with an outward friendliness, but he never knew when there might be some uprising against him. The reception he received varied upon the locality, the time, the presence of secret societies hostile to all foreigners, and the particular state of relations between China and the West. The Chinese have been widely accused of antiforeignism. The charge is correct if one means that they were unalterably opposed to foreign interference but it is not valid if interpreted to mean that they would not accept foreigners.

Chinese antiforeignism stemmed from their unhappy experience with the imperialistic spirit manifested by Westerners. Sir Robert Hart, dean of old China hands, once described China's experience with the Westerner:

> He [the Westerner] is a Christian—therefore it is a sacred duty to attack every other cult and preach the Gospel; he finds consumers keep alive a demand for opium—therefore it is right, if not his duty to supply it; he learns that China has an immense population—therefore he inveighs against every restriction, and claims liberty to sell to all who will buy, and to buy from all who will sell; he is told by some one that China has no laws, that Chinese judges are corrupt, that justice is bought and sold, and that torture takes the place of evidence on oath—therefore he demands and obtains extra-territoriality; he finds that China is not a military nation—therefore he pushes aside discussion, asserts his superiority, sees right in might, and has his own way; he has brought with him the idea that commerce knows only import and export duties—therefore he is indignant over the rapacity which levies revenue dues and inland taxes; he knows that such and such is the way of doing things at home—therefore he condemns all Chinese otherness, and would put four hundred millions of people in the garments of forty; in short, his doxy is orthodoxy, and everything else is heterodoxy, and so intercourse, instead of being mutually beneficial, is the reverse, and instead of fastening and cementing friendly relations, is producing discord, ill feeling, and even enmity.[1]

This one-sided picture reflects the fact that Hart wrote it shortly after the turbulence of the Boxer Revolt.

Clearly all the fault did not lie on the side of the Westerner, but the Chinese certainly saw it from this point of view. In

[1] Robert Hart, *These from the Land of Sinim* (London: Chapman and Hall, 1903), pp. 123-124.

fact, the question is not one of who was at fault but rather of the difficulties that arose because the Chinese political order and concept of foreign relations were so wholly different from those of the West. To the Chinese all foreigners were barbarians and none more so than the European and American. John Fairbank, in his *Trade and Diplomacy on the China Coast*, provides a scholarly account of Chinese knowledge of the West and of their attitudes toward the Westerner. He relates the story of a Britisher, Thomas Taylor Meadows, who had resided in China for several years. Mr. Meadows reported in 1852 that Chinese notions of Westerners were much like those the British entertained of savages—"They are always surprised, not to say astonished, to learn that we have surnames, and understand the family distinctions of father, brother, wife, sister, etc.; in short, that we live otherwise than as a herd of cattle."[2]

Ignorance of the West was only one of the difficulties standing in the way of the establishment of good relations. Another factor was the unusual paucity of political leadership in the Manchu dynasty at the time of the opening of relations with the West. There was the added difficulty that China had long adhered to the tribute system whereby all other states were considered inferior, a concept which grew out of China's long relations with tribal states along her borders. Her geographical position made for an extreme ethnocentricity and created a wall which barred the way to the working out of friendly relations.[3]

Nor would it be correct to note the use of force by the West and fail to record what Westerners saw in China. Obligations to one's neighbor ended with one's family and clan. A considerable degree of callousness toward human life prevailed, and, as we shall see, the Chinese were capable of extreme brutality.

Waves of violence threatened to inundate the missionaries from the very beginning. Until the Boxer Revolt of 1900 they

[2] John King Fairbank, *Trade and Diplomacy on the China Coast: The Opening of the Treaty Ports 1842-1854* ("Harvard Historical Studies" [Cambridge: Harvard University Press, 1953]), p. 19.
[3] *Ibid.*, see Chapter II, "Tribute and the Growth of Trade."

fought back, vigorously asserting their treaty rights, appealing to diplomatic officials, demanding indemnities, and support-ing the imperialistic policies of Western nations. The 1890's marked the climax of attacks against the missionary and, no less, it was the decade when the policy of retribution pursued by the West reached its high water mark.

In the winter and spring of 1891 secret societies in the Yangtze valley circulated the timeworn charge that mission-aries were kidnapping children and using their eyes for medical purposes. In May the American Methodist Girls' School at Nanking was destroyed by a mob.[4] Soon Charles Denby, Minis-ter of the United States in Peking, reported daily outbreaks against the missionaries. The violence in the Yangtze valley had no sooner come to an end than a missionary in Manchuria told that stories were being circulated of foreigners buying lice, poisoning them, and scattering them among the people—such stories usually heralded violence but nothing came of it in this instance.[5]

Minister Charles Denby acted with firmness, launched the usual demand for the punishment of those responsible for the destruction of the school, and in the following March justice was done—two of the rioters were arrested and decapitated, the others were imprisoned.[6]

Early in 1892 a discontent in Hunan stemming from a slack-ening of business vented itself in the distribution of slanderous leaflets, including one entitled "Death to the Devil's Religion." Denby now naïvely and belatedly reported that many intelli-gent Chinese believed that the Western intrusion had brought many unfortunate results—loss of territory, extraterritoriality, foreign manufactured goods, and the importation of opium. As if the admission might reflect unfavorably upon him, Denby

[4] Charles Denby to Secretary of State James G. Blaine, June 5, 1891, Inclosure, Clipping from *North China Daily News* of May 29, 1891, *United States Foreign Relations, 1891* (Washington: Government Printing Office), pp. 402-403. Hereafter these volumes are cited as *Foreign Relations*.

[5] *Ibid.*, June 28, 1891, Inclosure, Doctor Westwater to Mr. Bandinel, *Foreign Relations, 1891*, pp. 413-414.

[6] *Ibid.*, March 5, 1892, Inclosure, The Tsung-li-yamen to Denby, *Foreign Relations, 1892*, pp. 91-92.

hastened to assure the Secretary of State: "The chart that guides the foreign representatives is the treaty. He has only to see that its provisions are complied with. If those provisions work injury to China he can not help it. She must find her own methods of relief."[7]

In July, 1892, appeared a notice falsely carrying the signature of a local official who confessed that he had been worshipping the "Hog Ancestor, Jesus" and that in return he had received a generous salary from each of the Western powers. Placards called for attacks on foreigners while others threatened that any Chinese who sold land to foreigners would meet death.[8]

Three years later, in 1895, these routine occurrences increased in tempo. Extensive riots at Chengtu, the capital of Szechuan, resulted in the destruction of Protestant and Catholic mission buildings.[9] A diplomatic protest was still in preparation when, on August 1, eleven missionaries were brutally slain in the small village of Huashan in southern China. Miss Mabel C. Hartford, the only American present, was injured; she would have been killed without the intervention of the wife of her native teacher and her Chinese servant.

The Huashan tragedy represented the culmination of a chain of incidents bred by suspicion, fear, and poverty. A secret society, the "Vegetarians," had been defying the Chinese authorities and engaging in violence for over a period of a year when they became involved in an argument with a Christian convert and then looted his shop. He appealed to the authorities, thus further antagonizing the Vegetarians, and they retaliated by stealing his rice crop. In July, 1895, soldiers appeared on the scene, an unwelcome development which the Vegetarians attributed to the influence of an English missionary. Feeling threatened, they now secured arms and prepared for a revolt, and needing money and food, they attacked the offensive missionary settlement.[10]

[7] *Ibid.*, March 14, 1892, *Foreign Relations, 1892*, p. 92.
[8] Charles Denby to Secretary of State, July 27, 1892, *Miscellaneous Letter Files*, Department of State Archives.
[9] Charles Denby to Edwin F. Uhl, Acting Secretary of State, June 4, 1895, *Foreign Relations, 1895*, p. 87.
[10] Charles Denby to Secretary of State Richard Olney, December 18,

Although only one American had been injured and one American Methodist station destroyed, the missionaries in China, the boards at home, and many of the clergy demanded that the American government take strong action. Meetings of missionaries denounced Minister Denby who had at first agreed to join with the British in a commission to investigate the Chengtu riot. This, held the missionaries, was inadequate protest; they demanded that the United States defend its honor by conducting its own investigation.[11] The Corresponding Secretary of the Board of Foreign Missions of the Reformed Church urged Secretary of State Olney that immediate steps be taken to provide an adequate naval force at Amoy.[12] A similarly urgent note was received from the Methodists and Baptists.[13] At the same time the Presbyterian Ministerial Association of Chicago urged the government at Washington "to move at once with utmost promptness and decision and determination:

> First, to demand and enforce the proper punishment of all implicated in outrages, officials, private citizens, and soldiery alike. Second, to demand and insist upon full money indemnity for all damage done to property of Societies and private individuals. Third, to demand and require good guarantees from the Government of China for the protection of life, person and property of all foreigners for the future.[14]

1895, Inclosure, Report of Commander J. S. Newell, U.S.N., *Foreign Relations, 1895*, pp. 173-189.

[11] Charles Denby to Secretary of State Richard Olney, August 15, 1895, *Foreign Relations*, 1895, pp. 108-109.

[12] Henry N. Cobb, Secretary of the Board of Foreign Missions of the Reformed Church in America, to Secretary of State Richard Olney, August 7, 1895, *Miscellaneous Letter Files*, Department of State Archives.

[13] A. B. Leonard, Corresponding Secretary, Missionary Society of the Methodist Episcopal Church, to Secretary of State Richard Olney, September 17, 1895, *Miscellaneous Letter Files*, Department of State Archives, and Henry C. Mabie, Home Secretary, American Baptist Missionary Union, to Secretary of State Richard Olney, September 21, 1895, *Miscellaneous Letter Files*, Department of State Archives.

[14] George B. Laird, Secretary of the Presbyterian Ministerial Association

Judson Smith of the Congregationalists inquired of Olney what the government was doing to protect its citizens abroad.[15]

When Minister Denby was sharply criticized by the missionaries for committing the United States to a joint investigation of the Chengtu affair, he hastened to restore his standing by charging the Viceroy of Szechuan with encouraging the riot and demanding his dismissal before the facts had been determined.[16] The Department of State had decided to conduct its own inquiry but before this had been accomplished, the British and French had completed their investigation and the Viceroy had been removed.

The American government was more prompt in investigating the Huashan riot of August 1, appointing Commander Newell of the Navy to sit in on the trials of the accused and to get the facts of the riot. Thanks to foreign pressure the Chinese officials soon beheaded twenty-six of the Vegetarians.[17]

Up until the time of the Boxer Revolt missionaries and their denominational boards continued to enlist the power of their government to pressure the Manchu-Chinese officials into taking such crude measures. These appeals unto Caesar for assistance in promoting the Christian gospel were defended by the missionaries as necessary to bring the government to maintain order; and order, they declared, would benefit the Chinese quite as much as the missionary. Thereby the missionaries inextricably identified themselves with the governments of Western nations with the inevitable result that the Chinese considered them part and parcel of Western imperialism.

The aggressiveness of the missionaries, however, was completely overshadowed by the arrogance of secular powers. In

---

of Chicago, to Secretary of State Richard Olney, September 24, 1895, *Miscellaneous Letter Files,* Department of State Archives.

[15] Judson Smith, Foreign Secretary of the American Board of Commissioners for Foreign Missions, to Secretary of State Richard Olney, November 21, 1895, *Miscellaneous Letter Files,* Department of State Archives.

[16] Charles Denby to Secretary of State Richard Olney, August 31, 1895, *Foreign Relations, 1895,* p. 122.

[17] Charles Denby to Secretary of State Richard Olney, December 18, 1895, Inclosure, Report of Commander Newell, *Foreign Relations, 1895,* pp. 173-189.

1894 China and Japan engaged in a war and the result was a terrible humiliation of the Chinese. The West took careful note of the weakness of the Manchu-Chinese government and was soon engaged in exploiting that weakness to the fullest. Japan was likewise anxious to gather in the fruits of victory and demanded Formosa, the Liaotung peninsula, and an indemnity. Russia, Germany, and France intervened to prevent any cession of territory on the continent and Japan had to content herself with Formosa and an indemnity.

China paid heavily for this favor from the West. Russia led the way by gaining exclusive rights for the government-sponsored Russo-Asiatic Bank. Then in 1898 came the mad scramble for concessions. Russia secured a lease of Port Arthur and a sphere of influence in Manchuria. Germany, using the murder of two missionaries as a pretext, demanded Kiaochow and a sphere of influence in Shantung. China yielded to the German demands and then found herself confronted by French demands for a sphere of influence in Kwangtung. England, seeing the race for concessions, sought to halt it but finding herself unable to do so asked and received a lease of Wei Hai Wei and a recognition of a British sphere of influence in the Yangtze Valley.

The United States, having had so many illustrations of the scriptural passage "ask and ye shall receive" pondered on the problem of where her best interests lay. Not a few Americans were willing to take over some portion of the crumbling Chinese empire. Early in March, 1898, Minister Denby denounced the "tortuous treachery" of Russia and regretted Great Britain's failure to take action.[18] Before the concessions race was over, E. H. Conger had replaced Denby as Minister and he advised the Secretary of State that the policy of no territorial aggrandizement left the United States at a great disadvantage in the struggle for control.[19] The American Minister then suggested that "next to controlling a desirable port and com-

[18] Charles Denby to Secretary of State John Sherman, March 8, 1898, *Miscellaneous Letter Files*, Department of State Archives; *ibid.*, March 19, 1898, Department of State Archives.

[19] E. H. Conger to Secretary of State William R. Day, August 26, 1898, *Miscellaneous Letter Files*, Department of State Archives.

modius harbor in China, the permanent ownership or possession of Manila and vicinity would be most invaluable to us in securing and holding our share of influence and trade in the new era just beginning in this country." "It would," said Conger, "give a convenient and essential base of supplies, where American trade, capital and brains could and would be massed ready for the commercial conquests, which Americans ought to accomplish in China."[20] Conger supplemented this some months later with a recommendation from Consul John Fowler at Chefoo that the United States obtain a site for a coaling station in North China or in Korea.[21] The American minister returned to the subject in March, 1899. This time he said that while, in his own opinion, permanent ownership of territory was not desirable ("except for a coaling station if that is needed"), it was nevertheless true that if China was to fall into the hands of European powers, the United States would be in a better bargaining position if she had a strong foothold.[22] Conger reversed himself after the Boxer Revolt, and when Secretary of State John Hay suggested the acquisition of territory, he advised against it.

The missionaries did not share these sentiments as a group but neither did they voice any strong criticism. There was some inclination to believe that China might learn a lesson in humility and the need for better treatment of the foreigner. Only one small group of missionaries openly advocated territorial acquisition and they favored taking over the Spanish islands in the Pacific rather than any part of China.[23]

The net result of American expansionist feelings, as far as Asia was concerned, was the acquisition of the Philippine Islands, Wake Island, and Guam at the close of the Spanish-American War. Whatever lust entered the hearts of Americans

[20] *Ibid.*

[21] E. H. Conger to Secretary of State John Hay, January 7, 1899, *Miscellaneous Letter Files,* Department of State Archives.

[22] E. H. Conger to Secretary of State John Hay, March 1, 1899, *Miscellaneous Letter Files,* Department of State Archives.

[23] Judson Smith, Foreign Secretary of the A.B.C.F.M., to Secretary of State John Hay, January 9, 1899, *Miscellaneous Letter Files,* Department of State Archives.

as they witnessed the threatened partition of China, it seems to have been satiated by these acquisitions elsewhere.

The outside world had been amazed by the weakness of China illustrated so well in the war with Japan; the Chinese were equally impressed. The defeat made it clear to many of them that reform was necessary if China was to survive.

The reform movement, which began in 1895, was led by K'ang Yu-wei, a Cantonese scholar. Seeking to combine the merits of the ancient Confucian teachings with those of Western Christianity, he wrote a new commentary on the classics in which he incorporated the concept of God as a spirit. K'ang likewise drafted a memorial calling upon the Emperor to initiate a reform program and organized the Higher Learning Society. In this activity he had the support of Liang Ch'i-ch'ao. Both were friendly with Timothy Richard, the English missionary, who advised them. Liang soon became Richard's secretary. Gilbert Reid, an American missionary, was also close to the reformers and participated in the discussions.[24]

Several high officials were active in the reform movement and one of them, Weng T'ung-ho, asked Richard to outline a program. Richard's recommendations offer remarkable testimony to the typical Westerner's faith in the universality of his own political ideals and the notion that there was nothing wrong with China that good upright and efficient Westerners could not cure. There were to be two foreign advisers to the Emperor, a cabinet of eight, of whom half were to be foreigners, reform of the currency system, building of railroads and opening of mines and factories, establishment of a board of education to introduce modern schools and colleges, a modern army and navy, and a press guided by foreign journalists.[25]

Eventually K'ang Yu-wei became Secretary of the Tsungli Yamen and gained direct access to the Emperor. In the summer of 1898 came a series of sweeping imperial decrees. Almost overnight the essay examination system was ordered abolished,

[24] Meribeth E. Cameron, *The Reform Movement in China, 1898-1912* ("Stanford University Publications in History, Economics, and Political Science," Vol. III, No. 1 [Stanford University Press, 1931]), p. 28 and Timothy Richard, *Forty-Five Years in China: Reminiscences* (London: T. Fisher Unwin, 1916), p. 256.
[25] Richard, *op. cit.*, p. 256.

temples were to be converted into schools for Western education, Christianity was promised protection, a university to teach Western science was decreed, and other revolutionary innovations were promised. The reformers then realized the imminent danger of intervention by the reactionary Empress Dowager. They made plans to have her put aside, but before these could be carried out Yüan Shih-kái informed his sworn brother, Viceroy Jung Lu, a strong supporter of the Empress, of what was to take place. The Empress Dowager struck quickly, assumed the regency once again, placed the Emperor under close guard, and ordered the arrest of the leaders of the reform movement. It was now clear that Westernization must wait.

In March 1899 an imperial decree granted Catholic missionaries official status and the right to deal directly with officials of the government of the same rank. The action has been variously interpreted as a drastic concession wrung from the Chinese and as one granted by the Empress Dowager in the hope that it would arouse the people to a recognition of the unlimited ambitions of the West. Professor Gerald Nye Steiger thinks that the move was inspired by the hope of the Manchu court to have missionary questions settled on a local level, thus relieving it of some of the foreign pressure.[26]

The announcement of this decree caught the Protestants unprepared. At first their sense of rivalry inclined them toward asking that they also be given official status. Minister Conger suggested that the Protestants should ask for the same status as the Catholics, and in July 1899 the various missionary boards sent a memorial to Secretary of State John Hay to this effect.[27] However, the request was retracted after the boards discovered that the missionaries were decidedly opposed.[28]

[26] George Nye Steiger, *China and the Occident: The Origin and Development of the Boxer Movement* (New Haven: Yale University Press, 1927), pp. 98-99.

[27] Henry N. Cobb, Corresponding Secretary, Board of Foreign Missions of the Reformed Church in America to Secretary of State John Hay, July 8, 1899, *Miscellaneous Letter File*, Department of State Archives. The request was signed by Judson Smith of the American Board, Frank F. Ellinwood of the Presbyterian Board, A. B. Leonard of the Methodist Episcopal Board, Henry Mabie of the American Baptist Missionary Union, and Henry Cobb of the Board of Missions of the Reformed Church.

[28] Henry Cobb, Secretary of the Board of Foreign Missions of the Re-

In another development, in September 1899, John Hay dispatched the Open Door Notes to the major Far Eastern powers, requesting them to uphold Chinese territorial and administrative integrity and to maintain the free use of treaty ports within their spheres of influence (thus protecting American merchants against discrimination). Each of the major powers gave favorable replies but reluctantly and with reservations. American missionaries hailed the move and so did the American press, but the Hay notes had no quieting effects in China.

In that unhappy country a strong antiforeign movement was underway led by the so-called Boxers. The Boxers were most active in the provinces of Shantung and Chihli during the winter and spring of 1900. By March, Judson Smith, Secretary of the American Board of Commissioners for Foreign Missions, forwarded alarming reports to Secretary of State John Hay and inquired "what additional measures for the effective protection of the life and property of American citizens have been taken by our government?"[29] Judson Smith advised that proclamations by the throne would not be sufficient; the United States should insist on the despatch of Chinese troops to put down the rioters. He thought it might be necessary to make some demonstration of power.

Judson Smith's reports were outweighed by the accounts given by other observers. The Presbyterian missionaries said that there had been little actual violence.[30] Minister Conger's reports during the winter and early spring warned of a general uprising against the foreigner but W. W. Rockhill, adviser to Hay on Far Eastern affairs and an expert on matters Chinese, saw no reason to fear any general outbreak. Secretary Hay accepted Rockhill's estimate of the situation.

In late May and early June it became clear that the situation

formed Church, to Assistant Secretary of State David J. Hill, April 13, 1900, *Miscellaneous Letter File*, Department of State Archives.

[29] Judson Smith, Secretary of the American Board, to Secretary of State John Hay, March 24, 1900, *Miscellaneous Letter File*, Department of State Archives.

[30] *U. S. Foreign Relations, 1900*, Conger to Hay, December 7, 1899, Inclosure 9, Conger to Tsungli Yamen, December 2, 1899, quotes telegram from the Reverend Arthur H. Smith.

was serious, and in the next two months came the holocaust. No completely accurate figures of the number killed were ever compiled. One missionary placed the number of Chinese Christians at 30,000 but this figure seems high.[31] Arthur H. Smith reported 136 Protestant missionaries killed, forty-four Catholics, and fifty-three children of missionaries.[32] Even more shocking was the brutality displayed—heads severed by broad swords, burning of men, women, and children, mutilation, and every fiendish device was employed.

The terror was largely concentrated in three of the northern provinces. Shansi, where the reactionary Manchu, Yu Hsien, was Governor, suffered the most because of the encouragement he gave to the Boxers. Chihli, the province in which Peking is located, also experienced a general outbreak of violence.

All of China would have been swept by the terror if the orders of the Empress Dowager had been obeyed. Three Governors-General in South and Central China maintained peace, however, recognizing that China would pay heavily for seeking to wipe out the foreigner.

In Peking the foreign legations, badly overcrowded with foreign and native refugees, were under siege for nine weeks. The Western world heard the reports and were shocked. A force of two thousand marines and sailors from the Japanese and Western warships at Taku were sent to the rescue but proved inadequate and had to turn back. Japan, the only power in a position to send in effective forces at once, offered to send an expedition providing the other powers agreed. Precarious as was the situation at Peking, much time was taken up by the Western nations in reaching an agreement on the composition of the expeditionary force. Not until August 14 were the legations rescued.

The Boxer Revolt awakened a widespread public interest in the missionary question. Unfriendly critics asked what right American missionaries had to impose their religion on the

---

[31] Luella Miner, *China's Book of Martyrs: A Record of Heroic Martyrdoms and Marvelous Deliverances of Chinese Christians During the Summer of 1900* (Philadelphia: The Westminster Press, 1903), p. 16.

[32] Arthur H. Smith, *China in Convulsion* (New York: Fleming H. Revell Co., 1901), Vol. II, p. 613.

Chinese. This was a note that had been struck previously by some periodicals such as the *Nation* and the *Arena*. Now the matter took on more than academic significance. Missionaries were advised that if they felt the necessity of preaching to the heathen, they should do so at their own risk. Otherwise they would provide their home governments with a cause for taking military action and bring to the people whom they professed to serve unmerited punishment. What right did Americans have to assume that their system was better than that of the Chinese? The Chinese had the same moral convictions and the same imperfections as Christians.[33] They were satisfied with their theology, and it seemed better policy to let them alone. Who could know what religion was best? Obviously no one knew, and therefore it would be wiser to let each country and people work out its own salvation. These criticisms echoed the sentiments of Voltaire who had told the story of a Chinese who, having heard a dialogue between a Jesuit, a Jansenist, a Quaker, an Anglican, a Moslem, and a Jew, had terminated the argument by ordering them all to be locked up in a lunatic asylum in separate cells.

The critics also took delight in taunting the missionaries about demanding indemnities. They cited the report of General Chaffee who had been in command of American troops in Peking. The editor of the *Nation* held that it left the missionaries something to explain for they were proposing a sliding scale of indemnities, according to which one town was to pay $17 a life while another was assessed at $350 for each life lost. It seemed to the editor that the Japanese Buddhists in China, in refusing to collect indemnities, had shown a more Christian outlook.[34]

Mark Twain joined in the attack. His ability to draw cari-

[33] J. M. Scanland, "Our Asiatic Missionary Enterprise," *Arena,* September 1900, pp. 258-267.

The *New York Times* was critical of the missionaries throughout the summer of 1900. An editorial on June 10 said that the administration was under great pressure from the churches and quoted a government official as saying "They seem to think that the United States can post a regiment in front of every missionary in China."

[34] Editorial, *Nation,* August 15, 1901, p. 122.

catures found a natural target in the missionary and the indemnity question. "The Blessings-of-Civilization Trust," he
said, was made up of men of faith, zeal, courage, sentiment,
emotion, enthusiasm, mixtures of poet, devotee, and knight-
errant. "The head-piece of that kind of a man," thought
Twain, was likely to be of an inferior sort. One of these men
in Peking was reported to have collected fines from the Chinese amounting to thirteen times as much as the losses that the
native Christians, for whom he was seeking indemnification,
had suffered. The extra money was to be used for missionary
work.[35]

To rub the gilt off the symbols of righteousness is always an
occupation which pleases the human species, and the critics
had their amusement. Actually the indemnity claims of the
missionaries were modest, especially if compared with the
$52,707 claim filed by an American engineer of later political
prominence.[36] An interdenominational missionary conference
held in New York at the close of the Boxer Revolt laid down
the policy that claims for indemnities should not include suffering, loss of life, or interruption of work, but only the actual

[35] Mark Twain, "To the Person Sitting in Darkness," *North American
Review*, February 1901, pp. 161-176 and "To My Missionary Critics,"
North American Review, April 1901, pp. 520-534. He accused William
Scott Ament of collecting indemnities far beyond the amount of damage
suffered. The biographer of Ament states that Twain based his charges
on a story which appeared in the *New York Sun*. He explained that Ament
had not compelled payment and that the local officials were agreeable
to making contributions; that the *Sun* story had read "13 times as much
indemnity" but should have read "1/3"; and that all the money collected went to indemnify Chinese who had suffered losses and to a fund
for widows and orphans. However, the missionary had been aggressive;
for instance, he had taken over a Mongol residence and had sold all its
furnishings. See Henry D. Porter, *William Scott Ament: Missionary of
the American Board to China* (New York: Fleming H. Revell Co., 1911),
pp. 223-238.

[36] Herbert Hoover arrived in China immediately preceding the Boxer
Revolt. $48,833 of the claim was for salary he was to receive as an engineer
for the Mining Bureau of Chihli Province. He had to leave when the
revolt broke out. The project on which he was to work was dropped and
Hoover accepted another position. He filed a claim for the amount of the
salary provided by his three-year contract. The claims commission allowed
him only $10,759. *Boxer Indemnity Claims Commission*, Vol. II, Depart-
ment of State Archives.

value of destroyed or injured property, and extraordinary expenses involved.[37] This was not binding on the families of martyred missionaries, and some filed heavy claims. The administrator of the Horace Pitkin estate, for instance, filed a claim for $100,000.[38]

While the critics exploited the Boxer Revolt and the indemnity claims, missionary leaders sought to turn the experience to the advantage of their cause. Accounts of native martyrdom were collected from each mission station after the return of the missionaries and these were narrated in numerous books, usually in tones of effusive admiration when the simple facts would have sufficed. A woman missionary explained the firmness of faith manifested by native martyrs, as did Arthur H. Smith, as the product of a religious revival that had swept through the affected provinces in the spring.[39] So exciting was the revival that missionary schools had found their recitations turned into prayer meetings, for three weeks classes had not met, and one group of students had set forth for the countryside on an evangelistic tour. Writers told of how native Christians in many cases refused to make the slightest compromise in order to save their lives. One had gaily marched out to meet the Boxers as they approached his home. A Chinese family, apprehended by the Boxers, had marched to their execution singing the hymn "He Leadeth Me."[40] Others had refused to leave the missionaries even though they might thereby have escaped. Missionaries who for years had been taunted with the charge that their converts were "rice Christians" now felt that their work had been vindicated. Luella Miner, Presbyterian missionary and author of *China's Book of Martyrs,*

[37] Arthur J. Brown, "Future Missionary Policy in China: A Notable Conference of Missionary Secretaries," *Missionary Review of the World,* November 1900, p. 855. The meeting of mission secretaries voted in favor of indemnity "in exceptional cases, for loss of life which has destroyed the means of support for wife and children." *Ibid.*

[38] *Boxer Indemnity Claims Commission,* Vol. II.

[39] Luella Miner, *op. cit.,* pp. 32-33.

[40] E. H. Edwards, *Fire and Sword in Shansi: The Story of the Martyrdom of Foreigners and Chinese Christians* (New York: Fleming H. Revell Co., 1903), p. 9.

drew the moral that most shared: "The Church has been stirred as never before in modern times, and has heard in this record the call of God to more strenuous and devoted effort to redeem the lands thus purchased by blood and suffering."

CHAPTER IV

THE MISSIONARY MOVEMENT AT HOME
BECOMES A CRUSADE, 1890-1917

IRONICALLY, in the 1890's at the very time that the Chinese rose up in angry violence against the Western intruder, the missionary movement at home assumed the full proportions of a widely supported and highly respected crusade. The reasons for its remarkable growth are to be found primarily in the revivals set into motion by Dwight L. Moody and in the new political currents that were sweeping the United States into the vortex of world affairs.

The keynote of the Moody revivals was that men ought to live for God and do something. The Rev. Adoniram Judson Gordon, well-known Boston Congregationalist, told a meeting of missionary candidates at Cleveland in 1901 that they must become God-intoxicated men. "God wants that kind of men to-day," said Gordon, "men inebriated with the Holy Ghost; men that may be counted insane sometimes because of the tremendous earnestness of their fire and zeal."

Dwight L. Moody plumbed no new intellectual depths and his theology, to the degree that he had any, was no more complex than that he had learned as a schoolboy. Yet, no American of his generation had a larger audience. What he lacked in intellect and deep spiritual insight, he made up for in his unshakable grasp of religious stereotypes and an amazing ability to put into words the religious problems that troubled the average churchgoer. He was a powerful personality, tremendously practical in concentrating his attention on what was to him the main issue, namely conversion, and a born leader of men. Usually he went his own way, taking no note of the new intellectual currents that were disturbing churchgoers, but on occasion he took time out from his soul-saving campaigns to deal with the exponents of Biblical criticism. Before one of his great audiences he disposed of the intellectual problem by telling his hearers: "The Bible was not made to understand." In his theological satchel were all the dogmas of the orthodox but his passion for souls left him little time to engage in doctrinal controversies.

From one end of the United States to the other and in England and Scotland as well, Moody and his colleague, Ira Sankey, and many other lesser evangelists, revived the sagging spirits of churchgoers. In short crisp sentences Moody presented to his thousands of listeners the simple alternatives of damnation and salvation. He never stressed the former; he did not need to, for his listeners had a clear picture of Hell. His emphasis was on the compassion of Christ for sinful men. The greatest sin was to remain indifferent, to hold back from the offer of salvation. Moral living made no difference, every man was a sinner who did not deliver himself wholly into the hands of Christ. Only then would uncertainties vanish. Moody, Bible in hand, innocent of all the philosophical debates of the ages, seemed like the very epitome of certainty. Like a confident captain of a ship, he offered free passage to the Beautiful Isle of Somewhere. And as the ship waited while the undecided made up their minds, Sankey led the happy multitude of those who had already taken passage in the singing of his gospel songs, songs so popular that by 1900 the copyrights had netted more than $1,250,000.

Out of the revivals of the 1870's and 1880's came a group of young converts who spoke of having met God on a spiritual mountain top. Their dominant thought was that one must give himself to God for the salvation of the world. They were burningly interested in having everyone become a Christian. Among them was the Reverend Adoniram Judson Gordon. A young theological student at Boston University, Dr. Rollin Walker, later recalled how he had met Gordon at Northfield in the summer of 1886 and had later attended his church in Boston. Walker spoke of him as passionately fond of the Bible, a man who believed that Christ was vividly present and who loved God and his fellowmen so intensely that he was unaware of the problems of the higher criticism. Like Moody, he was dominated by a passion for having men accept Christ, and nothing else mattered. Moody, Gordon, and the great leaders of the missionary movement such as John R. Mott and Robert E. Speer all stressed dedication of oneself to God. None of these men were scholars and they never worried about definition of the terms of their formula; they believed their message to be divine, demonstrated, in the Bible, and verified by their own experience. Neither Mott nor Speer would have argued with the higher criticism; they knew, as did Moody, that the leaders of the higher criticism in Scotland, men like Marquis Dodds and George Adams Smith of the University of Edinborough, were also enthusiastic evangelicals who, like they, believed that men should be led to a crisis when they made a decision for Christ. This was the important thing; theological differences were unimportant. From such as these came the missionaries.

The atmosphere of the Moody revivals carried over into the meetings of the Student Volunteers for Foreign Missions, the organization of college and seminary students which provided the leadership for the foreign missions crusade. Speakers before the Student Volunteers never engaged in expositions of theology; their aim was to create a mood. Sermons stressed the obligation to rule out all selfish ambitions and to live a life dominated by Christ. To become transformed in Christ's image was the goal. All other ambitions were vain strivings; only in seeking Godlikeness, said one speaker, could one achieve abundant fulfillment. Bishop William McDowell told the Volunteers that God was standing before them waiting for each of them to take himself and all his powers and his sense of obligation up into unconquerable resolution and cry for time and for eternity, for weal or for woe, "*I will*." In 1906 Robert E. Speer pleaded before the Volunteers:

> I simply ask in this opening hour, quietly, each one alone, to forget everybody else, to be just as though Christ and you were alone here in this hall together and everything else just silence and emptiness round about us. . . . Would that here, during these first moments, we could realize

that there is the fact—that over against each one of us the Lord is standing, the Lord with a thorn-crowned head and the nail-pierced hands and the pleading voice of His infinite love calling to us, calling. Surely we can almost hear His voice calling to us. How can we hold back from that call?

The inner religious ecstasy of converts demanded that the world be given some outward manifestation of the inward joy. In 1898 the Methodist Bishop of Kentucky, T. U. Dudley, asked his listeners how, if Jesus "had touched my eyes and now I can see, yes, see the good hope that there is for humanity, see the open door and the Father's house and the welcome of the prodigal, and the feasting, and the joy of the universe because sinners are redeemed, how can I help going, that I may bring those that are blind as I was, that He may touch their eyes?"

The Moody revivals injected a new spirit into the evangelical churches. Yet the churches faced serious problems. The intensity of emotions of religious revivals was not easily sustained, and church leaders were well aware that some new challenge was needed. To the religious liberals there was the challenge of harmonizing religious teaching with the new science and with the cause of economic and social justice, but the orthodox and their leader, Dwight L. Moody, simply dismissed science as a new source of heresy and wrote off slums and other social problems as products of sin.

The answer to the problem of avoiding a relapse from revivals into apathy was found in foreign missions. Scores of writers echoed the opinion of the well-known Princeton University professor, Henry Van Dyke, who in 1896 said: "Missions are an absolute necessity, not only for the conversion of the heathen, but also, and much more, for the preservation of the Church. Christianity is a religion that will not keep."[1] The only thing that could save the church from the perils of luxury and materialism, warned one of the commissions at the

[1] Henry Van Dyke, "The Necessity and the Needs of Foreign Missions," *The Outlook.* February 1, 1896, p. 201.

world missionary conference in 1910, was a world-wide plan of conquest that would throw the church back upon God.[2]

Of all programs leaders might have chosen in the hope of perpetuating the vitality that the revivals had given to the churches, none was more in accord with the temper of the times than foreign missions. It was the religious counterpart of the new political forces that were stirring men's souls. The new generation of Americans was looking outward, and it was the young converts who directed Moody's revival campaigns from the goal of saving America to saving the world. Mott, Speer, and Eddy were contemporaries of the businessman with an eye to foreign markets and of the new statesman with an irrepressible urge to cast the weight of American influence onto the scales of international power politics. All felt the lure of playing life's role on the world stage.

The missionary movement was dependent on large-scale financial support. Its success required a climate of opinion in which missions could be linked to more earthly considerations than becoming inebriated with the Holy Spirit. From 1890 to 1917 the task was not difficult. Humanitarianism, nationalism, and imperialism had taken hold of the popular imagination; all three set up goals that the missionary movement could be interpreted as furthering. These cultural and political considerations explain in large part why the missionary movement gained the public support it did after 1890.

Missionary fervor reached a high water mark during the imperial years after 1890 and the first two decades of the twentieth century. New organizations were launched, the number of missionaries multiplied many times over, and missionary propaganda reached flood proportions. Conversion of the heathen became a part of the American credo and served as a vent for the pent up idealism of the younger generation.

The perfect embodiment of this new missionary enthusiasm was Robert Wilder, son of a former missionary to India. As a student at Princeton the younger Wilder sought to form a

---

[2] *Report of Commission I: Carrying the Gospel to All the Non-Christian World, Vol. I of World Missionary Conference, 1910* (New York: Fleming H. Revell Company, 1910), p. 46.

national organization of students committed to becoming foreign missionaries. That he should have been possessed by an enthusiasm for missions was not strange. Evangelical zeal for the heathen was a family passion. His father, for many years a missionary in India, had recently returned to Princeton to edit the *Missionary Review of the World* in the hope of freshening the springs of missionary enthusiasm at home. His sister, Grace, had organized a student missionary society while a student at Mount Holyoke College. In the Wilder household the ordinary mundane concerns of life had been pushed into a remote orbit, and all that mattered was the state of one's soul. Conditioned to believe that the richest and happiest experiences were religious revivals where the Holy Spirit made itself felt, Robert Wilder had only one purpose in life, a passion to bring to everyone the world over a knowledge of the power of Christian faith to free men's souls from the earthly bondage of sin and make of them vessels of God's spirit.

Robert Wilder and a group of young religious enthusiasts won over Dwight L. Moody to the idea of inviting a group of 200 college and seminary students to Northfield, Massachusetts, in the summer of 1886 for the purpose of Bible study. Northfield, the birthplace of Moody, had already become the summer capital of Protestant evangelicalism. Wilder was determined to use the occasion for making the missionary society he had founded at Princeton intercollegiate in scope. At every opportunity he and the other nine students from Princeton talked about missions and finally he called a meeting to be devoted to missions. The meeting, at which three missionaries' children, two Oriental students, four Europeans, and one American Indian spoke, came to be known as the "Meeting of Ten Nations." Indifference toward missions was now converted into the great issue confronting the church. Before the conference adjourned, one hundred had dedicated themselves to becoming foreign missionaries. Overflowing with enthusiasm, the students decided to send four of their number on a tour of colleges to awaken them to Christ's command to go and preach to all nations. The four first named found they were unable to go but Robert Wilder and John Forman, another missionary's son, went.

In July 1888, at another meeting at Northfield, the Student Volunteer Movement for Foreign Missions was formally organized. Because practically all of the students present were members of the Young Men's Christian Association, the Young Women's Christian Association, or the Inter-Seminary Missionary Alliance, it was decided that the administration of the Movement should be in the hands of an executive committee of three, one to be named by each of the three organizations. The first named were John R. Mott, Robert Wilder, and Nettie Dunn. This committee almost immediately established the practice of having three secretaries, one to travel, one to handle correspondence, and a third to take care of editorial work.[3]

The Volunteer Movement achieved immediate success. Interest in missions sprang naturally out of the religious excitement stirred up by revivals. Across the land Dwight L. Moody, A. J. Gordon, and A. T. Pierson had called on church people to pray for an outpouring of the Holy Spirit which would enable them to make a complete surrender to God. In this spirit of consecration, becoming a candidate for the foreign mission field seemed the ultimate denial of self. Here at last the restless soul would find freedom from selfish ambition and complete identification with the divine purpose. In such a climate of religious opinion the success of the Volunteers was assured.

No more appropriate time could have been chosen for the organization of the Volunteers. Several colleges had already become centers of missionary activity. A student missionary group had been organized at Oberlin, and the first members of the Oberlin band had gone to China as early as 1881. The American Inter-Seminary Missionary Alliance was organized in 1880. In the resolutions adopted at its organizational meeting were many of the phrases which later became watchwords of the Movement, "the opening doors of Eastern Empires," "the greatest enterprise that any age has inaugurated," "the

[3] *Report of the First International Convention of the Student Volunteer Movement for Foreign Missions held at Cleveland, Ohio, February 26, 27, 28, and March 1, 1891* (Boston: T. O. Metcalf and Company, 1891), p. 24. Hereafter cited as *Report of Student Volunteer Convention of 1891.*

reclaiming of the world for Christ."[4] A new sense of urgency was felt. In 1883 Robert Wilder organized the Princeton Foreign Missionary Society. If any doubts about the possibility of arousing interest disturbed the founders of the Volunteers in 1888, they were soon dismissed. Wilder and Forman recruited 650 members the first year. Many years later Wilder recalled: "It seemed as if the only thing needed in a college was to strike a match and the whole college blazed up with enthusiasm for the evangelization of the world."[5]

The Volunteers soon became active throughout the forty-eight states. In the very early years their greatest success came in the Middle West. Of the 6,200 listed in the directory of the organization between 1888 and 1891, more than half came from the area between the Alleghenies and the Rockies and north of the Ohio River. In 1892 Ohio had more volunteers in its colleges than any other state, a fact to be explained in part by the many denominational colleges within its borders, including such prominent centers as Oberlin, Wooster, and Ohio Wesleyan. But the movement was one of national scope. In 1904 the first five states in terms of Student Volunteers were Illinois, Massachusetts, Pennsylvania, New York, and Iowa. The Pacific coast states had 348 members by 1904, and the southern states had almost 1,000 members.[6]

The Student Volunteers led all other missionary organizations in creating enthusiasm. Most of the societies founded in later years came into being as a result of the work of Volunteers. It sent out no missionaries on its own but helped make available thousands of students to denominational missionary boards. By carefully avoiding competition with the established societies and seeking to arouse a public interest in missions helpful to these groups, it was able to gain support from most of the denominations. To some extent its success was based upon its close affiliation with the Young Men's Christian Association, the Young Women's Christian Association, and the

---

[4] William M. Beahm, "Factors in the Development of the Student Volunteer Movement for Foreign Missions" (Unpublished Ph.D. dissertation, Divinity School, University of Chicago, 1941), p. 36.

[5] *Ibid.*, p. 81.　　[6] *Ibid.*, p. 114.

Allied Seminaries Association. Officially it was an agent of these three groups which named the governing board. However, it gained such strength as to be able to carry on its crusade without depending on these three groups for support.

It was also fortunate in that, unlike many associations of the crusader type, it had at its head John R. Mott, a man with the zeal of a reformer but also blessed with great administrative ability, who was able to reconcile conflicting points of view. A young student from Scotland, John A. Mackay, after a brief interview with Mott in 1914 later recalled the awe with which he had met him: "I then understood what another young man felt when he came from an interview with that solemn and majestic figure with the impressive head and shaggy eyebrows, 'It was like being in to see God.' " Mott served as Chairman from the earliest years until his retirement in the 1930's. During all those years he was one of the most popular speakers to college students. His idealism and sincerity gained him respect and admiration long after his own causes had given way to the reforms of a new college generation, reforms too secular for him and beyond the range of his vision.

The Student Volunteers were the dynamo which set the whole organized denominational machinery of American Protestantism into motion in behalf of missions. It did far more than recruit missionaries; it was the chief promotional agency in the missionary movement. At the time of its organization, few ministers showed any enthusiasm for foreign missions, the young people knew almost nothing about the enterprise, and laymen were almost wholly indifferent. The Volunteers aimed at making every minister a zealous exponent and every church an active missionary society. Military terminology, so often employed by speakers at Volunteer Conventions, helped express this ideal of a church in arms. The Rev. A. T. Pierson, speaking before the first Convention, declared:

> This is a council of war. In the tent of the Commander we are gathered, and the Commander-in-chief is here. Here are his subordinates, the heads of departments, the under captains, and here are the volunteers in the army.

And the question for consideration is, How can the marching orders of this invisible Captain be carried out promptly and energetically?[7]

In this state of mind the Volunteers set forth to put the Protestant churches into battle array.

Indoctrination of college students received the first priority. By 1893 John R. Mott was able to report that the Volunteers had started a series of regular monthly missionary meetings in about 200 institutions. In addition the local Volunteer bands were holding weekly meetings for the study of missions. A few years before there had been only ten such study groups in the United States and Canada but by 1893 there were 136.[8] Outlines and textbooks for these classes were provided by the Volunteers. After 1900 the number of these indoctrination classes increased rapidly. By 1910 there were 2,084 with 25,208 students enrolled. Four years later there were more than 40,000 students.[9]

The Volunteers likewise set out to enlist the support of young people in the churches. Since the Civil War the major denominations had each developed a youth movement, and every local church had its Epworth League, Christian Endeavor Society, Young People's Union, or an equivalent. The Student Volunteers were determined to win these organizations over to the missionary cause. Small groups of Volunteers devoted their summers, and in some cases an entire year, to visiting churches. In June 1895, Horace Pitkin called on the leaders of Volunteer bands to "burn in the imperative need of using the opportunity of this summer. . . . We are to be missionaries *now*." The Yale

[7] *Report of Student Volunteer Convention of 1891*, p. 81.

[8] *The Student Missionary Enterprise: Addresses and Discussions of the Second International Convention of the Student Volunteer Movement for Foreign Missions Held at Detroit, February 28 to March 4, 1894* (New York: Fleming H. Revell Company, 1894), pp. 71-72. Hereafter cited as *Report of Student Volunteer Convention of 1894*.

[9] *Students and the Present Missionary Crisis: Addresses Delivered Before the Sixth International Convention of the Student Volunteer Movement for Foreign Missions, Rochester, New York, December 29, 1909, to January 2, 1910* (New York: Student Volunteer Movement for Foreign Missions, 1910), p. 21.

band sent out five students for a year. They "visited 70 cities, addressed 884 meetings and held 364 missionary conferences at which some 2,000 young people's societies were represented. They influenced 241 of these societies to organize missionary committees, 579 to secure a collection of missionary books, 392 to undertake missionary study, 518 to adopt a plan of systematic giving and 757 to use a missionary prayer cycle." In one summer the Volunteer band at Denison University visited 209 churches in Ohio and West Virginia. A member of the band at Northwestern University travelled 1,344 miles in thirty-two days during which time he gave missionary addresses in twenty-four churches, organized sixteen new missionary committees, started five missionary libraries, and sold missionary literature. The direct result of the Volunteers' activity in the churches was the organization of the Young Peoples' Missionary Movement in 1902, an organization which became an important agency in its own right.

In making available books on missionary topics at low cost the Student Volunteers did much to enlighten the public as to conditions in heathen lands, the problems encountered by missionaries, and the needs of the enterprise. Between 1898 and 1902 more than 100,000 copies of Volunteer literature were sold. In 1906 alone three of their textbooks sold over 20,000 copies.

The promotion of missionary interest at home received a great deal of emphasis but it was never permitted to become the primary function. From the first the major task of the Volunteer Movement was deemed to be the recruiting of missionaries. During the first eight years of its existence 686 Volunteers went to foreign fields. Others were preparing to go in unprecedented numbers. In 1894 there were three times as many men in the colleges expecting to be missionaries as there had been in 1886. By 1914, almost 6,000 had gone out as missionaries. Of these, 1,739 had gone to China.[10]

[10] *Students and the World-Wide Expansion of Christianity: Addresses Delivered Before the Seventh International Convention of the Student Volunteer Movement for Foreign Missions, Kansas City, Missouri, December 31, 1913, to January 4, 1914* (New York: Student Volunteer Movement

The Crusade at Home

The spectacular success of the Student Volunteers in the colleges was matched by a remarkable growth of missionary fervor among young people in the local churches. Missionary boards set up courses and suggested programs to tap their interest in far-off places. The Women's Foreign Missionary Society of the Methodists organized a whole hierarchy of societies for the youngest to the oldest—Little Light Bearer Circles, King's Heralds, and Standard Bearers. In several denominations the young people's societies gave over one meeting each month to a missionary subject.

The crusaders organized the Young People's Missionary Movement in 1902. Six years later more than 100,000 were enrolled in its mission study courses.[11] In one year alone it sold 143,592 textbooks and thousands of charts, maps, and pamphlets. Each summer it sponsored conferences where leaders were trained in the most effective ways of promoting missions. Large public expositions depicting native scenes, costumes, home life, religious practices, and recreation in heathen lands were one of the many facets of the program. From 3,000 to 15,-000 persons a day saw the Boston exhibits in 1911.

The new enthusiasm manifested by young people stirred the men in the churches into action. In 1906 a young business man from Washington, D.C., John B. Sleaman, attended the convention of the Student Volunteers in Nashville, Tennessee. Profoundly impressed by the willingness of students to dedicate their lives to the missionary cause, Sleaman concluded that the laymen ought to support the cause financially and take an active part in promoting missions. At an interdenominational missionary meeting in New York in November 1906, an invitation was extended to meet the next day for "A Call to Prayer." Here the need for laymen's support was presented, and the

---

for Foreign Missions, 1914), p. 18. Hereafter cited as *Report of the Student Volunteer Convention of 1914.*

11 *World-Wide Evangelization, The Urgent Business of the Church: Addresses Delivered Before the Fourth International Convention of the Student Volunteer Movement for Foreign Missions* (New York: Student Volunteer Movement, 1902), p. 47. Hereafter cited as *Report of Student Volunteer Convention of 1902.*

Laymen's Missionary Movement was organized.[12] Those present resolved to consult with the secretaries of the denominational boards with reference to a campaign to educate laymen, a comprehensive plan for "the sending of the Gospel to the entire non-Christian world during the next twenty-five years," and to form a Centennial Commission of Laymen to visit the mission fields.

In the course of the next fifteen years the Laymen's Movement made foreign missions a matter of respectability, civic and Christian duty, and even patriotism. The General Secretary, J. Campbell White, later President of the College of Wooster, called for investigation, agitation, and organization for the purpose of "enlisting the whole Church in the supreme work of saving the world." "Practicability and business-like administration," said White, must now be introduced into missions.[13]

The Laymen's Movement sponsored the National Missionary Campaign in 1909 and 1910. Seventy-five conventions were held in cities throughout the country with a total attendance of 71,000 registered delegates. The campaign reached its climax in a great convention in Chicago. "Here is a new sort of missionary meeting," wrote Lyman Abbott, editor of *The Outlook*. Leading business men in front and filling the ranks, observed Abbott, paid their own traveling expenses and a five dollar registration fee.

In 1913 the Laymen organized and directed the United Campaign for Home and Foreign Missions. Twenty teams of speakers, with four men on each team, were organized to conduct two-day conferences. The aim of these conferences was twofold: to educate laymen to the importance of missions and to prepare the way for general adoption of the "every member canvass" plan for raising funds. During the autumn of 1915 and the first few months of 1916, seventy-five conventions were held with a total registration of over 100,000.[14] The campaign

[12] *Interdenominational Conference of Foreign Missionary Boards and Societies in the United States and Canada* (New York: E. O. Jenkins' Sons' Printing House, 1893), p. 3.

[13] *Ibid.*

[14] *Students and the Modern Missionary Crusade: Addresses Delivered*

came to a climax with the Laymen's Missionary Congress in Washington, D.C., in April 1916. The editor of *The Missionary Review of the World* observed that the delegates were "men of large influence and big business responsibilities; manufacturers, merchants, lawyers, brokers, bankers, physicians, professors, editors, and heads of corporations."

Missionary leaders and clergy expressed greater enthusiasm over the support of businessmen than they did over the student volunteers who had dedicated their lives to the cause. Moreover, the leaders could not afford to ignore the affluent who were in a position to make generous gifts. In the 1890's missionary boards were heavily in debt and lack of money was the chief obstacle to expansion. When contributions increased, the Laymen's Missionary Movement received much of the credit. In 1905, the year before the organization of the laymen, contributions totalled $8,120,725; in 1915 they had risen to $18,-793,990.[15] The laymen undoubtedly accounted for a considerable part of the increase. Leaders of the Laymen's Movement frequently expressed the opinion that it would take $45 million to staff the mission fields adequately. At times so much emphasis was placed on fund raising that the impression was left that the only serious obstacle to the evangelization of the world was the lack of necessary funds. Even the support of some of the wealthiest men in America failed to remove the obstacle. The employees of these churchmen, who were receiving an average weekly wage in 1900 of less than $13 for a fifty-nine hour week, had little left over for the needs of the heathen.

The other major attempt to enlist the full support of laymen was the Men and Religion Movement. This campaign differed from the Laymen's Movement in that it aimed at giving glad tidings to the poor at home as well as abroad. Surveys of important urban centers were made for the purpose of bringing to light the harsh facts of the new industrial order. Raymond Robins, a man of considerable wealth who believed that the

Before the Fifth International Convention of the Student Volunteer Movement for Foreign Missions (New York: Student Volunteer Movement, 1906), p. 46.

15 *The Missionary Review of the World,* May 1908, p. 381.

relations between capital and labor should be democratized, was in charge of the social service aspect of the movement. His fiery speeches before large mass meetings aroused the fear of vested interests, for temporarily it seemed as if the church was embarked on a crusade to Christianize the economic and social order. When the survey in Hartford, Connecticut, had been completed, one enthusiast wrote an article entitled "In Hartford As It Is in Heaven." The Men and Religion Movement also gave considerable attention to foreign missions, and in this realm, too, Christian perfectionism was the dominant note. The commission on missions urged that every local church became a "center of intelligent interest and self-sacrificing effort on behalf of this inspiring missionary objective."[16] In this case the "inspiring missionary objective" was not simply evangelization. It was now maintained that it was the duty of concerned laymen to Christianize every phase of the Western impact upon the rest of the world. In its final report the commission observed:

> You cannot go out to the East and preach one doctrine to it by the lives of your missionaries, and another doctrine to it by the lives of your merchants. You cannot go out to the East and without great difficulty teach it a theoretical message which is not confirmed in the actual diplomacy and conduct of the Western peoples. In the interest of Christianity and our missionary enterprise, we must penetrate with Christian principle all those forms of our conduct with the non-Christian world with which, for good or ill, our Christian impact is inseparably intertwined.

Women's missionary societies had been organized just after the Civil War and before 1890 had furnished the bulk of financial support. With the general increase in fervor at the turn of the century, the women's societies took on new life. The Federation of Women's Boards of Foreign Missions launched

[16] *Report of Commission VI: The Home Base of Missions, Vol. VI of World Missionary Conference, 1910* (New York: Fleming H. Revell Co., 1910), p. 183.

a large scale publishing program in 1901 and sold a half million books in the next eight years. Interest reached its highest peak in the winter of 1910–1911 with the interdenominational Woman's Missionary Jubilee campaign. Women "caught missions as children catch the measles," wrote an enthusiastic reporter. Mass meetings, elaborate luncheons in the best hotels, drawing-room meetings in the homes of the rich and socially elite attracted thousands.[17] Missions received the benefit in the form of record-breaking donations. The Methodist women, who in 1890 had worked hard to raise $200,000, passed the million dollar mark in 1914.

The rapid growth of the missionary movement caused denominational boards to create the Conference of Foreign Mission Boards as early as 1893. This agency helped to coordinate the work of the many societies both at home and in the foreign field, encouraged the preparation of missionary literature, promoted courses in missions in theological seminaries, and brought the point of view of the churches on questions of foreign policy before the Department of State. One of its early achievements was the calling of the Ecumenical Conference held in New York in April, 1900. More than 3,000 delegates attended the ten-day series of meetings. Former President Harrison presided over one of the meetings where President William McKinley and Governor Theodore Roosevelt spoke.

When the "Meeting of Ten Nations" took place at Northfield in 1886, missions had the support of only a scattered few in the churches. In 1917 the extension of Christianity was generally accepted as a primary function of the church. Forty-eight per cent of the churches had missionary committees, forty-two per cent had mission study classes, and in fully one-third practically every member contributed.[18] In China there were more than twice as many societies carrying on religious activities as there had been twenty-five years earlier.[19]

---

[17] William T. Ellis, *Men and Missions* (Philadelphia: The Sunday School Times Co., 1909), p. 73.

[18] Delavan L. Pierson, "The Men's Congress of Missions When Twelve Hundred Laymen Took Washington by Storm," *The Missionary Review of the World,* June 1916, p. 419.

[19] *Ibid.*

CHAPTER V

MISSIONS AND HUMANITARIANISM,
NATIONALISM,
AND IMPERIALISM, 1890-1917

In 1910 Lyman Abbott attributed the new enthusiasm for missions to the fact that the missionary movement had been freed from the "grim doctrine of an endless hell for the unreclaimed heathen" and was now devoting itself to the introduction of a humane social order. The changing emphasis was very much a recent phenomenon for as late as the 1880's a candidate before the American Board of Commissioners for Foreign Missions was told that he must be as sure of the eternal punishment of the unconverted as he was of God; that to eliminate fear of eternal punishment was to cut "the nerve of missions."[1] Speaking before the Student Volunteers at Detroit in 1894, Hudson Taylor, founder of the China Inland Mission, pleaded:

> The gospel must be preached to these people in a very short time, for they are passing away. Every day, every day, oh how they sweep over! . . . There is a great Niagara of souls passing into the dark in China. Every day, every week, every month they are passing away! A million a month in China are dying without God![2]

A liberal group of Congregationalists, in the 1880's, revolted against the idea that the heathen, who had never heard the gospel, would nevertheless be held responsible. They now put forth the theory of future probation, teaching that those who had never heard of Christ might be offered the gospel sometime after their death when they would have another opportunity

[1] Lyman Abbott, *Reminiscences* (Boston: Houghton Mifflin Company, 1915), p. 473.

[2] *The Student Missionary Enterprise: Addresses and Discussions of the Second International Convention of the Student Volunteer Movement for Foreign Missions* (New York: Fleming H. Revell Company, 1894), p. 48.

to gain salvation. In this way they were able to reconcile their humanitarian sympathies and democratic sentiments against arbitrariness with their proclaimed adherence to the Bible as the supreme authority.

The orthodox party, who retained control of the American Board, rejected all missionary candidates who held to the theory of future probation. Led by the secretary of the board, Dr. E. K. Alden, the orthodox maintained that "future probation" was not Biblical and that any such theory made missions much less urgent. While denying future probation, the orthodox contended that a few heathen, although they had not heard of Christ, might have lived in harmony with Christ's teaching and be saved.[3]

There was more to this difference of opinion than met the eye. The progressive Congregationalists were adjusting their theology to changing fashions of thought. While they did not deny the authority of the Bible, they opened the door to significant revisions of theological dogma by according equal authority to "Christian consciousness," which they defined as the common feeling of the most enlightened and pious men in any age.[4] In this way they allowed for change from age to age as experience, learning, and piety cast new light on the true meaning of Christ's teachings. Thus did the "progressive orthodox" lower the sluice gate and into the stagnant water eventually flowed, as the conservatives had feared, all the new currents of thought.

From 1886 to 1893 this controversy dominated the annual meetings of the American Board. The liberals made no headway at the meeting in Des Moines in 1886. At the next annual meeting in Springfield, Massachusetts, it was apparent that the debate had boiled over into personal animosity and bickering. Leaders of both sides, proud and sensitive of their positions

[3] For a discussion of this controversy see David Everett Swift, "Conservative Versus Progressive Orthodoxy in Latter 19th Century Congregationalism," *Church History*, March 1947, pp. 22-31.

[4] Robert H. Wilcox, "The Ultimate Criteria of Christian Doctrine," *The Andover Review*, October 1887, pp. 345-346.

before their constituencies, connived in the very spirit of Satan in *Paradise Lost* as he set out to capture heaven.

Finally at the annual meeting in Worcester in 1893, Doctor Alden and two orthodox members of the Prudential Committee resigned. A resolution was passed that the committee for the nomination of new members should receive nominations from the various organizations of Congregational churches. The Board now became a denominational agency and therefore came to reflect the more liberal opinions that had gained ascendancy in the denomination.[5]

The future destiny of the heathen never became a matter of such controversy in the other denominations. Their missionary boards were more closely integrated into the denominational machinery. As opinion gradually changed in the churches, the missionary societies quietly moved toward the new view. Eternal punishment received literally no attention in the missionary literature after the turn of the century. In 1910 a commission reporting to the World Missionary Conference at Edinburgh found that among both volunteers and contributors in the United States, few seemed to have been influenced by the thought that the heathen would go to hell.[6] In fact, by 1910 Robert E. Speer, one of the chief spokesmen for missions, charged that the idea that missionaries were motivated by the thought of saving the heathen from damnation was an invention of the scornful stay-at-homes and that missionaries had never been primarily moved by this consideration.[7] Nothing demonstrates more clearly how unpopular the idea had become than this attempt to absolve all present and past advocates of having used this argument.

To gain support for missions it was necessary to adjust theology to popular sentiment—and apparently the public had developed such an aversion toward damnation that, while they

[5] Editorial, "Worcester Meeting of the American Board," *The Andover Review,* November 1893, pp. 715-717.

[6] *Report of Commission VI: The Home Base of Missions, Vol. VI of World Missionary Conference, 1910* (New York: Fleming H. Revell Company, 1910), pp. 133-134.

[7] Robert E. Speer, *Christianity and the Nations* (New York: Fleming H. Revell Company, 1910), p. 33.

did not want the Chinese to come to California, neither did they want them to go to hell. Yet, there were those like William Owen Carver, a southern Baptist theological professor, who, as late as 1910, confessed that he could find no satisfactory explanation as to how any other fate could await men who did not gain salvation through the gospel. Carver admitted that the changed concept of the nature of God and his relation to the world and to humanity had cooperated with the concept of religious evolution to discredit the notion that men who die out of Christ are doomed to death eternal.[8] Theology and public sentiment seem to have been partly at cross purposes, but theology was also adjusting itself to new currents of thought and few theologians found it difficult to believe that the heathen would be spared damnation.

The new emphasis was in accord with the rapidly developing humanitarianism of early twentieth-century America. Jacob Riis, crusading for children's playgrounds in New York, and Jane Addams, working to improve the conditions of immigrants on Chicago's west side, symbolized the movement to uplift the downtrodden. The popularity of Progressivism with its emphasis on the dignity of man, human welfare, and the possibility of progress is indicative of the spirit of optimism which prevailed. Missionary leaders were in tune with the age when they dropped the emphasis on hell and stressed the spiritual and physical benefits of the Christian gospel. It was their belief in the power of the gospel to emancipate men from degrading superstition and to introduce a higher concept of life that gave them a sense of urgency concerning foreign missions.

The turning point between the old stress on snatching the heathen from the jaws of hell, and the new view of missions as a humanitarian agency, was the publication in 1897 of the Rev. James S. Dennis' three-volume work *Christian Missions and Social Progress: A Sociological Study of Foreign Missions.*[9]

[8] William Owen Carver, *Missions and Modern Thought* (New York: The Macmillan Co., 1910), pp. 13-14.

[9] James S. Dennis, *Christian Missions and Social Progress: A Sociological Study of Foreign Missions* (New York: Fleming H. Revell Company).

The author had been a missionary in Syria. His book purported to be a sociological study of the role of missions, and much of the tremendous prestige it enjoyed was undoubtedly due to its supposedly scientific nature. The book had a scintillating tone of modernity and of authority, and it was welcomed by missionary enthusiasts as the definitive statement on missions.

Dennis described missions as a factor in the social regeneration of the world. The aims of foreign missions were to elevate human society, modify traditional evils, and introduce reformatory ideals. Underlying Dennis' approach to missions lay the assumption that Christianity had been the supreme force in the social regeneration and elevation of the Western world. Christian countries were different, said Dennis, in that while they were not free from evil there was a spirit of protest against all that degraded human personality. Among the heathen, dishonesty, thievery, vulgarity, and cruel customs not only prevailed but they were accepted and unchallenged. The task of Christian missions was to introduce a spirit of regeneration and a Christian conscience which would protest against moral laxity and social injustice. This would inevitably lead, in the case of China, to the abolition of the binding of little girls' feet, the granting of equality to women, the sharp censuring of those who were dishonest, and the lifting of life to a higher level. He believed that this spirit of regeneration could only be introduced as individuals were won over to Christianity.

Dennis' study, embodying the new view of missions, gained him a wide reputation. He was called upon to lecture at theological seminaries, and writers on missionary topics spoke of him as the authority on missions. He was elected to the Presbyterian Board of Foreign Missions and in 1910 was one of its representatives at the World Missionary Conference in Edinburgh. The recognition bestowed upon Dennis was in considerable part a tribute to the social view of missions.

The new view had many spokesmen after 1900. Speer declared: "The world needs to be saved from want and disease and injustice and inequality and impurity and lust and hopelessness and fear, . . ."[10] During the days of the Spanish-Ameri-

[10] Robert E. Speer, *op. cit.*, p. 29.

can War, John R. Mott asked "Where is the war?" and then proceeded to define it as a war against social evils around the globe.[11] In 1900 the most well-known of all missionary writers on China, Arthur H. Smith, told his American readers that Christianity could improve the position of the girl in the family, show Chinese parents how to train as well as how to govern their children, improve education, create an intellectual atmosphere in the home, abolish polygamy and concubinage, purify and sweeten the home, and promote patriotism.[12] The former president of Ohio Wesleyan University, Bishop J. W. Bashford, asked how Christians, when they saw "the unevangelized peoples of the earth . . . living in poverty and disease and ignorance and sin" could refrain from offering them "the key which will open to them the divine storehouse.[13] By 1915, one missionary leader on the home front looked back on the change in missionary emphases and noted:

> One of the most marked changes taking place in the foreign mission propaganda during the last century has been the shift of emphasis from the individual to society. The social aspect of Christianity was not given due recognition at home or abroad a generation ago. It is not strange therefore that while the missionaries were promoting great, sweeping social movements, international in character and fundamental in reach, they did not recognize them as such, but continued there as we did here to put supreme emphasis upon individual conversion.[14]

It is clear that Dennis, Speer, Mott, and the other leaders of the missionary movement were advocates of a program where-

[11] John R. Mott, "What of the War?" *The Student Missionary Appeal: Addresses at the Third International Convention of the Student Volunteer Movement for Foreign Missions* (Cleveland: Fleming H. Revell Company, 1898), p. 274.

[12] Arthur H. Smith, *Village Life in China: A Study in Sociology* (New York: Fleming H. Revell Company, 1899), pp. 342-345.

[13] J. W. Bashford, *God's Missionary Plan for the World* (New York: Eaton and Mains, 1907), pp. 44-45.

[14] James L. Barton, "The Modern Missionary," *Harvard Theological Review,* January 1915, p. 6.

by conversion of the heathen was gradually becoming a means to an end, namely an improved society.

Thus a new emphasis, more in harmony with current American humanitarianism, had replaced the traditional concern with rescuing the heathen from damnation. Yet, while the final aim had been readjusted to the climate of opinion in the United States, the means had remained the same. The goal of social regeneration was to be reached by conversion of individuals to Christianity. In this respect the new missionary program was true to tradition. It involved no sharp break with the past to the degree that the Social Gospel did at home. Speer, who did more to formulate the new program and to win it adherents than anyone else, argued strongly against seeking to introduce Western institutions. To him, the backwardness of heathendom was not so much a product of heathen institutions as it was due to the absence of a Christian spirit within these institutions. His prescription called for changing Chinese society by changing individual men.[15]

This approach had a tepid quality from the point of view of those who looked forward impatiently to a new social order. They had come to the conclusion that there could be no significant improvement in China until the institutions and customs that shaped men to be slaves of disease, ignorance, and exploitation were replaced. But there were very few missionaries who went this far in their thinking about the social evils they encountered. Not until 1912 did any missionary or any advocate of missions espouse any all-out social reform program. In that year a missionary in China, the Reverend H. K. Wright, wrote—apologetically—that there was no contradiction between the Scriptural views of individual salvation and of social salvation. Going a step further, he maintained that the social views

[15] Speer wrote: "The West and Western nations, which owe all their good to Christianity, are under a heavy debt to the rest of the world, which it is not the function of the Christian church to discharge. It is the function of the Christian Church to inspire the Christian nations to do justice and to give help to the non-Christian nations, but there are many great and truly Christian services with which the foreign missionary enterprise is not charged. They are to be rendered through other forms of international relationship." *Christianity and the Nations*, p. 57.

found in the Bible led to religious work in behalf of social and economic amelioration and regeneration and sometimes of revolution. Too much missionary work in education and missions, he observed, had been "a mere exhibition of Christianity, or a clinic in which mental objections to it could be removed." Missionaries had acquiesced in a social system that allowed the existence of coolies, "beings beside whose position that of the American slaves was enviable." Or, if any note was taken of these miserable souls, missionaries had usually said, " 'Be ye warmed and fed with the Gospel,' not stopping to consider that Christianity is for beings in their position a simply impossible thing." Wright thought that China must change, that missionaries must help in providing leadership, and that they would do well to examine the proposals of the Christian Socialists.[16]

Missionaries who held such aims for the missionary movement were certainly rare, and among active supporters of missions at home there is no record that any held such views. This does not alter the fact that the missionary program was humanitarian in emphasis, a fact largely responsible for its widespread public support, including the praise of leaders outside of the church.

Edward Alsworth Ross, the eminent sociologist, found much to praise in missionary work after a trip to China. He wrote of the influence of mission schools on the new government educational system, of the advance of female education, and of the influence of missionary translations of the great books of Western learning. Ross thought that the achievements of the missionary were not to be counted in the number of Christian converts but in the changed attitudes toward opium-smoking, foot-binding, concubinage, slavery, "squeeze," torture, and the subjection of women.[17] He observed that what the missionary was teaching was not so much the gospel but Western

16 H. K. Wright, "The Social Message and Christian Missions," *The Chinese Recorder*, March 1912, pp. 147-155.

17 Edward Alsworth Ross, *The Changing Chinese: The Conflict of Oriental and Western Cultures in China* (New York: The Century Company, 1911), p. 245.

ideas of right and wrong. Another sociologist, Franklin Henry Giddings, spoke of the Christian missionary enterprise as devoting itself to the diffusion of knowledge, to the improvement of conditions, and to the upbuilding of character and considered it one of the most important factors in uniting the classes and the races of men in a spiritual humanity.[18] That the humanitarian motive struck a responsive chord in large parts of the population is also attested to by the many endorsements of missions by American presidents and diplomats.

Humanitarian aims were dominant in the missionary literature of the day. There seems to be little reason to question the sincerity of missionary enthusiasts in proclaiming that their only motive was to help the Chinese. They believed that Christianity accounted for what they considered the superiority of Western, and particularly American, society. To them this superiority was manifested in a greater concern for human life, in the rights of women, in free public education, in the treatment of children, and in superior moral virtues. They were more than willing, they were anxious, to supplant Chinese ethical systems and native religions with their Western counterparts. In attributing the supposed superior advantages of the West wholly to Christianity, they simplified the history of the West to fit their own predilections. In concluding that Western institutions were superior, they measured institutions against a set of values that was also a product of Western history. In assuming that Western institutions could be engrafted on an Oriental civilization, they did not anticipate the "culture concept"—a concept that was then only beginning to develop in the minds of historians, anthropologists, and other scholars concerned with human affairs. All of this is easy to understand in a generation brimming over with confidence. And it must be said that missionaries were not unique in this confidence in the universal application of Christianity and democracy—most Americans seem to have shared this faith.

The second great appeal employed in developing an interest in missions to China related to American nationalism. How

18 Franklin Henry Giddings, *The Principles of Sociology* (New York: The Macmillan Company, 1928), p. 360.

Christian missionary work in China was made to fit in with American self-interest may not be apparent at first but it was a consideration that is prominent in the missionary propaganda.

When missionaries first went to China from the United States, individual heathen were the focal point rather than China as a nation. Once the missionary program envisaged the regeneration of Chinese society, there developed an interest in the future of China as a country. The salvation of individual Chinese was linked to the progress of the nation, its political reform, and most important, to the question of what kind of a China would eventually emerge. That China was changing was clear, and to the highly nationalistic Americans who viewed China through paternal eyes there was no little uneasiness concerning China's future. That she would be powerful, no one doubted. Whether the new China would be a force for peace, democracy, and world brotherhood or a yellow dragon employing Western technology and her vast human resources to destroy Western civilization was considered an open question.

The question of China's future role made possible the dramatizing of the missionary enterprise as the agency determining the fate not only of isolated individuals but of a whole nation. A picture of four hundred million Chinese caught in the throes of revolutionary change excited the most prosaic of imaginations. Observing the changes in China after 1900 one writer described what was happening as "a political revolution, a moral advance, an intellectual renaissance, a religious reformation, and a nineteenth century of scientific and industrial development all combined."[19]

Missionary leaders anxiously asked what was to be the final outcome as China rushed headlong through the many stages of historical development that had transformed the Western world since the decline of feudalism in the thirteenth century. Marshall Broomhall, a representative of the China Inland Mission, asked the question that was uppermost in the minds

[19] S. Earl Taylor and Halford E. Luccock, *The Christian Crusade For World Democracy* (New York: The Methodist Book Concern, 1918), p. 64.

of Westerners: "Shall Asia experience merely an Intellectual Renaissance or a Spiritual Reformation? Shall the East merely conform to Western scientific principles or be transformed by the renewing of the Holy Spirit?"[20] John R. Mott, leader of the Student Volunteers, described the non-Christian nations as plastic and changing. These nations, he wrote, were examining the West to see what had made it rich and powerful. Should these people fail to see that religion "is the most fundamental thing in our civilization" the result would be moral disaster. This, then, said Mott, was the decisive hour.[21]

Thousands of church-going folk now turned their eyes to the struggle going on in the great China arena. The fetters of ancient thralldom were being sundered by missionaries, commerce, and the forces of the modern world. Would the awakened Chinese dragon emerge from his long sleep only to threaten the world or would he employ his immense powers to further the realization of Western ideals of universal brotherhood and the welfare of mankind? In a book entitled *Our Share in China and What We Are Doing With It*, George J. Bond, a China missionary, held that the "yellow peril" could be avoided if the Christian church did its duty. He wrote: "China is moving indeed, and as Napoleon truly said, she will move the world. But how?"[22] The Methodist Bishop, Charles Henry Fowler, reduced the problem to terms calculated to wrest the most indifferent from apathy. The Bishop told his listeners:

> Her very numbers is God's promise of perpetuity. The Yellow Race will remain the menace of the world. It lies on the shore of Asia, a huge club, only waiting to be picked up by some Hercules. China is the world's problem for the twentieth century. Who will seize this club? . . .
> It is a Bear standing on the trail. His posture does not

[20] Marshall Broomhall, *Present Day Conditions in China* (New York: Fleming H. Revell Company, 1908), pp. 1-2.
[21] John R. Mott, *The Decisive Hour of Christian Missions* (New York: The Student Volunteer Movement for Foreign Missions, 1911), p. 34.
[22] George J. Bond, *Our Share in China and What We Are Doing With It*, p. 27.

change his nature. If Russia appropriates and assimilates China, we are face to face with the most powerful Empire ever known among men. The world problem is this: Shall Russia be allowed to absorb China? This problem is full of dragon's teeth, teeth enough to seed down the world with century-long strifes.[23]

Nor was this opinion confined to the churches. Captain Alfred T. Mahan, noted historian of the influence of sea power in history, took the position that the Western world had a common interest in bringing the Asian peoples within the compass of the family of Christian states: ". . . not by fetters and bonds imposed from without, but by regeneration promoted from within." He warned of danger should China become Westernized technologically without accepting the mental and moral forces "which have generated, and which in large measure govern, our political action."[24] Mahan praised the work of missionaries because he believed they were inculcating the guiding moral principles of the West. A similar view was expressed by a sociologist who held that it was the Bible more than blood that united the English race and that it would unite China with the English race in bonds more deep than those of any political convention.[25] Americans generally looked forward with confidence to China becoming a democratic nation guided by Christian ideals and closely allied with the United States, and they believed that this process would be largely a product of the missionaries, those noncommissioned ambassadors of the great American republic.

The blending of nationalism and enthusiasm for foreign missions found expression in presidential speeches. Theodore Roosevelt called for support of the missionaries because their work helped to avert revolutionary disturbances in China and

[23] Charles Henry Fowler, *Missionary Addresses* (Cincinnati: Jennings and Graham, 1906), pp. 44-45.

[24] Alfred T. Mahan, "Effects of Asiatic Conditions Upon International Policies," *North American Review*, November 1900, p. 615.

[25] Henry William Rankin, "Political Values of the American Missionary," *The American Journal of Sociology*, September 1907, p. 172.

to lead her into a position for peace and righteousness.[26] Collectors of old phonograph records may have discovered William Howard Taft's plea for foreign missions on one side of a recording and an equally strong plea for a stronger army and navy on the other. Taft confessed that he had not realized the immense importance of foreign missions until he went to the Orient, when there was thrust upon him "the responsibilities with reference to the extension of civilization." No man, he thought, could "study the movement of modern civilization from an impartial viewpoint and not realize that Christianity, and the spread of Christianity, are the only basis for hope of modern civilization." He explained that he wished to speak of foreign missions "from the standpoint of political, governmental advancement, the advancement of modern civilization." He thought he had some experience "to know how dependent we are on the spread of Christianity for any hope we may have of uplifting peoples whom Providence has thrust upon us for our guidance." "National altruism of this sort," though not specifically authorized by the Constitution, was not prevented by the Constitution. Taft thought it was clearly the duty of a nation to assist another nation—"the Constitution authorizes it because it is a part of national well being."

Of all the political leaders none manifested a more complete faith in missions than did Woodrow Wilson. Speaking to a group of ministers, Wilson said:

> This is the most amazing and inspiring vision—this vision of that great sleeping nation suddenly awakened by the voice of Christ. Could there be any greater contribution to the future momentum of the moral forces of the world than could be made by quickening this force, which is being set afoot in China? China is at present inchoate; as a nation it is a congeries of parts, in each of which there is energy; but which are unbound in any essential and active unit, and just as soon as unity comes, its

[26] Theodore Roosevelt, "The Awakening of China," *The Outlook*, November 28, 1908, p. 666.

power will come in the world. Should we not see that the parts are fructified by the teachings of Christ?[27]

Wilson's enthusiasm for missions was part and parcel of his whole attitude toward America's role in world affairs. The United States had a duty to lead the world in the ways of peace and righteousness. His strong disapproval of the balance of power system, his refusal to support the bankers because the conditions of their loan to China infringed on the sovereignty of that nation, his promise to the Latin American people in his famous speech at Mobile that they had nothing to fear, all these reflected Wilson's moral approach to foreign policy. A year after he spoke the words quoted above, Wilson led the nation into war on the basis of an idealistic vision of a new order among nations. Wilson's approach to foreign problems and the new missionary zeal were in complete harmony.

The missionary movement's link to the strong nationalism of Americans expressed itself in the belief that China would follow them in the paths of righteousness and become, in turn, a guiding star for humanity at large as it sought the way into the land of Canaan with its promise of brotherhood and the life abundant. The alignment of missions with national self-interest invited support from people who otherwise would have been indifferent. China was not viewed as any immediate threat but there was a deep feeling that sometime in the distant future she would either be a firm and valuable friend or a difficult enemy. Certainly hope outweighed fear. The danger seemed remote and there was never any real alarm. The vision of a friendly and democratic China converted to Christianity provided a stronger motive than any lurking fear of a remote future when a powerful and hostile China might be thrown into the balance against the United States.

Granted that a Christian sense of oughtness inspired the missionary, it is also true that the missionary movement and imperialism were wheels driven by the same explosive energy generated by a sense of superiority, moral duty, and the ego satisfaction to be gained in developing the underdeveloped

[27] *Missionary Review of the World,* February 1916, p. 97.

areas of the world in the image of one's own society. The difference lay not so much in the nature of the generating forces which gave the impetus to the two movements but rather in their aims. American imperialism aimed at a goal circumscribed by a nationalistic faith in American institutions; the missionary movement in general accepted these goals but also, at its best, transcended them and envisioned a world brotherhood where human values would take precedence over national loyalties. Yet, to draw a sharp line between the secular movement of imperialism and the religious movement of the missionary is hazardous, for American imperialism, though economic gain was a basic element in it, owed much to psychological drives. These had their roots in the moralistic tendencies of American life and cannot easily be separated from religious traditions, which help to explain the traditional moralistic fervor.

Missionaries and secular advocates of expansion took similar positions on questions involving China and colonial areas. The German occupation of Shantung was described by one missionary as "doubtless one of the judgments of an all-wise Providence, intended to humble the colossal pride of this nation, and, by showing the utter insufficiency of their present beliefs and methods, lead to an acceptance of Christ and His truth."[28]

When the United States went to war with Spain, the editor of *The Methodist Review* wrote: "We shall be much disappointed if the final outcome of the war does not show that it was one of God's most efficient agencies for the advancement of true Christian civilization and the ushering in of brighter times for the human race." Nor did duty end with the emancipation of the Cubans. During the hostilities, Admiral Dewey had defeated the Spanish naval squadron at Manila and Spanish land forces on the islands had surrendered on August 13, 1898. With the American flag flying over the islands, it was difficult to withdraw. A series of factors combined to make for annexation. Business groups hailed annexation of the

[28] Henry M. Woods, "China—Some Events of the Past Year," *The Missionary Review of the World,* September 1898, p. 684.

islands as the key to the China market. The manifestation of an interest in the islands by Germany whetted the American appetite. Encouragement from leading British statesmen helped overcome any hesitation. Those supporting annexation in the public press felt compelled to justify it in terms of moral responsibility. Charles Denby, former minister to Peking, asked: "Why shall we not take the people of the Philippines kindly by the hand and lead them into the blessed light of perfect freedom?" Denby admitted that "in other lands and other wars the condition of the conquered people has been hard and deplorable" but in "our case we march bearing gifts, the choicest gifts—liberty and hope and happiness." Another writer deplored the terms "imperialism" and "expansion" as used in the debate over the Philippines and preferred the phrase "'extension of civilization' for it expressed the motive and controlling principle of the war and of the treaty by which, when ratified, it is to be concluded." The McKinley administration committed itself to annexation of all the islands while the peace conference was in session in Paris and was adamant when Spain sought to retain the islands. Spain finally yielded. In the Senate a great debate ensued and the treaty was ratified by a margin of only one vote.

In January 1899, Judson Smith, Secretary of the American Board, forwarded to Secretary of State John Hay a series of resolutions adopted by a number of missionaries in China calling for the acquisition of the entire Carolines, Pelew and Ladrone islands. The missionaries contended that the Spanish had never granted religious freedom on these islands and that the natives favored the Americans. They likewise pointed to the value of the islands as bases for a cable line and warned that if the islands should fall into the hands of an enemy, he would have a decisive advantage in the event of war.[29]

After the Boxer Revolt missionaries refrained from interpreting acts of imperialism as acts of God, and a new attitude developed toward indemnities and the old gunboat policy. More and more missionaries and advocates of missions came

[29] Judson Smith to John Hay, January 9, 1899, *Miscellaneous Letter Files*, Department of State Archives.

to share Speer's conclusion that the motives of European governments and of missions were irreconcilable.[30]

In China antagonism between foreign merchants and missionaries was traditional. The latter held that businessmen as a group had no sympathy with missionary aims and that their behavior reflected unfavorably upon Christianity. The businessman in China, in turn, often looked upon the missionary as a hopeless zealot. There were exceptions to this feeling of mutual distrust but there can be no question that there was little cooperation between them.

It was on the home front that the missionary crusade received the support of a great many business leaders. The Laymen's Missionary Movement was almost wholly a businessman's organization, and every important denominational missionary board had a number of prominent business leaders. John T. Underwood, President of the Underwood Typewriter Company, served on the Presbyterian Board, C. Edgar Welch, President of the Welch Grape Juice Company, was a member of the Methodist Board, J. Edgar Leaycraft, a prominent New York real estate dealer, worked with the American Bible Society, and S. W. Woodward, owner of a large department store in Washington, D.C., was a leader among the Baptists. John R. Mott, head of the Student Volunteers, took pride in his success in raising money among businessmen.

Missionaries never argued that their work would lead to an expansion of trade, but some of their supporters at home saw

[30] The father of Pearl Buck expressed grave concern over the building up of Chinese resentment by the imperialistic powers of the West. He thought a revolution would start in Russia because of the miserable conditions of her people. It would spread to Asia, "and because men of the white race have been the oppressors, all the white race must suffer." His daughter replied that Americans, having done so much good in China and having no concessions, would certainly not have to suffer. To this, he answered: "We must never forget that missionaries went to China without invitation and solely from our own sense of duty. The Chinese therefore owe us nothing. We have done the best we could, but that, too, was our duty and so they still owe us nothing. And if our country has taken no concessions, we have kept silent when others did, and we too have profited from the unequal treaties. I don't think we shall escape when the day of reckoning comes." Pearl Buck, *My Several Worlds* (New York: The John Day Company, 1954), pp. 89-90.

this as one of the much to be desired by-products of foreign missions. Charles Denby, former Minister to China, suggested that missionary leaders should use the argument, for "the statesman, the diplomatist, and the businessman look at this work with reference to its influence on commerce and the general prosperity of the world."[31] A prominent woman journalist who had traveled in the Orient and who lectured extensively, Margherita Arlina Hamm, argued that the missionaries' Western goods excited attention and created a demand for these things. "From this point of view," the writer said, "every missionary is a salesman for the manufactures of Christendom!"[32] The Rev. Francis E. Clark, President of the United Society of Christian Endeavor, saw among the many advantages of foreign missions the increase of trade and commerce and "the widening of our empire."[33] Theodore Roosevelt called for public support of missions in part because missions would help us commercially.[34] Chester Holcombe, in his early years a missionary to China and later Acting Minister in Peking, called the missionary enterprise in China "unequalled by any other, for the development of our commerce with that vast population."[35] In brief, there was an awareness of the missionary's role as a promoter of trade. Undoubtedly the economic benefits to be derived played some part in the marshaling of public support. Yet, there is no evidence to support any general thesis that the missionary enterprise was merely a tool of the middle class to prepare the way for the exploitation of China.

[31] Charles Denby, "The Influence of Mission Work on Commerce," *The Independent*, December 12, 1901, p. 2960.

[32] Margherita Arlina Hamm, "The Secular Value of Foreign Missions," *The Independent*, April 26, 1900, p. 1001.

[33] Francis E. Clark, "Do Foreign Missions Pay?" *The North American Review*, March 1898, p. 280.

[34] Theodore Roosevelt, "The Awakening of China," *The Outlook*, November 28, 1908, p. 666.

[35] Chester Holcombe, "The Missionary Enterprise in China," *Atlantic Monthly*, September 1906, p. 354.

CHAPTER VI

CHINA'S AWAKENING AND THE NEW EMPHASIS

IN MISSIONARY WORK, 1900-1917

In 1909 Arthur H. Smith observed that the Boxer cataclysm had shocked the Chinese into perceiving the "necessity of many changes in government, in education, in manners, in dress, in medicine, sanitation, in social appliances, etc., and hence presumptively in religion."[1] The general ferment, he noted, made a favorable culture-bed for religious changes.

Missionaries in all parts of China gave similar testimony. The Rev. A. L. Warnshuis of the Reformed Church mission at Amoy wrote that everywhere there was a spirit of inquiry.[2] A representative of the American Board in the Foochow Mission found that increasing dissatisfaction with the past was opening the way for "the truth."[3]

These judgments were based on the experience of missionaries who now, for the first time, spoke before large and attentive audiences. Compared to the earlier days when a sympathetic listener was rare and the overwhelming number of Chinese were hostile and almost at best indifferent, this was a highly favorable period for the missionary. Bishop Bashford on his arrival in China in 1904 traveled from one Methodist mission to another in various parts of the country. Everywhere churches were filled to capacity, and almost invariably a considerable number of Chinese publicly announced their decision to become Christians.[4] Another Methodist missionary

[1] Arthur H. Smith to Commission I, Carrying the Gospel to All the Non-Christian World, World Missionary Conference, 1910. The Commission sent questionnaires to scores of missionaries in China. The replies are located in the Missionary Research Library at Union Theological Seminary. All letters cited in this chapter are to be found in this collection rather than in the published report of the Commission.

[2] A. L. Warnshuis to Commission I, August 21, 1909.

[3] J. E. Walker, Shao-wu, Foochow, to Commission I, August 9, 1909.

[4] There are 54 volumes of Bishop Bashford's diaries. They provide a

told of the great enthusiasm at a district conference: "At the evening meetings which were of an evangelistic nature the people were more than could get into the church. All seats were packed, the windows were full, and many were standing outside. It seemed that the whole town had been aroused by the meetings."[5] Another Methodist missionary wrote of a great revival at Hingua in 1909 where there was an average daily attendance of nearly 2,000 and on Sundays between 4,000 and 5,000.

In 1908 missionaries expressed amazement at the success of the Canadian missionary in Manchuria, the Rev. Jonathan Goforth, who led a series of revival meetings. This was not an entirely new phenomenon; there had been a revival on a smaller scale in the months preceding the Boxer Revolt, but this one covered a larger area and seemed to reach people who had no previous connection with Christianity. Goforth continued his evangelistic crusade for many years with favorable results.[6] In November 1914, during a series of meetings at Soochow, scores of converts were made and many who had previously professed Christianity confessed their sins. The Presbyterian missionary in charge reported that Goforth placed the emphasis on letting the Holy Spirit have full control of heart and life and urged "confession and relinquishment of sin." In an emotional orgy students "broke down with uncontrollable weeping, until *the entire body*, about a hundred, were weeping aloud." The day following this meeting, stolen property of all kinds was returned to the rightful owners. Lamps, wash-pans, and other items, long missing from the dormitory, were returned; stu-

---

valuable commentary on happenings in China. Bashford was particularly enthusiastic about the prospects of Christianizing China.

[5] F. H. Trimble to Dr. John F. Goucher, Goucher Papers, Missionary Library, Union Theological Seminary. Goucher was one of the most prominent leaders among the Methodists in the missionary movement. He made a number of trips to China, gave large sums of money, and carried on an extensive correspondence with missionaries. He was also the founder and first president of Goucher College in Baltimore.

[6] "Forty-Seven Years Among the Chinese: The Fruits of the Labors of Dr. and Mrs. Jonathan Goforth," *The Missionary Review of the World*, September 1935, pp. 415-417.

dents who had broken window panes acknowledged their guilt; cigarettes and pipes were broken and trampled underfoot, and obscene books were torn to pieces.[7]

In February 1916 the Rev. Samuel Pollard, a missionary in Yunnan, told of the vast change in attitude. For thirty years missionaries had plodded on with very little success, but now conversions were frequent, services were crowded, native workers were enthusiastic, and even high officials attended worship.[8]

Indicative of the new day was the reception given Sherwood Eddy and John R. Mott on their evangelistic tours in 1914 and 1915. Both of them were relatively young men with a wide experience in working with young people in Europe and America. In 1915 they visited fourteen cities in China where they made a special effort to reach the student class. The ever enthusiastic Eddy, a man who radiated a deep love for humanity whether rich or poor, white or colored, cabled back to home base:

> Seven cities, 7,000 inquirers, average attendance, 3,000. President, officials cooperating. Mr. Wen (Commissioner of Foreign Affairs of Chekiang Province), Hangchow, baptized. . . . Opportunities double last year.[9]

In Tientsin 2,000 students filled the Guild Hall and several hundred had to be turned away. On the last day more than 1,000 signified a desire to join Bible classes. In Peking, President Yüan Shih-k'ai expressed an interest in the meetings, and the Vice-President requested Eddy to address his family and guests. Another official opened the Forbidden City as a meeting place, and the Minister of Education granted a half holiday to all government students so that they might attend the opening meeting. In Paotingfu, where Eddy's close friend, Horace Pitkin, had suffered a martyr's death during the Boxer

[7] Rev. M. B. Grier, "How the Revival Came in China," *The Missionary Review of the World,* March 1916, pp. 201-203.

[8] Rev. Samuel Pollard, "China—The Land of Surprises," *The Missionary Review of the World,* February 1916, p. 108.

[9] "Awakenings Among Chinese Students," *The Missionary Review of the World,* January 1915, pp. 5-6.

Revolt, some 500 indicated a desire to join Bible classes.[10] Eddy addressed an estimated 121,000 students during his tour.[11]

In no other twenty-year period did Christianity make as rapid an advance as from 1900 to 1920. The number of Protestant converts increased from 95,943 to 366,524.[12] A total of 337 mission stations were started, forty-eight per cent of the total number established by 1920.[13]

In harmony with the new humanitarian emphasis in the movement at home, missionaries established a great many new schools. J. E. Walker, of the Shao-wu mission of the American Board, advised the authorities at home that the great demand for English and Western sciences, coupled with the difficulty the Chinese government was having in securing competent teachers, presented a great opportunity to Christian schools and colleges.[14] John R. Mott told his readers: "It is Western education that the Chinese are clamoring for, and will have. If the Church can give it to them, plus Christianity, they will take it; otherwise they will get it elsewhere, without Christianity—and that speedily!"[15] Scores of missionaries stressed the importance of schools in providing Christian leaders for the new regime.

The establishment of Christian colleges seemed most urgent. A few were already in existence; Shantung Christian University founded in 1864, Yenching University founded in 1870, St. John's University founded in 1879, and Canton Christian College and the University of Nanking, which were both founded in 1888. These collegiate institutions had emerged from Bible schools and academies begun earlier. Six new colleges were

[10] *Ibid.*

[11] Willard Price, "The World's New Turning to Christianity," *The Review of Reviews,* June 1916 p. 719.

[12] *The Christian Occupation of China: A General Survey of the Numerical Strength and Geographical Distribution of the Christian Forces in China Made by the Special Committee on Survey and Occupation, China Continuation Committee, 1918-1921,* ed. Milton T. Stauffer (Shanghai: China Continuation Committee, 1922), p. 38.

[13] *Ibid.,* p. 34.

[14] J. E. Walker to Commission I, August 9, 1909.

[15] John R. Mott, *The Decisive Hour of Christian Missions* (New York: Student Volunteer Movement, 1911), p. 64.

established between 1900 and 1917; Soochow University, West China Union University, Shanghai University, Ginling College, Fukien Christian University, and Hangchow Christian College. By 1916 the Christian colleges had an enrollment of 2,103. Several of these achieved high standards. The University of Nanking did notable work in various fields but was particularly well-known for its contributions in agriculture. Yenching was the largest, had the best physical plant, and led in Chinese cultural studies. Ginling, a college for women, enjoyed a reputation for a strong teaching staff and excellent physical plant.

These schools resembled smaller denominational colleges in the United States in maintaining a strong Christian emphasis. Chapel services and courses in religion were compulsory but many religious activities were conducted on a voluntary basis. Most of the staff members were Christians and very often they had theological training. While these colleges undoubtedly rendered an important service, they were essentially foreign institutions and placed great emphasis on Western history, philosophy, and the English language. In many cases, while administrators sought to maintain high standards, the teaching staffs lacked the intensive graduate training of teachers in American universities. It must also be said that there were instructors of the very best caliber, who did distinguished work.

Even more important in the development of the missionary program in the years 1890 to 1917 was the expansion of elementary and secondary education. By the latter year the American and Canadian middle schools had approximately 20,000 students and the elementary schools 68,506. These schools placed an even greater emphasis on religious training, and the curriculum was almost entirely adopted to Western rather than Chinese needs.

That the schools, collegiate, secondary, and elementary, filled a need was suggested by the rapid expansion of enrollment. Whereas mission schools had less than 17,000 students in 1889, they had 169,707 in 1915. In the latter year the number of students was equivalent to 64 per cent of the total number of Christian communicants.

The establishment of schools on such a large basis raised

many questions. A number of conservative missionaries who were engaged in direct evangelism voiced scepticism about the efficacy of the schools as evangelizing agencies. As the schools increased in size and number, it was no longer possible to limit enrollment to students from Christian families and in some cases the Christian students were a distinct minority. With a majority of the students having no interest in the religious aims of the school they attended, it became difficult to maintain a religious atmosphere and the effort to do so had as its chief result widespread resentment among the students.

In 1910 Professor Ernest D. Burton of the University of Chicago, who was friendly to the missionary enterprise, had toured China and visited mission schools. He wrote to Commission III of the World Missionary Conference of 1910 that perhaps this was a time "when the wisest policy which the Christian church can pursue is to direct its efforts to the promotion of the general well-being of the nation . . . , assisting them to develop their educational, social and political institutions, in a sense without regard to the result of such effort either upon the spread of right ideas among the non-Christian community or of development in numbers and strength of the Christian community."[16] Burton considered the needs in China so great that these alone should provide an adequate philanthropic motive. To make this philanthropy secondary to proselytization might be self-defeating. He had found mission schools staffed by missionaries primarily interested in evangelization, and as a result the intellectual had been subordinated to the spiritual. There was serious danger, he thought, that this emphasis would lead to an obscuring of the fact that the schools were weak. Burton warned that the better moral tone of the schools was a dangerous excuse for low standards. The schools were already falling into disrepute and, said Burton, they "are in danger of becoming contemptible. . . ."[17]

Professor Burton questioned the practice of compulsory re-

[16] Ernest D. Burton to Edward C. Moore, Commission III, Education in Relation to the Christianization of National Life, World Missionary Conference, 1910. The correspondence of this Commission is available in the Missionary Library, Union Theological Seminary.
[17] Ibid.

ligious instruction. Coupled as this was with lower tuition rates than those of other Chinese schools, the net effect was to make students feel that conformity to the requirements of religious instruction was a price that had to be paid in order to take advantage of low costs. A student was likely to feel contempt for an institution that tempted him with such a bargain.[18]

Prior to World War I the boards at home were so engrossed in the promotion of missions and in expanding the mission schools that they paid scant attention to the problems posed by Professor Burton. China needed and welcomed schools, and missionary enthusiasts welcomed the opportunity that schools presented for evangelization. Leaders, excited by the vision of seizing hold of the new China and making it Christian, were in no mood for a critical analysis of the mission schools. Professor Burton's letter was ignored. Teachers in mission schools might have raised some of the same questions had they been consulted but they were generally ignored by the Commission on Education of the World Missionary Conference of 1910. In its report the commission spoke only of the opportunities for opening schools and their usefulness as an evangelizing agency. The report was an appeal for support rather than a study of the problems involved in carrying on an extensive system of education for religious purposes in a non-Christian country.

During the same period, 1890 to 1917, when a very large part of missionary work was becoming educational in character, there was a similar expansion of medical work. By 1916 there were 265 hospitals, 386 dispensaries, 420 physicians, and 127 nurses supported by Protestants. Almost half of these were American.[19] In 1914 the newly created Rockefeller Foundation took over Peking Union Medical College and began to plan for an institution that would train a Chinese medical profession of high standards. The new medical college formally opened in

[18] *Ibid.*

[19] *World Statistics of Christian Missions: Containing a Directory of Missionary Societies, a Classified Summary of Statistics, and an Index of Mission Stations Throughout the World,* edited by Harlan Beach and Burton St. John (New York: The Committee of Reference and Counsel of the Foreign Missions Conference of North America, 1916), p. 61.

1921. It became the finest medical center in China and it earned a reputation as one of the finest in the world.

Medical work on a large scale, like education, was costly. While Chinese medical facilities in the early years, and even in the later period in many areas, were either lacking or inadequate, it was none the less important that missionary hospitals and their staffs meet reasonably high standards. Often this was not possible as limited funds were dispersed among a large number of units. Sometimes hospitals were poorly located and in some few instances the limited demand for their facilities made them uneconomic. When the Burton Commission made a study of hospitals as nurses' training institutions, they reported:

> Many of the hospitals are models in every way, clean, well arranged, well conducted, and thoroughly creditable. On the other hand, there are others which reflect little credit upon the missions which are supporting them or the doctors who are directing them. Some of the buildings are of such a character that no Christian mission ought to permit their continuance. They are unsafe and unsanitary. The westerner is accustomed to associate the idea of cleanliness with a hospital, but some of these hospitals are little less than filthy. It is difficult to understand how representatives of the medical profession can permit the existence of some of the conditions we have noticed.[20]

Western standards should not be applied in judging Chinese hospitals, but missionary doctors themselves sometimes expressed concern over their inadequacy. Dr. Harold Balme, an Englishman, made a survey of two-thirds of the hospitals in 1920, which told the harsh facts. Thirty-four per cent had no nurses and 60 per cent not more than one nurse. Sixty-five per cent had no isolation block for patients with contagious diseases. Thirty-seven per cent had no protection whatever against flies or mosquitoes; 67 per cent had no screening for

[20] *Christian Education in China* (New York: Committee of Reference and Counsel of the Foreign Missions Conference of North America, 1922), p. 163.

their kitchens; and 71 per cent had no screening for the latrines. Only 8 per cent had a pure water supply, and only 6 per cent had running water throughout the hospital. Fifty per cent seldom or never bathed their patients. Seventy-three per cent had no means of sterilizing bedding or mattresses.[21]

Yet, it was the Christian missionary who first put forth the idea of preventive medicine in China. At first individual doctors prepared leaflets and distributed them. In 1912 the YMCA employed a medical missionary to give his full time to this work and a few health lectures were given in Peking. In 1915 the China Medical Missionary Association set up the Council on Public Health, and a year later the National Medical Association, made up of Western-trained Chinese physicians, joined it in forming the Joint Council of Public Health Education. By 1922 it had a staff of eighteen full-time and four part-time workers. In 1920 the Council distributed 5,963 books, 404,758 bulletins, 404,758 leaflets, and a similar number of posters. It also prepared lantern slides and moving picture films. Considering its limited financial means and the lack of an effective government to support the program, this was no mean achievement.[22]

A generous spirit at home in the face of crying need in China led to the establishment of medical institutions, but the support necessary for making them the best possible agencies was never forthcoming. Fewer hospitals and schools, better supported—they never reached more than a pathetically small percentage of the people anyway—might have been more useful to the Chinese.

When the missionaries in China were asked by a commission of the World Missionary Conference of 1910 about what was being done to improve social conditions, the vast majority replied that all types of missionary work contributed to that end.[23] Converts treated women with respect, they abstained

21 Dr. Harold Balme, "Enquiry into the Scientific Efficiency of Mission Hospitals in China," quoted in *The Christian Occupation of China: A General Survey of the Numerical Strength and Geographical Distribution of the Christian Forces in China*, p. 433.

22 *The Christian Occupation of China*, ed. Milton T. Stauffer, p. 38.

23 Commission I, in the questionnaire sent out to the missionaries, asked

from gambling and opium smoking and thereby improved their
economic condition, and they manifested a greater public
spirit. The missionaries also pointed to the contributions of
schools and hospitals to social welfare. The Rev. Henry Noyes
of the Presbyterian mission at Canton cited as beneficial results: "Evident in making the relation of husband and wife
more a relation of real companionship; in greater care in bringing up and educating their children and endeavouring to lead
them to Christ—in greater neatness in dress and care of the
home, and in more refinement generally." The Rev. A. H. Butz-
bach of Shenchow listed as beneficial results a more tender concern for family, the removal of idolatry, greater purity of life,
hopefulness, and decency in appearance. These typical testi-
monies as to the social benefits of Christianity, plus the ever
recurring emphasis on strict Sabbath observance, reflect the
highly individualistic ethic of the typical missionary.[24]

Only rarely did missionaries sense that they were witnessing
the collapse of a civilization, that the impact of the West was
undermining the basic Chinese institutions: the family and
clan, the guild, and the decentralized government. With the
revolution of 1912 a few more became aware of a new kind
of antiforeignism indicative of the beginnings of a Chinese
nationalism and of the Chinese groping for a new society based
on new political institutions and for a better economic order.
Missionaries who sensed the beginning of a vast social revolution saw the answers to Chinese needs in the Western forms
of society with which they were familiar, in terms of public
education, an improved technology, in scientific experimenta-

what was being done to improve social conditions. This statement is based
on an examination of the replies of the missionaries.

[24] The China Continuation Committee, established by the World Missionary Conference, set up a subcommittee on social and moral welfare.
In 1914 this committee carried on an extensive correspondence with missionaries to get their opinions and also to learn what was being done
along lines of social service. Most missionaries thought that evangelistic work, schools, and hospitals led to improved social conditions. Their
letters make clear that only an extremely small percentage had ever contemplated experiments along the lines of social service work in the United
States. The correspondence of the China Continuation Committee is at
the Missionary Research Library at Union Theological Seminary.

tion in agriculture, and Western democratic political institutions. That they did not perceive the full scope of difficulties standing in the way of Westernization—the need for a complete reorientation of political power, the obstacles that would be put in the way by vested interests such as the landlords, the difficulty of building a national spirit on some other basis than hatred of the foreigner—is not to be wondered at. They were trained and oriented in a Western society committed to gradual evolutionary growth, blessed with great wealth, and with a powerful middle class.

The striking fact is that there were some missionaries prior to World War I in whom the commitment to Christianity extended to an improvement of the economic and social conditions of the Chinese.

Although the first agricultural missionary, G. Weidman Groff, a representative of students at Pennsylvania State College, arrived in 1907, nothing was done in the way of rural reconstruction or of urban social work before 1913. In that year the College of Agriculture was established by the University of Nanking and it was soon engaged in extensive research and in training agricultural leaders. The YMCA led the way in seeking to improve urban conditions. The Peking "Y" organized the Students' Social Service Club in October 1913, which sponsored a playground for children and taught them games and calisthenics. The following year the Social Study Department of the Peking YMCA initiated a program of tours, which included trips to an insane asylum, some poor houses, an orphanage, and an industrial school.[25] The YMCA at Chengtu, in the interior province of Szechuan, launched a similar program and also sponsored classes where "methods of social progress" were discussed. The secretary of the Chengtu "Y" reported that efforts had been made to interest the governor and other officials in the need for better housing, public parks, and city planning.[26]

[25] Secretary, Peking YMCA, to Social and Moral Welfare Committee. See files of the China Continuation Committee at the Missionary Research Library, Union Theological Seminary.
[26] R. J. Davidson to Social and Moral Welfare Committee.

In the fall of 1914 an important social service work was organized at Changsha in Hunan. The emphasis was on the promotion of hygiene through instruction in the causes of tuberculosis and infant mortality. A school of midwifery and three milk stations for the free distribution of milk were established. During the summer, playgrounds were opened on school grounds.[27]

Similar enterprises were being started at Chuchow in Anhwei, in Hinghwa, and in Tientsin.[28] A YMCA leader wrote to the China Continuation Committee (see footnote 24) in 1914 that a new vision was being given to self-centered students and "a new conception of Christianity to many 'mission-compound-limited' Christians."[29] Actually this type of missionary work was in its infancy. Not until the 1920's and 1930's was there any significant effort to help the Chinese solve some of their economic and social problems.

The dominance of the evangelical psychology of converting individuals persisted in spite of a whole series of fundamental economic problems of a tremendous magnitude. On every hand there was terrible poverty. In the rural areas, where more than 80 per cent of China's millions lived, there was great hardship. Neither the missionary nor anyone else had yet studied the deep-rooted causes of the farmer's poverty. In the cities, working conditions in the new factories were probably the worst in the world, but little attention was given to the labor problem. China was desperately in need of help in solving these economic problems, but the great majority of missionaries, at least prior to World War I, were of the opinion that the solution to the economic problem lay in individual improvement.

Missionary prospects appeared relatively bright in the years after 1900, but new forces of hostility were now making their appearance. The first of these was the rising spirit of nationalism. At the very time that opposition to Christianity on grounds of its enmity to native faiths began to decline, patriotic Chi-

---

27 Lotta C. Hume to Social and Moral Welfare Committee.

28 See letters written by Elliott I. Osgood, William N. Brewster, and R. M. Hersey to Social and Moral Welfare Committee.

29 Secretary, Peking YMCA, to Social and Moral Welfare Committee.

nese began to charge that Christianity denationalized its converts. As early as 1902 W. A. P. Martin was dismissed as chancellor from the government-sponsored Tungwen College and an order issued for the dismissal of all missionaries from teaching positions.[30] Graduates of Christian schools were barred from the civil service examinations in 1904. Arthur H. Smith noted "a renewal of race antagonism owing to the growing national self-consciousness of China, and the recognition that she must in a way stand against the World."[31] For a time in 1909 there was discussion of establishing a Chinese Christian Church under the direction of a government official, a proposal aimed at ridding the church of foreign control.[32] However, nationalism did not become a mass movement until after World War I.

The missionaries expressed their greatest concern over the rise of agnostic materialism. A missionary in Hunan reported that young men came to Christian chapels, freely challenged the preachers, quoting Herbert Spencer and Western agnostics.[33] Other missionaries observed that book stalls were full of Chinese translations of the writings of Rousseau, Comte, Huxley, and Spencer. The thousands of Chinese students who went to Japan and the West exalted science while deprecating the superstitions of religion.

John R. Mott, after reading the testimony of scores of missionaries who had been questioned by Commission I of the Edinburgh Conference, expressed alarm over the anti-Christian character of government education. Formerly, wrote Mott, most of those opposed to religion were ignorant, and it was comparatively easy to meet their difficulties. Now there was a new kind of opposition. Students had adopted the watchword "Science without Christianity."[34] In their anxiety for Western

---

[30] Meribeth E. Cameron, *The Reform Movement in China, 1898-1912* ("Stanford University Publications in History, Economics, and Political Science," Vol. III, No. 1 [Stanford University Press, 1931]), p. 69.

[31] Arthur H. Smith to Commission I.

[32] D. L. Anderson to Commission I.

[33] W. Westwood to Commission I.

[34] John R. Mott, *op. cit.*, pp. 47-48.

learning, the young Chinese were quick to accept agnostic explanations of the universe.

In Chinese intellectual circles there was a desire to find the best in contemporary Western thought and to apply it to Chinese traditions and problems. The scientific method was much easier for the young Chinese to absorb than Christian theism, for there was in Chinese culture much that harmonized with Western scepticism. Life after death and theological speculation were foreign to Chinese tradition, but an empirical approach could easily be reconciled with the Chinese conviction that it was the earthly life that mattered. A group of professors of the National University in Peking, among them Dr. Hu Shih, were aggressive in their attacks on Christian theism while strongly advocating the pragmatism of John Dewey and secular humanism. By 1917 their students had established magazines disseminating these views. Shortly after the war both Dewey and Bertrand Russell lectured in China and were widely acclaimed. Thus the Christian missionary encountered a formidable enemy in the spirit of Western secular enlightenment at the very time when the old paganism was making its retreat.

With the coming of the revolution in 1912, there arose a Chinese demand for control of the Christian church. The revolution was widely interpreted by the Chinese as a triumph of nationalism, and such it was. The Manchu dynasty was foreign and most government officials in the higher echelons were Manchus. There was also a strong feeling that the revolution represented a popular uprising in which the people were for the first time assuming control of the nation. The French Revolution offered a popular analogy and, in many respects, an accurate one. The revolution was a revolt against something resembling feudalism and drew its inspiration from the ideal of nationalism even though it failed to achieve that ideal in the years immediately following the establishment of the republic.

The immediate effect of the political uprising was a demand by Chinese Christians that they be given control of their church. Christianity was a foreign enterprise in every respect.

Chinese pastors and lay workers were accorded an inferior status in the enterprise. The terms "native workers" and "native helpers" carried the connotation of subordination to the foreign missionary. The foreigner in general was usually a strong-willed person likely to impose his own opinions, and this trait could be found as often in the missionary compound as in the market place. The missionary was separated from the convert by race and color, by a better education, by a feeling that he represented a country which had demonstrated its superiority, by economic status usually quite superior to that of the convert, as well as by a feeling that in the Chinese Christian community, he was the teacher while the Chinese was the pupil. The Chinese resented this attitude although they were usually too polite to state openly to their foreign mentors that this was the case. By 1912, encouraged by the popular demand of "China for the Chinese," they became more outspoken. In a meeting in Peking, when a missionary asked how "can we ensure a wider and more fruitful effort to influence the people of this field to become Christians," a Chinese pastor retorted: "Remove the barrier of racial prejudice existing between missionaries and Chinese Christian workers, and then see to it that the Christian workers are properly placed."[35]

Missionaries underestimated the resentment Chinese felt at being accorded the status of serfs in the community of saints but they were not unaware of the problem. They paid lip service to the ideal of an indigenous church and repeatedly proclaimed that foreign missionaries must be only temporary workers in fostering the growth of a Chinese Christian church. "The end for which we are here is to make ourselves unnecessary as soon as possible," wrote one missionary. They indulged in considerable scolding of themselves for assuming too much authority. Probably all of them would have agreed with the Rev. D. L. Anderson, a missionary of the Methodist Church, South, who was attached to the Soochow mission, when he said:

[35] Conference in Peking sponsored by the China Continuation Committee from February 25 to 28, 1913. Letters and Minutes are available in the Missionary Research Library.

The urgent need in this field to-day is, that the Chinese Church be relieved as soon as possible of foreign domination, . . . and encourage Chinese Christians to think, plan, and act for themselves. . . . The established plan is, to say the least, unscientific and unnatural. It is an attempt to establish Christianity throughout the Empire by foreigners, or by native workers under foreign control and direction. It is a plan that if persisted in will hinder Christianity from ever being "at home" in China. Get the Chinese in the lead as soon as possible, and the result will be better methods of work sought out by Chinese themselves for the Gospel.[36]

The difficulty, wrote Anderson, was that the missionaries treated the Chinese Christian as a "babe in Christ," never consulted him, and made all the decisions as to plans themselves.

Although acknowledging that the establishment of a vigorous Chinese Christian church must be the work of the Chinese themselves, the missionaries believed that the transition must be gradual. One difficulty standing in the way of a transfer of control was the dependence on foreign financial support. The Rev. George Douglas contended that no church could be truly independent until it achieved self-support. "It may call itself so," he said, "and the aid-givers and aid-receivers may use many artful contrivances to bury the dependence out of sight, but the fact remains."[37] Practically all missionaries were agreed that control could not be delegated to the Chinese until they became financially independent, for the mission funds were a trust from the constituency at home that must be administered in accordance with the wishes of the givers. Missionaries feared that if the Chinese assumed control they would make the church something scarcely recognizable to Western eyes. In the years before Chinese resistance became implacable, they gave no thought to the added difficulty that

[36] D. L. Anderson to Commission I.
[37] George Douglas in a paper before a conference in December 1912, sponsored by the China Continuation Committee.

foreign money had created institutions on such a costly scale that it was impossible for the Chinese to shoulder the financial burden.

Missionaries were convinced that Chinese Christians were not yet prepared to shoulder the tremendous responsibility of transmitting to their fellowmen the faith once delivered unto the saints. Little was heard from missionaries on furlough in America of the problem of making Christians out of the converts but to Commission I of the World Missionary Conference of 1910, they unburdened themselves. They somehow expected that the Chinese would, or at least should, become like the most pious, understanding, and wise Christian laymen at home. Cut off from the home churches by six thousand miles of ocean, they were insulated from daily reminders that even good American Christians sometimes failed to measure up to Saint Paul's admonition that they walk not as other gentiles walk, in the vanity of their mind, and put on the new man, which after God is created in righteousness and true holiness.

The missionaries learned the hard way that Chinese converts could be disillusioning. On occasion, wrote a representative of the American Board at the Shao-wu mission, illness and inadequate supply of foreign workers had left the native workers without supervision. While in many cases their behavior had been gratifying, serious defects had also developed. The converts, he said, inherited predilections, prejudices and misconceptions which were a hindrance to their "growth in grace and to the formation of symmetrical Christian character," and which seriously marred "their fitness for independent leadership among their own people."

A great reverence for authority made the Chinese excellent workers when under supervision, but this same trait led them to abuse those subordinate to themselves. The American Board missionary at Shao-wu cited the case of a talented Chinese pastor who, shortly after his ordination, overruled a local lay preacher and received a man into the church. Not long afterwards the new church member "mauled one of his employees so severely that the injuries proved fatal."[38]

[38] J. E. Walker to Commission I, August 9, 1909.

There was also great concern that Chinese in positions of authority in the church would be influenced by loyalty to clan and filial piety. This would "interfere seriously with fair and effective administration of church discipline."

What the missionaries feared most was that some Chinese Christians, impatient to discard foreign control, would also discard the essence of Christianity. George Douglas summed up a common feeling when he wrote that they were there to found a Chinese Church, not a semiforeign one but "it is *to be a church*, that is, a uniquely Christian thing, composed of living members of the living Christ,—not a mutual improvement society founded on some 'tao te' [a way of life]." The Chinese must accept the gospel that Christ died for man and that there was no other way of salvation.[39] Given this objective, perhaps the missionaries were justified in their fear that the heathen environment was still such a compelling factor in the life of the Chinese convert that he could slip back into its way of life even without sensing any wrong-doing. But the hard fact remained that unless they were willing to permit the Chinese to take over control of the Christian church in China, that church would suffer the obloquy of being foreign, and this the missionary acknowledged was to invite certain defeat. He was caught in a dilemma from which there appeared to be no simple escape.

Uneasy over the problem that faced them, missionaries took comfort in the fact that they could point to some degree of Chinese control. The Methodists made much of the fact that China had its own bishops and district conferences. Episcopalians cited the authority vested in their bishop and the powers exercised by the Chinese through the synods. The Presbyterians pointed with some pride to thirty-three presbyteries where the Chinese were in a majority and the fact that in 1908 the Union Presbyterian Church of China had been organized. All these arrangements gave the Chinese some voice, but final authority still resided in foreign hands. Both the Methodist and Episcopal bishops were foreigners. More im-

[39] George Douglas in a paper before a conference in December 1912, sponsored by the China Continuation Committee.

portant, the missions—as distinguished from the native local churches—controlled policy, and in the missions the Chinese had no voice.

A new trend, nevertheless, was discernible. Some few missionaries, born and educated in China, developed a new point of view. Among them was Dr. Lucius Porter, later distinguished Dean at Yenching and visiting lecturer in Chinese studies at both Harvard University and Columbia University. Upon his return to Tungchau, station of the American Board near Peking, after attending college in America, his boyhood Chinese friends and other Christian leaders talked to him frankly about the attitudes of the older missionaries. He and others came to realize that unless the Chinese were given more responsibility and control of the work, the younger ones would leave Christian work.[40]

Largely through the influence of these sons of missionaries the North China Mission of the American Board took the unprecedented step in 1914 of combining the mission and the local churches in an association in which missionaries and Chinese had equal representation.[41] As members of local churches missionaries could be elected to the governing board and they might also be entitled to membership on that board by virtue of an administrative position. Under this arrangement missionaries still wielded considerable control but more by virtue of their own personal ability or appeal than by the authority vested in them by the Board in the United States. No other mission went this far, and the other two missions of the Congregationalists in southern China did not take this step until 1927.

[40] Lucius Porter to author, February 10, 1956.
[41] W. E. Strong to Paul G. Hayes, March 29, 1927, American Board of Commissioners for Foreign Missions, General Letters. The archives of the American Board are now in the Houghton Library at Harvard University.

CHAPTER VII

THE MISSIONARY'S PICTURE
OF CHINA, 1900-1917

THE large yellow blotch in the grade school geography denoting the strange land of China held a fascination. A thousand pictures moved before the mind's eye—Buddhas of angry mien in pagoda temples, rivers loaded with yellow silt and carrying junks, endless terraces of rice, cities crowded with yellow-skinned men in long black robes, women with bound feet, men sucking endlessly at opium pipes, a country rich in minerals yet untouched, strange people who ate with chop sticks, concubines, and inscrutable gods and spirits. From pulpits all over the land the returning missionary told his story of the evils of heathenism. It was a picture of somber shadows but through it, like streaks of light, ran lines telling of a remarkable people who, if converted to Christianity, might even surpass the Anglo-Saxons.

Many years after volunteering for the mission field, Fletcher S. Brockman recalled the picture of China given to Student Volunteers.

As most, of those who spoke or wrote about missionary work were more familiar with the Bible than with conditions in foreign countries they used the Old and New Testaments, especially the Old, as their source books on religious life in heathen lands. The passage most frequently used to describe the people in non-Christian lands was from Paul's letter to the Romans: "And even as they did not like to retain God in their knowledge, God gave them over to a reprobate mind, to do those things which are not convenient; unrighteousness, fornication, wickedness, covetousness, maliciousness; full of envy, murder, debate, deceit, malignity; whisperers, backbiters, haters of God, despiteful, proud, boasters, inventors of evil things, disobedient to parents, without understanding, covenant-breakers, without natural affection, implacable, unmerciful."[1]

Missionary criticisms sometimes were not unlike the negative reactions of the novice in music who finds in Bach nothing but incomprehensible noises and, in dismissing the composer as of no account, reveals his own incapacity of appreciation. Few missionaries were psychologically prepared or trained to make an analysis of social institutions and consequently, in reporting their experiences, dwelt on the strange and the unusual. Having gone to China dedicated to building a new society, they found in the old nothing but arguments to justify their cause. The audience at home readily listened, contrasting what they heard about China with their own idealized picture of America.

Not all missionaries succumbed to easy generalizations about the character of the Chinese. A very few were jarred loose from their American small-town moorings and set out to seek an understanding of the complexities of a very different people. They soon learned that here was a civilization far removed from the primitive tribal life so often associated with heathenism at home. Here was a civilization built on the experience of a thousand years, with cultured literati whose manners and learning were such as to create in a sensitive Westerner moments of uneasiness when he himself was made to feel like a crude rustic. It soon became apparent that if China were to be won to Christianity, some missionaries would have to acquire enough knowledge of Chinese culture to meet the literati on their own grounds. To these few it was not enough to crusade against the practice of binding the feet of little girls and the smoking of opium. They probed into the Chinese classics and discovered a world that demanded admiration. Their attitude toward China changed from one of petty criticism and condescension to one of respect and understanding.

Pearl Buck's picture of the transplanted American distributing tracts and preaching obscurantist sermons needs to be coun-

[1] Fletcher S. Brockman, *I Discover the Orient* (New York: Harper and Brothers, 1935), pp. 14-15.

terbalanced by attention to men of such catholic tastes, learning, and scholarship as Dr. W. A. P. Martin, Samuel Wells Williams, Gilbert Reid, and James Legge. Their world was not bounded by a narrow ethnocentrism excluding appreciation of a foreign culture. James Legge, translator of the Chinese classics, exemplified the cosmopolitan outlook of the scholar when on a visit to the Temple of Heaven in Peking, he removed his shoes in awe as he contemplated the altar where for centuries the emperors had stood in obeisance before the supreme deity *Shang Ti*.

These missionary scholars wrote in a spirit of suspended judgment, deeply aware of the vulgar criticisms foreigners had so often proclaimed out of ignorance. S. Wells Williams confessed that it was a difficult task to understand the religions of China for "their real belief—that which constitutes their religion, their trust in danger and guide in doubt, their support in sorrow and hope for future reward—is not quickly examined nor easily described." The inquirer into Chinese religions was further embarrassed by "his own diverse views, his imperfect knowledge, and misapprehension of the effect which this tenet or that ceremony has upon the heart of the worshipper." Williams thought that no one had "very satisfactorily elucidated the true nature of their belief and the intent of their ritual."[2]

W. A. P. Martin, who served as President of the Imperial University, and whose book, *The Lore of Cathay*, is marked by its fairmindedness, observed:

> Never have a great people been more misunderstood. They are denounced as stolid, because we are not in possession of a medium sufficiently transparent to convey our ideas to them, or transmit theirs to us; and stigmatized as barbarians, because we want the breadth to comprehend a civilization different from our own. They are represented as servile imitators, though they have borrowed less than

[2] S. Wells Williams, *The Middle Kingdom: A Survey of the Geography, Government, Literature, Social Life, Arts, and History of the Chinese Empire and Its Inhabitants* (New York: Charles Scribner's Sons, 1914), II, p. 191.

any other people; as destitute of the inventive faculty, though the world is indebted to them for a long catalogue of the most useful discoveries; and as clinging with unquestioning tenacity to a heritage of traditions, though they have passed through many and profound changes in their history.[3]

Not that either Williams or Martin lost faith in the missionary enterprise, for both insisted that Christianity had a contribution to make. The learned Dr. Martin had no wish to sweep away the old civilization but he did hope that Christianity would produce an intellectual revolution. Science would then be a free agent cutting away gross superstitions and a Christian conscience would stimulate inquiry in the spirit of the precept "Prove all things, hold fast that which is good." He looked forward to a great intellectual emancipation enabling China to benefit from Western learning in those areas where the Chinese mind had been closed to investigation.

The three great religions of China, Confucianism, Taoism, and Buddhism, received detailed treatment in many missionary writings. This was particularly true of Confucianism probably because many of the teachings of the Great Sage agreed with many of the highest ethical precepts of Christianity, a fact often recognized. This led to the frequently expressed hope that an emphasis in missionary preaching on the points common to the teachings of Confucius and of Jesus would make Christianity more acceptable to the Chinese.

The more learned of the missionaries agreed with W. A. P. Martin that the "real sage" as distinguished from the Confucius of apocryphal myth was modest, reverential, an apostle of forgiveness, and humane.[4] Bishop James W. Bashford ranked Confucius along with Socrates, Epictetus, Marcus Aurelius, and Moses as one of the great teachers of mankind.[5] Confucius, wrote the bishop, had denied himself and accepted the duty

[3] W. A. P. Martin, *The Lore of Cathay or The Intellect of China* (New York: Fleming H. Revell Co., 1912), p. 8.

[4] *Ibid.*, pp. 104-105.

[5] James W. Bashford, *China An Interpretation* (New York: The Abingdon Press, 1916), p. 195.

that "God imposes on each through his conscience." Consequently he had gained that freedom of which Christians spoke, a freedom that had enabled him to say: "If I examine myself and find I am upright, I will go forward against thousands and tens of thousands."[6] To some of the missionaries who had reportedly told their Chinese listeners that Confucius was in hell, this must have suggested that the Bishop was making salvation a matter of right conduct rather than faith.

Taoism and Buddhism fared less well at the hands of missionary writers; both religions were looked upon as having degenerated into rank superstition. Arthur H. Smith, popular missionary writer, thought that Buddhist monks fully deserved their ill repute and particularly objected to their withdrawing large tracts of land from the use of the community "in order to support in idleness, gambling, opium-smoking, and vice social vampires who add nothing to the common weal, but suck the life-blood of China." As for the Buddhist nunneries, Smith observed that "there may be virtuous women among them, but the shrewd adage runs:

> Ten Buddhist nuns, and nine are bad;
> The odd one left is doubtless mad."

A Chinese might be either Buddhist or Taoist but he was quite likely to be both and to be a Confucianist as well. Regardless of his religious persuasion, he invariably practiced filial piety. Worship of ancestors was obligatory on all, and failure to do so the only ground for being considered impious. It was, moreover, the basis for all social relations. Under its sway, each individual felt that his successes and his failures, his virtuous acts and his transgressions, brought either honor or disgrace to his ancestors of thousands of years. Only in China was it possible for a distinguished son to lift his deceased parents out of obscurity and to grant to them the honor earned by the living. And ancestor worship knitted the individual to his family and the family, in turn, to the clan and village, while the filial piety of the Emperor served as the

6 *Ibid.,* p. 207.

bond between the whole of the Chinese people. The Emperor, too, referred his conduct to the judgment of his ancestors finding in his awareness of their judgment the greatest motive for virtuous rule. W. A. P. Martin saw in it all a spectacle that partook of the sublime.[7]

Martin thought that all that was good and beautiful in the institution of ancestor worship should be retained, but in this opinion he stood almost alone. Ancestor worship was almost invariably considered a species of heathenish idolatry and the source of many evils. Arthur H. Smith said that because filial conduct required that one have children, the Chinese had fallen victim to early marriages, polygamy, and concubinage. It was likewise responsible for the problem of overpopulation and resulting poverty.[8] The Rev. Francis E. Clark, founder of the United Society of Christian Endeavor, in an article for the *North American Review* held that ancestor worship accounted for "the pitiable state of weakness and decay to which China has been reduced, and, indirectly, for the revolution [Boxer Revolt] and massacres which have recently horrified the world."[9]

China was complex, but to Westerners viewing her from far off ancestor worship seemed to be the key that explained all her shortcomings. The Rev. Francis E. Clark entitled one of his articles on China "The Empire of the Dead." Another missionary spoke of the Chinese as having his eyes on the back of his head. To all it seemed that China was backward, lagging far behind the West in the march of progress. This backwardness was easily explained in terms of ancestor worship, which had caused the Chinese to look to the past rather than to the future.

To the Americans of Theodore Roosevelt's era, this was a most plausible key to the China problem. All eyes were focused on the brave new world of tomorrow. Heralds of progress in

[7] W. A. P. Martin, *op. cit.*, p. 275.

[8] Arthur H. Smith, *Chinese Characteristics* (New York: Fleming H. Revell Co., 1894), pp. 183-184.

[9] Frances E. Clark, "The Empire of the Dead," *The North American Review*, September 1900, p. 376.

The Missionary's Picture of China

American Protestantism proposed to bury the dead dogma of the past including a considerable portion of orthodox Christian theology so that the church might proceed with the ushering in of the Kingdom of God. This outlook did not make for patience with Chinese reverence for the past.

Missionaries did not limit their reports to the religious beliefs of the Chinese. They had much to say about the characteristics of the people, a subject leaving room for considerable differences of opinion. The Rev. John L. Nevius, a missionary in Shantung, found the Chinese honest and having high moral standards in sexual matters. One found what one was disposed to find, thought Nevius, and as for himself, he believed the differences in standards and practice of virtue in the United States and China were not such as to form any marked contrast or "to render it modest or prudent for us to designate any particular vice, or class of vices, as peculiar to, and especially characteristic of the Chinese."[10] In view of the religious and spiritual privileges and training of Americans, he thought them more to blame for their shortcomings than the Chinese. Nevius candidly confided that he had some hesitancy in expressing these opinions for it seemed quite probable that "the views which I have presented will be regarded by some as prejudicial to the interests of religion and missions." "Indeed," said Nevius, "I have been expostulated with by some worthy and pious people, who have told me that if I represented the Chinese as, on the whole, 'so well off,' and in many respects 'a very good sort of people,' Christians would not care to do anything for them."

A similarly friendly estimate of the Chinese was given by Gilbert Reid whose special missionary assignment was to work with the literati. He thought no nation stood as high in its ethical system as did China although the people were generally immoral and the ruling class very corrupt. He struck a new note for Student Volunteer Conventions when he said:

[10] John L. Nevius, *China and the Chinese: A General Description of the Country and Its Inhabitants; Its Civilization and Form of Government; Its Religious and Social Institutions; Its Intercourse with other Nations; and Its Present Condition and Prospects* (Chicago: Missionary Campaign Library Number Two, 1882), pp. 289-290.

The Missionary's Picture of China

I do not know whether my friends here on the platform will agree with me in what I am now going to say—but, I say, you will not find in the cities of China such vileness and debauchery as you can find in the slums of any of our large-cities in the United States of America. You will not find in China such crime and slime as you find here. I have lived in New York and other large cities in this country, and in large cities in China, and I have found it so. I have never come across there such repulsive, exceedingly pitiable crime as I have seen in the cities of this land.[11]

Yet, Reid thought that he had never seen in China "any such delicacy, kindness, sympathy, goodness and holiness" as one could find among Christian people in any city or town in America.

The Rev. F. F. Ellinwood of New York, a frequent contributor to *The Missionary Review of the World*, while portraying China as a land where crude animism reigned supreme, praised the character of the Chinese. They were aggressive and cosmopolitan like the Anglo-Saxons, their industry reaching out over the world. The Chinese were remarkable for their thrift and a wonderful race that was sure of great future influence in the world. He considered China the most frugal and the most industrious of all nations.[12]

Bishop Bashford extolled the Chinese qualities of virility and industry, intelligence and reasonableness, adaptability and cheerfulness, solidity, common sense, and religion. He was even more impressed by their readiness and cheerfulness in adapting themselves to their environment.[13]

These eulogies gave a certain sweetness to a picture where there was very little light. The scholarly might indulge in contemplation of the sublime insights of China's moral philosophers and the more sensitive missionary wonder at the cheer-

---

[11] *The Student Missionary Appeal: Addresses at the Third International Convention of the Student Volunteer Movement for Foreign Missions* (New York: Student Volunteer Movement for Foreign Missions, 1898), p. 328.

[12] F. F. Ellinwood, "The Religions of China," *The Missionary Review of the World*, February 1890, p. 148.

[13] James W. Bashford. *op. cit.*, p. 24.

fulness of the villager in the face of unkind fate, but the rank and file missionary traversing the village street saw with the eyes of one who came not to bring peace, but a sword. The missionary engaged in evangelization saw little of the literati and less of the Chinese classics. The poverty and the superstition and the brutality of life were ever present. Omnipresent hostility erupting at times into physical attack conditioned him against viewing the strange world in which he found himself with intellectual repose. He had come to be a doer of the word and not a hearer, and only in the doing could he achieve serenity.

A young missionary after one year's stay at a station thirty miles inland from Amoy wrote home of the horrors of idolatry. He had seen thousands of dollars spent every month on theatricals and other demonstrations in honor of gods. "Even small, poor villages," he said, "have several thousands of dollars filched from them every year." He had concluded that idolatry was a gigantic form of robbery.[14]

Bishop Henry Fowler of the Methodists, who gave a great many addresses on missionary work, seems to have represented a considerable body of opinion. His condemnation of the Chinese abounded with the most derogatory analogies. China, he said, was the supreme dissembler of all the races and of all the ages, a compound of Judas Iscariot and Ananias. It lacked the conscience of Judas or it would have committed suicide. The Bishop maintained:

> This moral mummy is embalmed and wrapped in superstitions four thousand years old, and more than ten thousand layers deep. These superstitions touch every act of life, and every word, and every secret thought. They are victims of luck, fortune-tellers, and necromancy. They live in a world packed to the very stars with powerful spirits, which must not be offended. All ranks and classes, from the emperor down to the poorest coolie, are steeped and boiled and parboiled in superstition. By these supersti-

[14] Letter from John G. Fagg, *The Missionary Review of the World,* January 1890, p. 51.

tions the university men and the priests govern and rob and torment all classes.[15]

The Bishop appeared most troubled by the priestly exploitation of the poor.

Missionary talks and many of the writings of persons with no firsthand information mirrored the views of Arthur H. Smith. His several books were widely read, finding a place on the reading lists of both missionary societies and college courses in the Far East. The more than thirty years he spent in China as a missionary, his wealth of firsthand observations, and his lively style of writing help account for his popularity. On one furlough alone Smith delivered 170 addresses in less than six months.[16]

The books of this influential writer were informative, especially as regards the daily lives of China's millions. Interspersed with his sharp indictments was restrained praise, giving his writing at least an appearance of being well-balanced and fair. Yet, on occasion, his sprightly pen left the impression that the Chinese were stupid in all matters except the art of deceit.

This is particularly true of his book, *Chinese Characteristics*, the tone of which is reflected in such chapter titles as "The Disregard of Accuracy," "The Talent for Misunderstanding," "The Talent for Indirection," "Intellectual Turbidity," and "The Absence of Sincerity." He found the lack of sincerity particularly deplorable. Not only the present generation but even Confucius and Mencius had employed the art of deception, both of them having falsely pleaded illness when for a variety of reasons they wished to avoid keeping engagements. Deceit was so deeply ingrained that the Chinese did not consider the term "liar" opprobrious.[17] Straightforwardness was considered to be rude, and some fictitious reason was always given to explain an action. Politeness was a cardinal virtue to which frankness and honesty were readily sacrificed. The same

[15] Charles Henry Fowler, *Missionary Addresses* (Cincinnati: Jennings and Graham, 1906), pp. 32-33.
[16] "Dr. Smith a 'Traveling Bishop,'" *The Missionary Review of the World,* September 1906, p. 706.
[17] Arthur H. Smith, *Chinese Characteristics,* p. 271.

lack of honesty was common in business affairs and in foreign relations. The Chinese readily made promises that they had no intention of keeping. Smith flippantly concluded: "We by no means intend to affirm such a proposition as that there is no honesty to be found in China, but only that, so far as our experience and observation go, it is literally impossible to be sure of finding it anywhere."[18]

In his description of the Chinese intellect, Smith declared that the Chinese were able to hold their own with any race but that a number of factors in their environment had combined to make for intellectual turbidity. An education restricted to the classics was partly responsible because it discouraged intellectual vigor. The Chinese language, likewise, because of the difficulty of conveying ideas or facts precisely and accurately, made for muddled thinking. A further explanation of Chinese intellectual deficiencies lay in their complete concentration on matters relating to the stomach and the money bag, a product of the extreme poverty of the country.

Smith observed that to an uneducated Chinese any idea whatever came as a surprise and usually caught him so unprepared that it took him "an appreciable time to get such intellectual forces as he has into a position to be used at all." The Chinese mind was like a rusty old smooth-bore cannon mounted on a decrepit carriage, which required much hauling about before it could be pointed at anything, and then was sure to miss fire. Smith illustrated this weakness.

> Thus when a person is asked a simple question, such as "How old are you?" he gazes vacantly at the questioner, and asks in return, "I?" To which you respond, "Yes, you." To this he replies with a summoning up of his mental energies for the shock, "How old?" "Yes, how old?" Once more adjusting the focus, he inquires, "How old am I?" "Yes," you say, "how old are you?" "Fifty-eight," he replies, with an accuracy of aim, his piece being now in working order.[19]

[18] *Ibid.,* p. 281.
[19] *Ibid.,* pp. 84-85.

Among Smith's other books, particularly *Village Life in China: A Study in Sociology*, the stress on Chinese foibles was likely to leave the impression that the Chinese were fools. Much was made of the Chinese belief in spirits and the pains taken not to offend those spirits. Villages were irregularly laid out in order to protect the good spirits, and the gates in the village wall were never opposite each other for fear of an evil spirit sweeping through. In some regions grape vines were taboo because the branches point down, an ill omen.

These illustrations would seem to indicate that the author had a uniformly low opinion of the Chinese. In a certain limited sense this is correct, but his praise of the Chinese belies this. He admired their industry, perseverance, patience, and good humor. He wrote:

> The Chinese have many and conspicuous virtues, among which are their faithfulness to duty, their sobriety, their unfailing industry, their unequalled patience, their inextinguishable cheerfulness, manifesting itself in blooming flowers, in warbling birds, and smiling faces, even in the midst of deep poverty, gloomy prospects, and heavy hearts. All these are wonderful and admirable endowments.[20]

Smith devoted much less attention to the supposed virtues of the Chinese than to their failings, but no reader was permitted to forget that he considered them a superior people.

His final summary analysis in *Chinese Characteristics* reflects Smith's combined admiration and disapproval.

> What the Chinese lack is not intellectual ability. It is not patience, practicality, nor cheerfulness, for in all these qualities they greatly excel. What they do lack is Character and Conscience.[21]

The introduction of "the funded civilization" of the West with its science, technological achievements, and popular government would not suffice to meet China's deficiencies. These

[20] Arthur H. Smith, *Rex Christus: An Outline Study of China* (New York: The Macmillan Co., 1903), pp. 105-106.
[21] Arthur H. Smith, *Chinese Characteristics*, pp. 136-137.

developments in the West were the fruit of Christianity: before China could enjoy the advantages of Western civilization it was necessary to plant the tree of Christianity that had brought them forth.

Two aspects of Chinese life that were prominent in the missionary's picture of China were the inequality of women and particularly the practices of foot binding and infanticide. In the United States, where there was a strong popular movement to give equal rights to women, the inferior position of the Chinese woman seemed deplorable. Moreover, women were extremely active in the missionary crusade, and it was but natural that they should take a particular interest in the welfare of the women of China.

The greatly inferior position of women in China was attributed to the influence of Confucius and Buddha. Confucius was quoted as saying that man was the reproduction of heaven and therefore a woman must always remain subordinate in the making of decisions, tend to her duties in the preparation of food and wine, and not leave her own apartments. The Buddhist scriptures taught that women were hopelessly inferior and impure and that the most that a woman could hope for as a reward for religious devotion was that in some future transmigration she might be born a man.

One woman writer described the position of woman in China as follows:

She is not desired at birth, is subject to father, husband, and son, and is denied the privileges of education. To destroy girl babies at birth was formerly exceedingly common, and not regarded as crime by the majority. Often no name, simply a number, is given to the girl baby, and a father in counting his family mentions only sons. Girls are simply sold as bondmaids to relieve poverty; and a wife may be legally sold or rented by her husband to another man for a fixed period. The binding of the feet is but an outward and visible sign of the crippled lives and energies of one-half of the Chinese people.[22]

[22] Helen Barrett Montgomery, *Western Women in Eastern Lands: An*

A similar report was presented at the Student Volunteer convention in 1902 by Harriet Noyes, a missionary in Canton. She told of the selling of girls into slavery, the unfortunate position of the young Chinese bride married to a man she did not know and subjected to the arbitrary rule of a mother-in-law, foot binding, and infanticide.[23] The frequency of such descriptions suggests that Americans who knew anything about China had some knowledge of the unequal status of Chinese women.

The binding of little girls' feet was a particularly popular subject. Several theories have been advanced as to the origins of this practice. Some have attributed it to a desire to prevent Chinese women from getting out of the home and indulging in gossip. Another explanation is that bound feet showed that the women did not have to work. Still others have expressed the opinion that small feet were considered aesthetic.

S. Wells Williams observed that the practice extended to all classes, the only exceptions being the Manchus and the Tartars, but that in some areas, especially in Canton and Fuchow, one saw very few bound feet. The pain endured by young girls during the early stage when their feet were first bandaged was described in considerable detail by Williams and many others.

The disposing of infant females was also emphasized in missionary accounts. The Rev. W. S. Ament, for many years a missionary in Peking, maintained that he had seen the cart that in the early morning hours carried away the lifeless bundles of infant girls. He attributed the practice to the mother's fear that a demon inhabited the body and the belief that exposing the body would cause the evil spirit to go down into the earth.[24]

Outline Study of Fifty Years of Woman's Work in Foreign Missions (New York: The Macmillan Company, 1911), p. 48.

[23] Harriet Noyes, "The Claims of China's Women upon Christendom," *World Wide Evangelization, the Urgent Business of the Church: Addresses Delivered before the Fourth International Convention of the Student Volunteer Movement for Foreign Missions* (New York: Student Volunteer Movement, 1902), pp. 338-339.

[24] W. S. Ament, "The Unevangelized Millions in China," *Addresses*

The Missionary's Picture of China

S. Wells Williams thought that the reports of infanticide were probably greatly exaggerated. He cited investigations showing that it was comparatively rare about Canton, and he denied the story of the much discussed black cart in Peking. The cart had been found to contain infants of both sexes, who had presumably died of natural causes. Williams thought that poverty was the chief cause of infanticide.[25]

One American missionary, Isaac Taylor Headland, a professor at Peking University, denied that Chinese women were as abused as most missionary reports indicated. Headland's wife served as physician to the Empress Dowager, and he was personally acquainted with several members of the ruling family, facts that may help account for his description of China as a land of sweetness and light. He thought girls were only slightly less welcome than boys and that the disappointment was not very different from that of a Western family hoping for a boy after having several girls. To be sure girls in China were a cause of expense rather than a source of income, and there was no opportunity for a girl to bring honor to the family ancestors, but he had seen too many Chinese fathers manifesting great fondness for little girls to accept the traditional story.[26]

After 1900 there was increasing emphasis in missionary writings on China as a country in revolution. The establishment of public schools, the founding of a republic, increased participation of women in public life, the progress of the anti-foot-binding campaign, and the building of railroads were hailed as the dawn of a new day and as evidence refuting the argument that missionary work was futile.[27] Chinese criticism of long-venerated institutions was hailed as "China's Divine Discontent."

---

before the Fourth International Convention of the Student Volunteer Movement, pp. 100-101.

[25] S. Wells Williams, op. cit., p. 241.

[26] Isaac Taylor Headland, Home Life in China (New York: The Macmillan Company, 1914), p. 63.

[27] There were numerous articles in which the writers hailed the changes taking place. See William Ayer McKinney, "The Chinese Awakening: An Interpretation," World To-Day, September 1909; W. A. P. Martin, "China

The Missionary's Picture of China

The missionary's traditional picture of China caused deep resentment among the Chinese. A Chinese student who had been converted to Christianity wrote to his former teacher in a missionary school that the missionaries had done more harm to China than good, and the greatest harm was "that China has been made unknown, and much worse, misunderstood." He thought that the missionaries had given an unfair picture, in part because they came into contact with the worst element of China's citizenship and morality, but also because of their attitude of "egotistic faultfinding." Missionaries usually told the people at home of abnormal and unusual cases. In this they were influenced by a desire "to arouse and revive their missionary spirit and work up and stir up missionary enthusiasm."[28]

Another Chinese had many serious criticisms to make but thought that the greatest harm the missionaries had done was to make China misunderstood. He observed: "Their experience of China may be lifelong; their information accurate. But their viewpoint is never that of the people they describe. Underlying everything that is written or spoken about China is the foregone conclusion that the Chinese are 'inferior' and that their ways of doing things are wrong."[29] While a few missionaries were well-educated and behaved with courtesy and tact, he found most of them narrow in their theology and wholly deficient in their understanding of China. These missionaries spread ludicrous estimates of China's weakness.

That the Chinese should have resented what the missionaries said about them and about their institutions is not surprising. The missionary reports were one-sided and too often lacking in understanding. Yet Westerners would have known little about China had it not been for the missionaries. Those who would dismiss them with scorn out of a feeling of revulsion

---

Transformed," *World's Work,* August 1906; Courtenay Hughes Fenn, "China's Divine Discontent," *The Independent,* June 27, 1907.

[28] "The Nationalism of a Chinese Student," *American Journal of Sociology,* July 1908, pp. 52-63.

[29] Lowe Chuan Hwa, "The Christian Peril in China," *The Nation,* February 7, 1923.

for their obscurantist theological views do them an injustice. Anyone seeking to understand the Orient will find in the many articles written by missionaries, for instance those published in journals of the Royal Asiatic Society, excellent scholarship and will likewise benefit by a reading of their books. That the missionaries should have exhibited a bias in most of their writings is much less surprising than the healthy intellectual curiosity some of them manifested in things Chinese.

Yet, the quality of the missionary writings is of only secondary interest. The primary question is what impact did they make in the United States. That they reached a large audience at home has already been made clear. There are likewise a number of reasons for believing that what they had to say was favorably received.

The analysis of China in terms of a moral problem fitted in well with American predilections. The reform movement at home reflected the same tendency. To a considerable degree the central problem continued to be viewed as one of individual behavior. Right morals would solve all problems. By 1900 the reformers were giving increasing attention to social injustice; child labor, poor housing, and the exploitation of labor were widely discussed. But the chief focus of attention was on corruption. The crooked political boss was more offensive to the majority of people than was a system that permitted shameful exploitation of children. With such a climate of opinion prevailing there was no reason to disagree with the moral approach of the missionary.

The presentation of the China problem in terms of morals was only one factor assuring the missionary of a friendly hearing. His appeal is also to be explained as a natural human response to the strange and unknown. The person who has traveled far from home usually has no difficulty in gaining an audience. But above all else, the major factor assuring the missionary a friendly hearing was the heroic status he enjoyed in the eyes of American churchgoers. He had sacrificed all in order to spread the gospel. To leave America and go any place was a sacrifice; to go to China was tantamount to offering life itself, the last full measure of devotion. He spoke not only with the authority of a firsthand observer but with the authority of an ambassador of Christ.

Although the missionary painted a dark picture of Chinese heathenism, he elicited a great degree of sympathy for the people of China. If they were portrayed as victims of false religions, this also provided an explanation that freed the Chinese of blame and left the pagan system the target of criticism. Consequently there developed in the United States a highly sentimental feeling toward China. Having no vital interests in that area, this altruism did not often come into conflict with national self-interest. Moreover, the very weakness of China invited a charitable feeling toward her. Much the same attitude had been taken toward Japan until she gave rise to a chilling fear as a result of her decisive victory over Russia in 1905.

The attitude toward China, which the missionaries did so much to cultivate, confused the issue. It was first of all an attitude of superiority that made it difficult to treat China as an equal. Probably more serious was the fact that Americans had come to think that the philanthropic work of the missionary in establishing schools and hospitals provided the basis for permanent friendly relations. There came a time when foreign schools and hospitals, in spite of the good they accomplished, became the targets of attack for highly nationalistic Chinese. Poverty, which the missionaries largely ignored, became the problem of first importance to the Chinese. Accustomed to think in terms of the moral problem, Americans underestimated the importance to the Chinese of an improved standard of living. Practically nothing was done to help China rehabilitate herself economically. Nationalism probably ranked next in importance to the Chinese. Here, likewise, the old sense of superiority was a factor in delaying American recognition of China's claims to equal status among nations.

CHAPTER VIII

THE MISSIONARIES AND DIPLOMACY,
1900-1919

THE missionaries' insistence on their treaty rights, acquired by either force or threat of force, began to change to an attitude of uneasy and reluctant apology in the years after 1900. China, according to the new gospel, was to be won over by Christian love exemplified in selflessness and brotherhood. Many missionaries, of course, continued to believe that to spare the rod was to invite further exhibitions of heathen recalcitrance, but the new point of view gained more and more adherents in the decade before World War I. The Rev. George Alexander, a member of the Presbyterian Board of Missions, told his Washington congregation in November 1900: "The obstacles to the Gospel have not been melted away by the fervor of love, christian love, but blown down with cannon." The open door in China, according to this herald of the new dispensation, bore "the marks of bloody fingers." He prayed that in the days to come missionaries would no longer insist on their rights as citizens but follow in the footsteps of Jesus and by patient endurance give proof that there were foreign angels as well as devils.[1]

In the pulpits at home and among the new generation of missionaries there were many who shared in the new idealism. Reflecting the optimism of the early twentieth century, these evangelical liberals fervently believed that the Kingdom of God was to be actualized in history. Their blueprint for the new social order was the Sermon on the Mount. Their exhilarating faith grew out of their confidence in the principles of evolution, the efficacy of education, and the general technological advance. It was a faith that made all things possible,

[1] A copy of the sermon was forwarded to President McKinley by James B. Murray, November 2, 1900. *Miscellaneous Letter Files,* Department of State Archives.

even the evangelization of the world in one generation. In this climate of religious opinion a new importance was attached to the phrase in the Lord's Prayer, "Thy Kingdom come, on earth as it is in Heaven" and Jesus' enjoinder to turn the other cheek was exalted as a guide to individual and social behavior.

The harsh facts of anti-Christian feeling and the chaotic political situation in China provided a hazardous testing ground for such idealism. Although Chinese opposition declined somewhat after the Boxer Revolt, there were many instances of violent attacks upon missionaries. The hazards of applied Christian idealism, to be sure, were somewhat reduced by the sheltering hand of the United States government, the willingness of most missionaries to evacuate troubled areas, and an increasing spirit of tolerance on the part of more and more Chinese.

Early in 1902, thousands of armed marauders disturbed the peace of the province of Szechuan. These armed bands, successors to the Boxers, had as their motto: "Uphold the Ch'ing, exterminate the church, kill foreigners."[2] While they were particularly hostile to foreigners and Christian converts, they did not spare others, and they defied the authorities who were unable to muster sufficient troops to maintain order.

In June 1902, two families of converts were attacked but managed to escape personal harm. However, their property was destroyed. A few days later, about June 17, the same unruly elements brutally murdered seven converts, destroyed their dwellings, and burned a Christian chapel at T'ien Ku C'hoe. Other converts were wounded, and the danger to Christians caused them to flee.[3] By September the Boxers were threatening Chentu. In December a small remnant of twenty or thirty entered that city and threw the inhabitants into panic. At the close of a day of violent threats, they were finally met

[2] H. L. Canright to Minister E. H. Conger, August 6, 1902, *Papers Relating to the Foreign Relations of the United States, 1902* (Washington: Government Printing Office, 1903), p. 176. Hereafter cited as *U. S. Foreign Relations.*

[3] *Ibid.*, p. 177.

by soldiers who killed five of the Boxers and dispersed the rest.[4]

While no missionary was injured, the danger led to requests that the government of China protect both converts and missionaries. The Chinese government did take steps that satisfied both Minister Conger and the missionaries of its good faith. A new Viceroy was sent to Szechuan in December 1902. He received a letter of welcome from the missionaries at Chentu and, in turn, he entertained them at dinner in the company of several high officials. An amicable spirit prevailed and the missionaries hailed the friendly cooperation they received.[5]

In 1903 a new treaty between the United States and China was negotiated. Article XIV referred to the status of both missionaries and native converts. The latter were to enjoy complete freedom of religion and were not to be discriminated against but they were also declared to be subject to the same responsibilities as other citizens and subject to Chinese jurisdiction. The missionaries, in turn, were enjoined not to interfere with the jurisdiction of Chinese authorities over converts. The treaty likewise spelled out a right that missionaries had long claimed, the right to rent and lease buildings and land in all parts of the empire. For years missionaries had urged that this right be incorporated in a treaty.[6]

The absence of any violent attacks on missionaries in 1903 and 1904 was the more remarkable in view of numerous other disorders. In many parts of the empire secret societies aiming at the overthrow of the Manchus were active and they had in the past found it useful to attack missionaries. These attacks not only strengthened their position with villagers but they involved the central government in difficult controversy with foreign powers.

The lull in the storm came to a close in 1905. In the summer

[4] H. L. Canright to Conger, December 13, 1902, *U. S. Foreign Relations, 1903*, p. 80.

[5] *Ibid.*, p. 80.

[6] The treaty of 1903 was published in *U. S. Foreign Relations, 1903*, p. 98.

of that year resentment at American treatment of Chinese who had come to the United States and the proposed extension of the treaty excluding Chinese led to a widespread boycott of American goods and enthusiastic meetings of protest. Missionaries were almost uniformly sympathetic with the Chinese cause and used their influence, without success, to get a revision of the exclusion features of the treaty.

There were other disturbances, too, in 1905. Minister Rockhill, who arrived at his post in June 1905, sought to discourage the President and Department of State from interpreting the various outbreaks and the boycott as a concerted antiforeign movement. Reviewing the events of 1905 he pointed out that the disturbances were remote from one another and that the causes were in most cases unrelated. Rockhill found that there had been nineteen antiforeign disturbances during the year. Seventeen, he noted, were antimissionary. Two of these had been occasioned by enmity between Catholic and Protestant Christians, and one other was merely an affray with robbers. That left fourteen, he said, to be accounted for by dislike of missions.[7]

By far the most serious of the antimissionary outbreaks occurred on October 28, 1905, when the American Presbyterian Mission station at Lienchou was attacked and destroyed and five missionaries were killed by a mob of several hundred Chinese. The massacre resulted from the kind of misunderstanding that so often arose between natives and missionaries and, in this case, the missionary in charge of the station had contributed to the hostile feeling by taking unwise steps. He had bought a temple adjoining the mission property and then stored the idols from the temple in an outhouse. When, in preparation for a festival, the villagers had built a mat shed extending over on the mission station land, the missionary had called them together, and they had agreed not to do so again. When they did so again in violation of their agreement, the missionary took three of their small cannon. He returned these, but not all of the villagers learned of the return and they

---

[7] W. W. Rockhill to Elihu Root, April 21, 1906, *Numerical File, 1906-1910,* Department of State Archives.

invaded the hospital in search for them. Another factor in promoting hostile feeling was that the missionary had bought clan property from some unscrupulous middlemen who sold it without getting the consent of all members of the clan. The big attack came after the invasion of the hospital. Finding an unborn infant preserved in alcohol, the mob had carried it through the streets and shown the people how the missionary doctor murdered their infants.[8]

The American Consul, Julius Lay, faced a recalcitrant Chinese Viceroy who was extremely reluctant to agree to the payment of any indemnity. Lay, feeling the necessity of reaching an acceptable agreement with the Viceroy, pressed for payment for property losses but made no mention of American demands for indemnity for loss of life.[9] The Viceroy held that the missionaries were responsible for arousing the mob and that it was scarcely reasonable to place all the blame on the villagers. He agreed to pay the indemnity for property losses but warned that in order to meet this obligation, some of the people would have to sell their property or even their children. This, he thought, was likely to make for future trouble.[10]

When the Viceroy paid the claim, he asked Lay to inform the Yamen that the compensation demanded had been received and that the case had been settled. Lay now, for the first time, told the Chinese official that the government of the United States would also file claims in behalf of the next of kin of those who had been murdered. Lay had known of these additional claims for a long time but had withheld the information. He was sharply censured by his superiors in Washington for treating with the Viceroy in this deceitful manner.

The trick employed by Lay was in sharp contrast to the way in which the Presbyterian Board of Missions proposed to treat the Chinese. Arthur Judson Brown informed the Department

8 Julius Lay to W. W. Rockhill, December 7, 1905, *Rockhill Papers*, Harvard University.

9 Julius Lay to Viceroy Tsen, July 13, 1906, *Numerical File, 1906-1910*, Department of State Archives.

10 Viceroy Tsen to Julius Lay, July 12, 1906, *Numerical File, 1906-1910*, Department of State Archives.

of State that the Presbyterian Board would make no claim beyond reparation for property damages.[11] When the next of kin filed claims to the extent of $50,000 and the Department of State decided to support these claims, Brown notified both the Chinese and the Department of State that the Presbyterian Board would not support the claims. Washington criticized this action, but the Presbyterians replied that excessive claims were already creating a painful impression in China and doing harm to the cause of missions. The Presbyterian Board held "that the value of the blood of those who laid down their lives for Christ's sake should not be estimated in dollars and cents." The claims would injure the very cause for which the missionaries had given their lives and the Board expressed the belief that those who had been killed would not have countenanced such claims.[12]

The Department of State at first asked for $50,000 for the loss of lives but reduced this to $25,000 when it learned of Lay's deceit and after a captain in the Navy reported anti-American feeling at Canton and attributed it in part to Lay's handling of the case. The claims would probably have been withdrawn entirely, but Rockhill had already filed the claims with China's foreign office. Rockhill had earlier advised that it would be a mistake to present them and that such indemnities were invariably collected from poverty-stricken villagers, many of whom were wholly innocent.[13]

Another reminder of Chinese hostility occurred in November 1905, when an attempt was made to burn the Baptist mission station at Ying Te in Kwantung province. Again the

[11] Arthur Judson Brown to Robert Bacon, August 16, 1906, *Numerical File, 1906-1910*, Department of State Archives.

[12] This action was taken by the Presbyterian Board of Foreign Missions on September 17, 1906. The resolution was forwarded to the Department of State. *Numerical File 1906-1910*, Department of State Archives.

[13] There is a great deal of correspondence on Julius Lay's handling of the case in the *Numerical File 1906-1910*, Department of State Archives. Lay had been criticized by Minister Rockhill earlier, and another American consul who had been sent to Canton by Rockhill to investigate reported that Lay had antagonized the Americans living there. Lay took a cavalier attitude toward the Chinese Viceroy and boasted of outsmarting him. He was removed from Canton after the Lienchow incident had been closed.

Chinese responded quickly to requests for protection, and there was no further disturbance in that locality.[14] Early in 1906 there were a number of other outbreaks. A riot at Changpoo and another at Nanchang created great uneasiness among American missionaries, but they were not directly involved and suffered no injuries.[15] Six French and several British missionaries were killed in the Nanchang riot.

On October 28, 1907, a Chinese mob attacked the launch "Morning Star." The launch belonged to the American Scandinavian Free Mission at Canton and was in charge of two women missionaries. They did not suffer injury, but the launch was damaged and a Chinese woman and a girl, who had been on the launch, were detained by the local magistrate for months. Rockhill sought a settlement but met with a rebuff. Secretary of State Elihu Root and Rockhill took a firm stand, holding the Chinese to pay the last cent, until it became clear that it was hopeless. After a delay of almost two years the Viceroy donated $1500 but the remainder of the claim for $2900 was never paid. In this case the American government took the old position that China must be taught a lesson. In fact, the major consideration seems to have been that the Chinese must be shown that they could "not get away with it." The case left a great deal of ill feeling. The Chinese Viceroy was extremely bitter and at one point in the negotiations, he completely lost his temper. The insistence of the American government on defending the rights of the missionaries did not help them to build up a reservoir of good will.

The missionaries became involved in a case of a different type on January 12, 1907, when a Chinese professor at the Boone Divinity School at Wuchang, Liu Ching-an, was arrested and charged with being a revolutionist. The unfortunate Chinese professor was treated with barbarous brutality at his trial. The judge, who insisted that the Salvation Army was a revolutionary military organization, demanded that Liu so testify. When he refused, he was sentenced to 400 stripes with a

[14] W. W. Rockhill to Elihu Root, March 7, 1906, *Numerical File, 1906-1910,* Department of State Archives.
[15] *Ibid.*

bamboo. He was beaten until he fainted and then beaten again, but he remained firm in his refusal to state that the Salvation Army was a military organization and that the mission station was engaged in revolutionary activity.[16]

Logan Roots, Bishop of the Episcopal Church, had asked that someone be present at the trial to defend the good name of the mission. The Consul-General had refused to support the Bishop's request, but Rockhill at Peking made a vigorous fight, showing more feeling in this case than in any other involving missionaries. He took the position that the case was of "vast importance to Christian Missions generally" and immediately wrote to China's foreign offiece insisting that the Consul-General at Hankow be allowed to attend a rehearing of the case. Rockhill wrote to the Secretary of State that this was the first case of its kind so far as American missions were concerned and warned: "If our Missions can be freely calumniated and misrepresented by Chinese officials, and made out to be hotbeds of revolutionary propagandism, and held up to the people as centers of agitation hostile to the peace of the country, the lives of the missionaries will be put in jeopardy and their usefulness destroyed."[17] This time the government at Peking turned a deaf ear to American demands, a fact Rockhill attributed to the fear of giving orders to such a powerful Viceroy as Chang Chih-tung.

The old question of the right to lease property continued to be an issue between the missionaries and the Chinese. The missionaries added to the difficulty by being strangely insensitive to Chinese feelings. In 1909 two Methodist missionaries in Shantung were intent on acquiring land in the county where Confucius had been born, an area sacred to the Chinese. When some land was leased, the Chinese officials imprisoned the seller and refused to stamp the deed. The two missionaries protested to Consul John Fowler at Chefoo and demanded that he intervene and compel the Chinese to abide by the treaty of 1903. The Consul refused, advising the persistent missionaries, "Were

[16] W. W. Rockhill to Elihu Root, April 2, 1907, *Numerical File, 1906-1910*, Department of State Archives.
[17] *Ibid.*

we to force this to the end, we would have all China in arms against us." He maintained that it was not the intention of the treaty "to give them the right to lease land against the reasonable wishes of the government, or people."[18] In this decision, Fowler was upheld by both the legation at Peking and the Department of State.[19] The missionaries, still not satisfied, assumed a haughty attitude, asking why the United States should permit the Chinese to violate the treaty.

Another missionary of the Southern Presbyterian church, Hugh M. White, displayed similarly unwise zeal in pressing for the right to lease property in the city of Yen Cheng in Kiangsu. White followed the custom of employing a Chinese agent. In this case, the Chinese agent deliberately misled the people as to how the property was to be used. Opposition was further aroused by the missionary's attempt to buy four separate properties. When the truth became known, the officials refused to approve the sale. The disappointed missionary complained to the American Consul: *"Granted that he* [Chinese agent] *did lie, that would not vitiate his right to purchase property, nor would it justify the conduct of the magistrate."*[20] But the Chargé d'Affaires, Percival Heintzlemann, concluded that this attitude on the part of the missionary "imparts a bad odor to the whole case." He thought that the whole transaction, moreover, showed a spirit that should not be encouraged— missionaries "should carry the olive branch rather than the club."[21]

Another missionary was similarly rebuked by the legation when he asked for his government's support in a disagreement with the Hukuang Viceroy over the right to hold worship services "in buildings not specially created for the purpose, . . ."

[18] John Fowler, Consul at Chefoo to the Department of State, August 10, 1909, Inclosure John Fowler to the Rev. George W. Verity, August 10, 1909, *Numerical File, 1906-1910,* Department of State Archives.

[19] Alvey A. Adee, Acting Secretary of State, to John Fowler, September 18, 1909, *Numerical File, 1906-1910,* Department of State Archives; Henry P. Fletcher, Chargé d'Affaires to the Secretary of State, November 19, 1909, *Numerical File, 1906-1910,* Department of State Archives.

[20] Percival Heintzlemann to Philander Knox, July 13, 1911, *Numerical File, 1906-1910,* Department of State Archives.

[21] *Ibid.*

Minister Calhoun held that the United States was not bound to insist on the right to preach "in any obtrusive fashion in violation of regulations adopted by local authorities." The Chinese, he said, were not acquainted with the right of free assemblage and the United States should recognize this.[22]

Most missionaries exercised greater discretion, but there were those who became impatient with the forbearance shown by the American government. In 1914 Woodrow Wilson wrote to a missionary he had known at Princeton, Charles E. Scott, and asked for information. The reply bristled with the imperialistic spirit that had been so common before 1900. Scott reported how missionary work in his area had been interrupted by robbers. Consul Fowler had asked the Peking government to protect the missionary work and to make reparations. He attributed the failure of the Chinese to make amends to the soft policy of the United States. Sterner demands would bring results. He then cited the effectiveness of Japanese methods.

> But when a Jap. barber-spy *stirs up* a fuss there & gets himself *into trouble,* a Jap. flying squadron appears & gives them *five days* in which to make apologies & reparation & pay indemnity & give valuable trade concessions—and the Chinese authorities at once produce the brigands for Japan that *in 5 months* they could not find for America; & in addition cough up all else that is demanded, and mighty quick too it makes Americans out here feel cheap. For less outrages other nations have seized Chinese territory, and *kept it.*[23]

This attitude was by no means typical, but Charles E. Scott was not the only one who thought that the best way to deal with the Chinese was by the dispatch of gunboats.

In the same period, 1900 to 1917, officials of the American government continued to take a sympathetic view of missions. In fact, as they became more world conscious in their outlook,

[22] Minister W. J. Calhoun to R. B. Mosher, Consul General, Hankow, January 21, 1911, *Decimal File,* Department of State Archives.

[23] Charles E. Scott to President Woodrow Wilson, March 4, 1914, *Decimal File,* Department of State Archives.

the importance they attached to the work of the missionaries increased. William McKinley had been content to bestow words of praise and Theodore Roosevelt endorsed the missionary movement in much the same spirit that he lauded any project for strengthening civic righteousness. William Howard Taft and Woodrow Wilson went further than their predecessors in giving their support. Taft was always willing to listen to a missionary leader and seems to have had a genuine interest in helping the missionaries. In August, 1908, Bishop Bashford had interviews with President Roosevelt, William Howard Taft, the Republican nominee for president, and Secretary of State Elihu Root. The Bishop obtained satisfactory assurances that the Chinese would receive fair treatment and that the United States would do everything short of war to maintain the integrity of Manchuria. Taft went beyond Roosevelt in expressing the hope that he would be able to get other powers to join the United States in an effort to support Chinese control of Manchuria. He also stated that he thought it might be wise to announce the United States' intention to support China by arms if necessary in maintaining her integrity. The Bishop was invited by Taft "to write him freely in regard to Consuls and to [the] Minister in China."[24]

In June 1912, President Taft sent a note to Secretary of State Philander C. Knox stating he was very much interested "in the plan of Mr. John R. Mott of the Young Men's Christian Association to go to China and organize some religious movements over there." If the Secretary of State saw no objection, wrote Taft, he would like to help by giving some letters. Knox saw no objection, and Mott went to China with the endorsement of the President.[25]

During his early days in office Woodrow Wilson invited John R. Mott to become American Minister to China.[26] In addressing an assembly of clergymen in 1916, President Wilson

[24] James W. Bashford, *Diary*, Vol. 27, pp. 18-19, Missionary Research Library, Union Theological Seminary.

[25] President William Howard Taft to Philander Knox, June 1912, *Decimal File*, Department of State Archives.

[26] "John R. Mott Refuses Ambassadorship," *The Missionary Review of the World*, May 1913, pp. 389-390.

referred to the awakening of China to Christianity as "the most amazing and inspiring vision." He expressed the hope that the imaginations of Christian people would not fail to take fire when they faced the tremendous possibility of Christian missionaries making this new nation a moral force in the world.[27]

The endorsements that the missionaries received from American presidents was supplemented by sympathetic assistance from American consuls in China. Of these, John Fowler, Julian Arnold, and Nelson T. Johnson were the most helpful but by no means alone.[28] E. Carlton Baker, Consul at Chungking in 1914, wrote glowing reports of the medical and educational work that American missionaries were doing in Szechuan. Their activities, thought the Consul, reflected great credit upon the societies they represented and upon the United States.[29]

Many consuls and diplomatic officers were undoubtedly irritated by the zeal of the missionaries and disagreed with their religious opinions, but they did not choose to jeopardize their careers by making these sentiments public. Criticism in diplomatic notes was limited to the failure of an occasional missionary to leave a danger zone.[30] W. W. Rockhill had antagonized

[27] *The Missionary Review of the World,* February 1916, p. 97.

[28] The opinion here expressed is based not only on the records studied but also on an interview with Nelson T. Johnson. The author found former Ambassador Johnson extremely sympathetic with the missionaries. He recalled a journey into the interior with a missionary when the villagers flocked about him as a close friend.

[29] E. Carlton Baker, Consul at Chungking, to William Jennings Bryan, Secretary of State, December 16, 1914, *Decimal File,* Department of State Archives.

[30] In 1912 Baker complained that the missionaries failed to heed his advice not to go to the interior. In notifying the missionaries he quoted from the Book of Proverbs: "A prudent man forseeth the evil and hideth himself." Two years later he said: "It will always be a mooted point as to whether missionaries are more secure in their own community than they would be in fleeing to the coast or to some distant point which is thought to be safer." He was now inclined to believe that a missionary who had refused to follow his advice two years earlier had been safer at the outlying station where he was among friends.

The only complaint from a consul in this period, other than those cited elsewhere, was made by Samuel L. Gracey who was stationed at Foochow. He reported that fully half the work of a consul in China consisted of protecting the missionaries. He said that this made it impossible

the missionaries, and, in turn, they helped block his appointment as Minister to China in 1897. They protested mildly in 1905 when Theodore Roosevelt did appoint him, and Rockhill had to assure the President that he would do his best to defend missionary interests. On occasion diplomats expressed privately a degree of amusement. Cecil Spring Rice told the story of how the Chinese Minister asked the Secretary of State about a rumor in the press. The Secretary denied its truth. The Minister said, "Then he lie." "Yes," said the Secretary. "Then," said the Minister, "he make one much good missionary." The incident, Spring Rice related, "delighted the State Department."

There was no wide gulf between missionaries and public officials on the question of what the China policy of the American government ought to be. The Open Door Notes of 1899 and the lenient policy of the United States during the negotiations following the Boxer Revolt evoked the praise of the missionaries. Now that China gave promise of reforming herself, missionary opinion sought to strengthen the hands of the reformers and no longer called for Western nations to overcome Chinese obstinacy by occasional use of threats of force or resort to interventionist methods of solving the Chinese political problem. The new attitude, in the process of formation during the first decade of the century, did not find expression in pressure on the Department of State during the remaining years of the Manchu regime. American policy was generally believed to be friendly to Chinese nationalistic aspirations, and the missionaries felt no need of trying to influence a policy that was already in accord with their point of view. In 1905 they spoke out against the Chinese exclusion policy and called for better treatment of Chinese living in the United States. This was the only time during the decade when they expressed

---

"for a man to do all that is desirable in the matter of trade and commercial reports." Samuel L. Gracey to Assistant Secretary of State, June 20, 1908, *Numerical File*, Department of State Archives.

The author discussed the complaint of Gracey with Nelson T. Johnson, for many years a Consul in China and later Ambassador to China. He said that missionary cases had never taken more than a very small proportion of his time.

themselves on a political question. The Root-Takahira agreement and Knox dollar diplomacy aroused no interest among the missionaries and passed almost without notice in missionary periodicals.

Passive acquiescence in the China policy of the American government gave way to a lively interest in reshaping that policy after the overthrow of the Manchus and the establishment of a republic in China. No political change in China elicited greater enthusiasm than did the revolution of 1912. "That regime is now, happily, shorn of its power to cripple the development of a virile people. It can never again chill China's hot yearnings after freedom, nor stand in the way of its peoples' intelligent hearing and unfettered choice of the truth as presented in the message of our gospel," wrote two missionaries.[31] In a letter to the students at Mount Holyoke College, Miss Alice Browne of the American Board wrote that the Manchu dynasty "had made itself so thoroughly and cordially hated" that even the princes of the blood would not come to its defense. The new regime was doing momentous things, and Yüan Shih-k'ai, the new President, had promised religious freedom. She went on to tell how at a mass meeting of Christians in Peking a message from the President had been received with enthusiasm and the large audience had said in concert, "Ten thousand years to the republic! Ten thousand years to President Yuan! Ten thousand years to the Church of Christ!" In the excitement of the moment she wrote:

> As I sat there and listened to the patriotic speeches and hymns and prayers and looked at the two thousand Christians that made up the enthusiastic audience, and thought of the significant words sent by President Yuan,—stop to think? *President,*—and in millenniums—old China,—well,— the world seemed a rather wonderful place to be living in, just now. I wished that those old heroes, Xavier and Mor-

[31] M. J. Curnaw and J. O. Curnaw to John F. Goucher [letter has no date], Goucher Papers, Missionary Research Library, Union Theological Seminary.

rison, could have walked into that church and felt with
us the thrill of the new hope.[32]

These expressions of welcome for the republic were typical.
Bishop Bashford had noted at the very beginning of the revolution in October 1911: "I find also that the missionaries, the
American Consul-General and all foreigners with whom I
conversed are in sympathy with the revolution, though wisely
taking no part in the struggle."[33]

Viewing the new republic with the fondness of parents for
a newborn child, the missionaries had no doubts at first that
the United States would welcome it into the family of nations
by according it speedy recognition. They were soon to learn
that ways of diplomacy can be tortuous. By April 1912 Bishop
Bashford was in Washington pressing for recognition. On April
14 he saw President Taft who plied him with questions for
three-quarters of an hour and then said: "I will recognize the
Republic." He also explained to the Bishop: "But I have tied
up to five powers [Great Britain, Russia, Germany, France, and
Japan] in an agreement that no one of us is to intervene alone
& I owe it to them to notify them in advance of our proposed
action."[34] Bashford immediately urged the President to induce
the other powers to recognize the Chinese republic. Taft
thought this would be difficult but agreed to try. Before the
Bishop left, the President asked him to put his views in writing and to return four days later to meet Secretary of State
Knox. When the Bishop saw Knox, the Secretary of State said
that "in case the other five powers would not act soon, the
U.S. would recognize China alone."[35]

If there was an agreement in April 1912, historians have
yet to discover it. There may have been a tacit understanding,
but the documents suggest that Taft and Knox were governed
not by any agreement but by their desire to push through the

[32] Alice Seymour Browne to Students at Mount Holyoke College, February 27, 1912, Collection of Letters from Alice Seymour Browne, Missionary
Research Library.
[33] James W. Bashford, *Diary*, Vol. 37, p. 39.
[34] *Ibid.*, Vol. 39, pp. 2-3.   [35] *Ibid.*, p. 7.

bankers' consortium. This proposed scheme, successor of the ill-fated Knox neutralization plan, had as its aims the preservation of Chinese sovereignty in Manchuria and the introduction of American capital into the area. Russia and Japan had joined hands to prevent its realization. At the time Bishop Bashford was in Washington pressing for recognition of China, Taft and Knox still had hopes of success, and they did not wish to jeopardize their chances by offending Russia and Japan. To have granted China recognition without that nation having to agree to certain conditions in regard to Russian and Japanese interests in Manchuria and Outer Mongolia would have deprived them of an important leverage. In the months after the Bishop's unwary entrance into the complicated labyrinth of diplomacy there were charges that the bankers were using recognition as a club by which they hoped to compel China to agree to guarantees for the proposed loan.

The Committee of Reference and Counsel of the Interdenominational Conference of Foreign Missionary Boards and Societies in the United States and Canada studied the question and presented its report to the parent organization early in 1913. At the meeting at which this report was discussed, alternate statements for public release were prepared. One of these placed the blame for the delay in recognition of China on the six-power group of bankers. The second called for recognition but omitted any reference to the financial interests. A majority of the Conference voted in favor of the first but the Chairman, Arthur Judson Brown, successfully argued that it should not be released unless there was a unanimous vote in favor of it.[36]

The first proposal—the one not released—came to the attention of the banking group through a missionary who was a brother-in-law of Mrs. H. P. Davison, wife of one of the principals of J. P. Morgan and Company. He had been present at the meeting and the same evening, while at dinner in the Davison home, related the story of the criticism that had been directed at the bankers. Mrs. Davison then got in touch with Robert E. Speer and complained that there was a misunder-

[36] Copy of letter from Arthur J. Brown to Henry P. Davison, January 31, 1913, Goucher Papers, Missionary Research Library.

standing of the aims of the Six-Power group. Speer wrote to the Chairman of the Reference and Counsel Committee who, in turn, wrote to Davison.[37]

By letter the Chairman, Arthur Judson Brown, invited Davison to a meeting. In this letter he went on to explain that he had never questioned the motives of the American bankers—"Their character as Christian gentlemen is so absolutely above question on this subject that no one would dream of discussing such a phase of the matter."[38] Brown added that it was regrettable the Americans were tied up with the European and Japanese bankers whose governments were guided by political plans for China. The United States should be free to follow its own interests and to act justly with the new Chinese republic.

Willard Straight, long the principal agent of the group of American bankers in arranging China loans, attended the meeting with the missionary leaders in place of Davison. After the meeting, which lasted three hours, Straight, in accordance with a request from Arthur Judson Brown, wrote a summary of his views.[39] Straight denied that the American bankers or any of the other bankers had ever taken any step to interfere with recognition. This was the work of the governments, not of the bankers. Straight went on to explain that the bankers had gone into China at the request of the Department of State, which hoped thereby to increase American political influence and to develop the market for manufactured goods, particularly for railroad equipment. The country that made the loans for Chinese railroads, he explained, usually sold the equipment and Americans had therefore been at a disadvantage. Straight took issue with Brown on the latter's criticism of the agreement with the other powers. It was only through such a joint agreement that individual nations could be prevented from taking aggressive action in China.

[37] Copy of letter from Robert E. Speer to Arthur J. Brown, January 21, 1913, Goucher Papers.

[38] Copy of letter from Arthur J. Brown to Henry P. Davison, January 31, 1913, Goucher Papers.

[39] Copy of letter from Willard Straight to Arthur J. Brown, February 18, 1913, Goucher Papers.

The major reason why other nations were fearful of what the United States might do in China was that the missionaries had built up a moral influence that it would be easy for the American government to exploit.[40] This was one reason why the United States must cooperate with other powers, as Straight saw it.

Brown's position changed in only one respect as a result of Straight's arguments; he was now more inclined to place the blame on the governments than on the bankers. It still seemed to him "that the Six-Power Loan is a political as well as a financial proposition designed not merely to obtain sound security for a loan but to obtain virtual control over the new Republic so that it will be an Asiatic Egypt, . . ."[41] He concluded that "the problems of China are being handled by Western nations, not in the interest of the Chinese people and Republic, but in the interest of the political plans of the European and Japanese Governments. Whether this is to the advantage of China or not is a disputed question; but if it is, the advantage is incidental and not objective. The Governments are not thinking primarily of China but of themselves. . . ."[42] Brown deplored the situation.

The Taft administration failed to recognize China and the question was left for a decision by Woodrow Wilson who took office on March 4, 1913. The American banking group who were members of the consortium advised the new administration that it would continue only if requested to do so by the government. On March 19, 1913, Wilson announced that he would not make such a request because the "conditions of the loan seem to us to touch very nearly the administrative independence of China itself. . . ." The bankers, dissatisfied with the slow progress of negotiations, were glad to withdraw from the consortium. On May 2 the Wilson administration recognized the Chinese republic.

The decision was not only welcomed by the missionaries; they had undoubtedly had some part in shaping the Presi-

[40] *Ibid.*

[41] Copy of letter from Arthur J. Brown to members of Committee on Reference and Counsel [undated], Goucher Papers.

[42] *Ibid.*

dent's policy. Arthur Judson Brown had sent copies of his correspondence with Willard Straight to Wilson a week prior to the President's announcement that he would not support the consortium.[43] The day after the announcement, Brown congratulated Wilson on his "clearness of vision, breadth of statesmanship and high moral tone."[44] A few days later Wilson received a resolution passed by the Federal Council of Churches urging early action in recognizing the republic of China.[45] Not long afterwards there arrived a letter written on March 1 by the President's good friend and regular correspondent, C. E. Scott of the Presbyterian mission at Tsingtao in Shantung. The missionary described the suspicion and ill will among the Chinese because of Taft's dollar diplomacy and the failure of the United States to recognize the republic. He said that the missionary's work and his testimony "to the interest of the American public in the welfare of China" had been offset "by the Taft-Knox-Morgan 'dollar diplomacy.'" "The Chinese officials & educated leaders," Scott wrote, "look upon it, and rightly, as of a piece with the European *'chemin de fer'* diplomacy in the Turkish domains; with the English-Russian policy in Persia; and with the action of the Great Powers in China."[46]

In the winter and spring of 1915 the missionaries in China became alarmed over Japan's presentation of the Twenty-One Demands. Japan had entered the war that broke out in Europe in July 1914, only a few weeks after its beginning. She immediately set to work to root out the Germans in the province of Shantung and to take over the islands north of the equator that had been German colonies. The haste with which Japan entered the war and carried out these self-appointed assignments served notice that she was prepared to realize her own aims in the Far East while the other powers were busy with hostilities in Europe.

[43] Arthur J. Brown to Woodrow Wilson, March 20, 1913, Wilson Papers, Library of Congress.
[44] *Ibid.*
[45] Shailer Mathews to Woodrow Wilson, March 25, 1913, Wilson Papers.
[46] Charles Ernest Scott to Woodrow Wilson, March 1, 1913, Wilson Papers.

On January 18, 1915, Japan presented to President Yüan of China a set of demands that, if granted, would have left China little more than a protectorate. The demands were accompanied by threats and by an injunction that Yüan was to maintain complete secrecy. The President of China had only one possible weapon at hand for counteracting Japan and that was to let the demands become known and thereby arouse public opinion against Japan. This he did. Minister Paul Reinsch learned of the specific nature of the demands by January 22.[47] Within two weeks, while the exact points were not generally known, there was public discussion of the demands.

The first reaction of the Wilson administration was one of caution. Minister Reinsch, on the other hand, quickly concluded that Japan's demands, if granted, would rob China of her sovereignty and independence. Consequently, he kept up a blast of despatches to Washington citing specific points in the Japanese demands that would contribute to the weakening of Chinese sovereignty, emphasizing Group v of the demands particularly. Group v called for a considerable degree of Japanese control of China's armaments, industry, and police system. Reinsch was seeking to counteract any tendency toward equanimity in Washington induced by the incomplete nature of the information given to the Secretary of State by the Japanese Ambassador. The point to be made is simply that Washington had full, if somewhat contradictory information early in the negotiations.

Wilson and Bryan, deeply immersed in the Mexican imbroglio and in European problems, were not prepared to embark on a crusade to save China. While the traditional American stand in behalf of China's territorial and administrative integrity and independence and their own interest in China required some form of protest, Wilson early confided to Reinsch that diplomatic intervention might serve to sharpen the Japanese appetite for some of the Chinese melon.[48] Finally, on March 13, Bryan handed a note to the Japanese Ambassador

---

[47] Paul S. Reinsch, *An American Diplomat in China* (Garden City, N.Y.: Doubleday, Page & Co., 1922), p. 131.

[48] *Ibid.*, p. 137.

that stated that several of the demands seemed to threaten China's sovereignty. Both the United States and Japan, Bryan observed, had on numerous occasions declared that they would support China's integrity and independence. It is true that Bryan removed the stinger in part by acknowledging "that territorial contiguity creates special relations between Japan and these districts." Yet the note taken as a whole certainly reflected concern on the part of the American government.[49]

The responsibility of office that led Wilson and Bryan to restrain any feeling of indignation was absent in the case of the missionaries. They were thoroughly aroused and at least one of them, Bishop Bashford, was to go directly to the American President and Secretary of State. The Bishop learned of the exact nature of Japan's demands from Reinsch and from the correspondents of the Associated Press and the London *Times*. Sometime early in March, according to his diary, Bashford wrote a twelve-page letter to the Secretary of State asking him to notify Japan that "she could not close the case by secrecy & threats of force with China." The United States should inform Tokyo that "these Demands must come up for final adjudication at close of present European war."[50] The Bishop also wrote a four-page letter to Wilson citing the danger to Christian missionary work in China if Japan should have her way, and he named "old & responsible missionaries who urge action on our government."[51]

Wilson received a lengthy cable stating China's case on April 8 from seven of the most well-known missionaries in China. The petitioners asked that the United States and Great Britain demand that they be represented in the negotiations between China and Japan and that Japan be asked to withdraw the "unusual bodies of Japanese troops on Chinese soil" that "constitutes an outrage on the rights and a serious menace to the peace and safety of Americans and foreigners generally."[52]

[49] James W. Bashford, *Diary*, Vol. 46, p. 37.
[50] *Ibid.*
[51] *Ibid.*, pp. 65-66.
[52] The cable was sent under the signatures of Charles F. Hubbard, W. A. P. Martin, Chauncey Goodrich, H. H. Loary, John Wherry, Courtenay Fenn, and Edward W. Thwing, Wilson Papers.

By April 19 Bashford was in San Francisco on his way to plead China's case in Washington. He stopped in New York where he explained Japan's demands to John R. Mott, and that leader soon shared the views of the bishop-diplomat.[53] Bashford also saw Dr. Sidney L. Gulick, a former missionary in Japan, who was now in the employ of the Japanese government as an adviser and propagandist. Gulick had already read some of Bashford's letters and had presented Bashford's version of Japan's demands to Viscount Chinda, Japan's Ambassador, who had pronounced them false.[54]

On April 26 the Bishop arrived in Washington and had a long interview and lunch with Secretary Bryan. The Secretary said that the Bishop was correct in his report of what was included in Japan's demands but that he, the Secretary, had been assured by Japan's Ambassador that "part of them were requests put forward as expressing the wishes of Japan & in order to enable Japan later to make concessions." The Bishop retorted that there was nothing in the "demands" indicating what were demands and what were requests and that Japan was employing threats to exact China's agreement on all of them.[55]

In his letter to Wilson, the Bishop had charged that Japan was prohibiting mission schools in Korea from giving religious instruction. Bryan thought this charge revealed an anti-Japanese bias and that the charge was unfounded, whereupon the Bishop promised to provide a copy of a Japanese decree issued on March 30. According to Bashford, the interview closed with the Secretary of State stating that the Bishop "had interpreted the situation more correctly than President Wilson & himself."[56]

Actually the Bishop's interpretation of events did not differ

[53] James W. Bashford, *Diary*, Vol. 46, pp. 65-66.
[54] *Ibid.*, pp. 68-69.
[55] *Ibid.* Bashford apparently expected Japan to go to war against China. He wrote in his *Diary*, "I then did my utmost to impress upon Mr. Bryan that the only human agents who could prevent a war between Japan and China were President Wilson and himself and that they must promptly let Japan know the sense of injustice which the U. S. would feel over any use of force by Japan to secure these 21 Demands from China."
[56] *Ibid.*

essentially from the interpretation Reinsch had already placed before the Secretary of State. The most that can be said for the Bishop's information is that it confirmed what the American Minister was saying and that it added to the pressure already being exerted on the Wilson administration. That Wilson was influenced to any significant degree seems unlikely. The President's position was essentially the same in late April as it had been in March, several weeks before he saw Bishop Bashford. On April 19 Wilson wrote a note to Secretary Bryan in which he referred to the letter he had received from Bashford. He was perplexed, he wrote, "just how to answer friends like this without going into a long and full and perhaps not very wise exposition of just how the thing stands as a matter of international politics."[57]

China finally signed a treaty with Japan incorporating all of the demands except those of Group v. In 1919 China made a desperate effort to have the peace conference at Versailles restore her full sovereignty in Shantung. The missionaries energetically strove to have the United States use its influence in China's behalf. A relative of President Wilson, missionary Samuel I. Woodbridge, wrote to him expressing disappointment over his failure to insist on Japan's getting out of Shantung. The President impatiently replied:

France and Great Britain absolutely bound themselves by a treaty to Japan with regard to the Shantung settlement as it stands in the treaty with Germany. What would you propose that we should do? To refuse to concur in the Treaty with Germany would not alter the situation in China's favor, unless it is your idea that we should do that? By the exercise of what sort of force?

Japan, as you know, has promised to retain much less than the terms of the treaty give her. She has consented to bind herself by all the engagements of the Covenant of the League of Nations, and if the United States is to be a party to this treaty and a member of the League, she will have an opportunity of serving China in all matters of

[57] Woodrow Wilson to W. J. Bryan, April 19, 1915, Wilson Papers.

international justice such as she has never had before, and such as she could not obtain by the course you suggest.[58]

The missionaries had created a strong feeling of friendship toward China, and they sought to influence American policy in the interests of China. Presidents and secretaries of state were reluctant to offend the missionary group and to lay themselves open to criticism from the large groups of people who were deeply interested in China. However, other considerations often weighed more heavily with those responsible for foreign policy. The missionaries identified Chinese interests with moral principles. No president was more sympathetic with the missionary movement than Woodrow Wilson, but he soon learned that he could not carry on foreign relations in accordance with the dictates of his missionary friends.

[58] Woodrow Wilson to Samuel I. Woodbridge, September 2, 1919, Wilson Papers.

CHAPTER IX

THE CRUSADE RUNS INTO STUMBLING BLOCKS
AT HOME BASE, 1919-1931

THE Christianization of heathen lands, so fashionable a cause before the first World War, encountered two major difficulties in the America of the 1920's. The first of these was the decline of interest in the church. The second posed an equally formidable problem, namely the reorientation of the missionary program to the Christian humanism of postwar liberal theology. Both undermined the missionary movement so decisively that it was not to recover fully until after the second World War.

The former hold of the church on the American community was now challenged by a number of rivals. The automobile, the radio, and the moving picture theater did more to create indifference to the church than the combined teachings of the natural and social scientists that challenged the intellectual validity of its teachings. The discontinuance of the traditional Sunday evening service and the mid-week prayer service testified to the difficulty that the clergy encountered.[1] The church was in retreat before an increasing secularism as religion came to seem out-of-date, and more and more people were content with the meaning their daily round of pleasures gave to their lives.

The resulting apathy had a delayed impact on the missionary enterprise, and in the years immediately after the war the movement continued along the lines of rapid development characteristic of the years before 1917. Indeed, from 1919 to 1925, the number of volunteers and the amount of contributions far surpassed the marks set in the peak years 1910 to 1916.

Beginning in 1926 the declining interest in the church caught up with missions. In that year the number of students decid-

[1] For a discussion of the decline of influence of the church see Robert S. Lynd and Helen M. Lynd, *Middletown* (New York: Harcourt, Brace and Company, 1929), p. 317.

[147]

ing to become missionaries was less than half the number six years earlier.[2] In 1920, 1,731 new missionaries had sailed, but in 1927 only 558 made the voyage to new mission posts.[3] The two following years saw a slight increase, 667 and 827 sailed, but missionary leaders were also forced to take notice of the fact that fewer college students were deciding to prepare for the mission field. In 1920, 2,783 had signed the Student Volunteer pledge but in 1925 the number dropped sharply to 764 and in 1928 to 252.[4]

In 1932 the Student Volunteer Convention attracted only 2,500 student delegates compared to the 5,428 in 1920 and the 4,526 in 1924. A similar decline of interest was manifested in the failure of the movement to produce any of the enthusiastic campaigns such as the men and women of the churches had sponsored in the years before American entry into the war.

Contributions likewise registered a lessening interest in the conversion of the heathen although the income of the boards was maintained at a high level due to added income from investments and some large endowments. The contributions of fifteen denominations reached $29,800,000 in 1921, but in 1927 it declined to $27,180,000 and in 1928 to $26,780,000. The slump was actually greater, for the 1928 figure included a special bequest to one board of $3,000,000.

State and private universities and colleges that had only tenuous denominational connections had provided a goodly number of missionary candidates in the years before the war. Though supposedly secular institutions, they had maintained a religious atmosphere conducive to the development of missionary interest. After the war it soon became clear that their environment had changed, and a student who decided on mis-

[2] Kenneth Scott Latourette, "What Is Happening to Missions?", *The Yale Review*, September 1928, pp. 76-77.

[3] Charles H. Fahs, "Recruiting and Selecting New Missionaries," *Laymen's Foreign Missions Inquiry Fact-Finders' Reports*, ed. Orville A. Petty, Vol. VII (New York: Harper & Brothers, 1932), p. 17.

[4] *Ibid.*; Jesse R. Wilson, "Missionaries Sent Out By North American Boards," *The Foreign Missions Conference of North America: Report of 34th Annual Meeting*, ed. Fennell P. Turner (New York: Foreign Missions Conference of North America, 1927), p. 214.

sionary work on one of these campuses did so not because of the atmosphere there but in spite of it. Ten leading New England schools, several of them once centers for recruiting, contributed only thirty-four of the 1,307 Volunteers who went to mission lands between 1926 and 1930. Williams College, famous as the birthplace of the American missionary movement, could not claim a single Volunteer during these years. The "Big Ten" schools contributed only twenty-four during this five-year period. Five large southern universities had only ten graduates among the Student Volunteers who went out to the mission fields.[5] Clearly, college students had lost interest in foreign missions.

The sweeping undercurrent of change in theological beliefs was an equally important factor in the undermining of missions. A great portion of the clergy was now surrendering many of what had once been regarded as the cardinal tenets of the faith once delivered to the saints.

In 1929 Professor G. H. Betts made a study of the beliefs of 700 ministers and theological students in the Chicago area. Indicative of the trend of theological opinion was the much larger number of students who no longer accepted the New Testament as an absolute and infallible standard of religious belief.[6] It was scarcely less significant that one-third of the ministers no longer thought the Bible was uniquely inspired. The creeping skepticism of the late nineteenth century was now clearly and boldly prepared to declare itself in complete ascendancy.

In this decade of skepticism it was easier to be certain of what one did not believe than it was to contend for any new beliefs. The emancipation was sufficiently exhilarating in itself for a time to make the business of denial of old dogmas seem a worthy end, but theologians were soon engaged in seeking to formulate a new position that would be intellectually respectable and yet provide the churches with a message. But, as wombs

[5] Charles H. Fahs, *op. cit.*, pp. 19-20.
[6] Winfred Ernest Garrison, *The March of Faith: The Story of Religion in America Since 1865* (New York: Harper & Brothers, 1933), pp. 269-270.

for a new theology, the seminaries seemed incapable of producing anything better than secular humanism.

In 1932 several of the leading liberal theologians explained
how they had arrived at their intellectual position in a volume
entitled *Contemporary American Theology* edited by Vergilius
Ferm. The most striking characteristic of the accounts was their
nontheological nature. The tendency was clearly away from
theology and in the direction of humanism. "Some dogmas,"
observed the editor, "seem to have suffered extinction." His
picture of the shifting sands in the new theological desert
would have been inconceivable in the age of positive assump-
tions of Dwight L. Moody. Ferm observed:

> In the controversy on miracles natural law seems to have
> come out victorious. Prayer as petition has found the area
> of its immediate and dependable effectiveness limited to
> moral and 'spiritual' spheres. Attempts are being made to
> set up a theory of the atonement which will have 'reality-
> feeling' for an age that has little or none for blood-sacri-
> fice or for the feudalistic ideas involved in the Anselmic
> theory.[7]

Ferm went on to say that other doctrines were being transformed "to meet different intellectual molds of the modern
mind." The doctrines of sin and guilt were being "worked out
as principles that do not offend the ethical sense or ignore the
best psychological knowledge." "In general," concluded Ferm,
"a much larger place is given to the hopeful possibilities of
human personality, individual and social, than in the old
Protestant dogmatics."[8]

With the old theology sheared away, the leaders of Protestant
thought found themselves subject to the call of a new age.
Their references to God, the church, and old dogmas were now
little more than attempts to solve the problem of communicating to the laity the meaning of their humanistic message. Shir-
ley Jackson Case of the University of Chicago Divinity School,

[7] *Contemporary American Theology*. ed. Vergilius Ferm (New York:
Round Table Press, 1932), p. XIV.
[8] *Ibid.*

when asked what a Christian should believe, could only reply, "What he thinks he ought to believe in the light of his own experience and knowledge." Theologies, he said, were man-made affairs. Hosts of Christian people still thought in terms of theologies, and it was now necessary for the clergy to give attention "to the raw materials out of which theologies are made."[9]

Professor Walter Marshall Horton of the Oberlin School of Religion examined his own beliefs at the conclusion of his preparatory studies and found "there was little enough of which I was positively sure, except that the whole intellectual orientation of Christianity stood in the need of a radical revision."[10] Among his teachers had been Professors Wieman and Macintosh who had taught him that the empirical method offered the best approach to theological questions. Professor Wieman in his own statement offered little in the way of beliefs except that God was to be studied by the scientific method, that is, by observation and reason, if any correct concept was to be derived.[11]

In their meandering through the intellectual world of psychology, anthropology, and modern philosophy, the religious liberals seemed to find only one justification for remaining within the institutional framework of the church. This justification lay in their faith that the new social order must be based on the principles of Jesus, an act of faith quite inconsistent with their avowed empiricism.

No wonder that the older motives of foreign missions no longer held sway. An inquiry of pastors, missionary leaders, and teachers in 1927 showed that of a long list of motives the three least important were "the evangelization of the world in this generation," "the salvation of souls from eternal death through faith in Christ," and "the overthrow of false religions which cannot save and which blind men to the truth." Missionary enthusiasm could only be mustered among men who held staunchly to religious convictions and these were now lacking.

9 *Ibid.*, pp. 117-118.
10 *Ibid.*, pp. 183-184.
11 *Ibid.*, p. 347.

In the absence of the old dynamics the missionary movement would have withered away had it not been for the strength it received from the liberal's firm faith that a new social order based on the ethical teachings of Jesus could be realized. World War I speeded the shift from theology to secular ideals. Feeling the inadequacy of the older motives, the younger missionary propagandists recast the arguments in favor of missions in terms of the wartime crusade for democracy. The goals of democracy and the ideals of Christianity were merged by them into a single program of social redemption.

President Wilson had skillfully summed up what they had only vaguely sensed earlier in their groping for a better world and a role for themselves in bringing it about. The crusader in the White House, with whom they had so much in common, had said: "We shall fight for a universal dominion of right, by such a consent of free peoples as shall bring peace and safety to all nations and shall make the world itself at last free." And Wilson himself, on another occasion, had said what was so close to their hearts: "The gospel of Christ is the only force in the world that I have ever heard of that does actively transform the life; and the proof of the transformation is to be found all over the world, and is multiplied and repeated as Christianity gains fresh territory in the heathen world."[12] The missionary-minded President saw the world in terms of a dramatic conflict between right and wrong, universal brotherhood and egotistical nationalism, a spiritual unity of mankind and a fanatical, self-destructive loyalty to local religions. The struggle had all the drama of the traditional Christian epic of damnation and redemption, of trivial aims that end in self and of union with a divine cause. So it seemed to Wilson and the new generation of liberal-minded young missionaries. The President had crystallized the issues under the impact of the tragedy of war and a new compulsion had gripped the missionary movement.

"The missionary enterprise is the Christian campaign for international good will," said Harry Emerson Fosdick, the

[12] S. Earl Taylor and Halford E. Luccock, *The Christian Crusade for World Democracy* (New York: The Methodist Book Concern, 1918), p. 30.

most well-known of the postwar liberals.[13] This was the common conclusion. Democracy was a way of life as well as a political system, and it was the Christian way of life. Jesus, wrote the authors of a popular book on missions, was "the world's first and greatest democrat."[14] It was Jesus, they said, who had introduced to mankind the infinite worth of every soul. From this had derived the concept of human rights. In hospitals around the globe missionaries, devoting their lives to caring for people of another race who were complete strangers, had demonstrated their belief in the sacredness of human personality. In schools in backward lands missionary teachers had lived out the principle of the dignity of man. The missionary movement was democracy at work. It was the force of the ideals of Christ, wrote one writer, that broke down slavery, that raised woman from the position of a chattel to that of a free being, that taught us to care for the sick, needy, and suffering, and that instilled the idea of human brotherhood.[15]

A democratic society was now held to rest on the diffusion of Christian ethics and ideals. The ideals of charity, mercy, of individual responsibility, of the worth of every individual must be implanted before any society could be free. These were the ideals the missionary was setting forth as no other representatives of Western societies in heathen lands were doing. Tyler Dennett, one of the most prolific and also one of the most able exponents of the new role of missions, sought to destroy the stereotyped picture of the missionary as a visionary and overly pious man who gave all of his time to the transplanting of abstruse theological dogmas. Dennett, writing in 1918, stated that he would place the missionary beside the soldier "as equally worthy of the confidence and support of those who are truly determined to safeguard the democracy of the world."[16] Only if a world democracy were underwritten with a world Christianity, said Dennett, could the results of

[13] *Ibid.*, p. 15.
[14] *Ibid.*, p. 26.
[15] Margaret Wentworth, "Oh, Missionaries!" *The Outlook*, May 20, 1923, p. 96.
[16] Tyler Dennett, *The Democratic Movement in Asia* (New York: Association Press, 1918), p. 241.

the war be preserved.[17] J. Lovell Murray, Educational Secretary of the Student Volunteer Movement in 1918, summed up the general view:

> So far we have been seeing that Christ is the only solution of the world's problem and the only hope of world democracy. He must be proclaimed to the nations. Democracy can be firmly established only where His spirit and teachings have been accepted.[18]

Young missionaries now became apologetic about conditions at home. Measuring American society against the highest Christian ideals, they found that much remained to be accomplished if a truly Christian society were to be achieved. American democracy fell short of the ideal. On every hand were examples of race prejudice, class distinctions, and economic injustice. Some critics pointed to the position of the workingman. He was little more than a commodity on the market place. He had no voice in determining his conditions of work and he could be fired at any time. The workingman enjoyed none of the freedom of which democracy boasted. The Rev. Walter Van Kirk held that Christianity and more particularly the missionary cause was being held back "by unchristian industrialism which is permitted to starve the souls of men." Christ could not reign in human society, he contended, until social inequities and economic maladjustments had been eliminated from the thoughts and actions of men.[19] Sherwood Eddy emerged from the battlefields of France a confirmed Socialist and his strong criticisms of the industrial order led some heavy contributors to the YMCA to protest.[20]

[17] *Ibid.*, p. 252. Among the articles by Dennett were: "Doctoring China: The Problems and Achievements of Medical Missions," *Asia*, February 1918; "The Missionary Schoolmaster Who Began With Outcasts, Now Teaches the Rajah's Sons," *Asia*, March 1918; "The New Type of Missionary," *Asia*, September 1918; "Nationalism and Church Unity in Asia," *Asia*, October 1918; "Democratic Tendencies in Asia," *Asia*, November 1918.

[18] J. Lovell Murray, *The Call of A World Task* (New York: Student Volunteer Movement, 1918), p. IX.

[19] Walter W. Van Kirk, "Stockholm Conference and World Missions," *Missionary Review of the World*, November 1925, p. 858.

[20] George Sherwood Eddy, *A Pilgrimage of Ideas or The Re-Education of Sherwood Eddy* (New York: Farrar-Rinehart, 1934), pp. 206, 257.

In his book *China's Challenge to Christianity*, Lucius Porter, the missionary educator, called for a fearless application to practical affairs of the principles of love and righteousness taught and lived by Jesus Christ. One of the most important things missions could do for China, wrote Porter, was to help her avoid the worst effects of industrialism. The rapid increase of factory production in China, he said, was threatening the destruction of the very best in Chinese culture, namely, her long heritage of humanism. Chinese pressure could be brought to bear on Chinese employers but Western owners of Chinese factories presented a different problem for they were unamenable to Chinese public opinion. Western Christianity must bring pressure to bear on these employers. But above all, said Porter, the battle with the industrial problem at home must continue so that China might have an example to follow in the Christianizing and humanizing of industry.[21]

Porter likewise called for a new approach to the rural problem in China. Christian service for the vast multitudes of Chinese peasants must be much more than the visitation of itinerant preachers. Very little else had been done but Porter urged the adoption of a completely new program. He wrote:

> Messengers must be sent to live with the country folk, to understand their life, to establish schools, to enter into the problems of husbandry and farming, to inspire regenerated individuality, and to organize social life for richer experience and expanding development. . . . The Christian preacher needs to minister to the farmer, not only spiritually, but agriculturally also.[22]

During the 1920's and 1930's agricultural missions received a great deal of attention. In 1920, for the first time, the Student Volunteer Convention had special sessions on agriculture and rural reconstruction. The President of Massachusetts State Agricultural College, Kenyon L. Butterfield, traveled through China and asked missionaries "what appeal formed the central

[21] Lucius C. Porter, *China's Challenge to Christianity* (New York: Missionary Education Movement, 1924), pp. 68-69.
[22] *Ibid.*, p. 102.

feature of missionary endeavor in lieu of the old appeal of saving the heathen from eternal destruction." The answers of the missionaries failed to satisfy him, but upon his return to the United States he talked to a Mr. Grant, who suggested to him the idea of rural missions with the simple thought of helping to build up in mission lands little Christian communities.[23] Butterfield soon became a leading exponent of rural missions, and the idea received wide acceptance, although for various reasons, which we will discuss later, the idea was never implemented on a large scale.

Many advocates of missions now arrived at the conclusion that one of the chief aims should be the improvement of social and economic conditions in China. Until this time no Student Volunteer Convention had been jarred by controversy, but at the meetings in Des Moines in 1920 there was a revolt against the old leadership and the old point of view. A few of the older leaders had already made the adjustment. Bishop Francis McConnell, a veteran of many years, called for reform at home. "Race discrimination in a nation going forth to proclaim the everlasting brotherhood of man, and a social order founded on a selfish form of competition, will not work," warned the Bishop. "Competition," he said, "may be all right in the realm of sport, even in the realm of scientific knowledge, but competition for daily bread is another thing."[24] Sherwood Eddy, after his first address on a conventional theme, was asked by some student delegates: "Why do you bring us this piffle, these old shibboleths, the old wornout phrases, why are you talking to us about the living God and the divine Christ?" He threw away his manuscript before his second address and launched

[23] Kenyon L. Butterfield to James L. Barton, November 29, 1925, General Letter File, American Board of Commissioners for Foreign Missions, Houghton Library, Harvard University.

[24] Francis McConnell, "Practical Christian Principles in National and International Life," *North American Students and World Advance: Addresses Delivered at the Eighth International Convention of the Student Volunteer Movement for Foreign Missions, Des Moines, Iowa, December 31, 1919 to January 4, 1920* (New York: Student Volunteer Movement, 1920), p. 125. Hereafter this volume is cited as *Students and World Advance*.

forth a plea for the League of Nations and the correction of the extreme inequalities of wealth in the United States.[25]

The new social ferment in the missionary movement after World War I almost transformed the Student Volunteer Convention of 1924 into a Christian revolutionary meeting aiming at reform at home rather than the Christianization of China. The pressure from the students who attended the meetings in Des Moines four years earlier had resulted in the setting up of a program emphasizing world problems. Dr. Walter H. Judd, Chairman of the National Student Council of the Student Volunteer Movement, opened the convention with a speech that set the tone:

> I think we are met today to consider with fair, sane, un-prejudiced minds this troubled world and its desperate need. We are met to ask what is wrong in the world and why. We are met to consider not only those things that are wrong over there but some of the things that are wrong over here at home. We are here to discover and then, after we have made the discovery, to admit that all the world, including the United States and Canada, regardless of what it may say it believes or professes to follow, in its actual life and living conditions is today essentially pagan.[26]

Not all of the addresses broke with the traditional approach, but there was ample evidence that the social gospel had become a part of the missionary movement.

Paul Blanshard, then Secretary of the League for Industrial Democracy and Educational Director for the Amalgamated Clothing Workers, sounded the ram's horn. He had recently seen a book entitled *Unoccupied Mission Fields*. Blanshard said the unoccupied mission fields were the silk factories in

---

[25] Sherwood Eddy, "The Gospel Indispensable to the Students," *Students and World Advance*, p. 192.

[26] Walter H. Judd, "The Purpose of the Convention," *Christian Students and World Problems: Report of the Ninth International Convention of the Student Volunteer Movement for Foreign Missions, Indianapolis, Indiana, December 28, 1923, to January 1, 1924* (New York Student Volunteer Movement, 1924), p. 2. Hereafter this volume is cited as *Christian Students and World Problems.*

China, the textile mills in North Carolina, the Five and Ten Cent stores in Indianapolis, and the New York Stock Exchange. Some churches, those that had failed to recognize "that there is such a thing in the world as a social system which can damn men's souls before they are born," he said, were unoccupied mission fields.[27] Throughout the United States few workmen had any rights. They were "bought and sold like cakes of soap and sacks of flour." When they fought for the right to organize, they were arbitrarily dismissed even though they had performed faithful service for twenty or thirty years. Had Jesus worked in a modern factory, Blanshard thought he would have been discharged as an agitator, "for He would stand firmly for the rights of the working class."[28] Blanshard did not call for any radical change of the economic order, but he did maintain that the workingman could have freedom only if he were represented by a union.

No one spoke with greater enthusiasm than the veteran of forty years of Student Volunteer work, Sherwood Eddy. In passionate tones, he painted a picture of the pagan world, a world that included the United States and Europe as well as China. Everywhere he had found selfish materialism, autocratic exploitation, and strife. Everywhere there was unrest and revolt against these evils. He described the awful conditions in Chinese factories where children worked fifteen hours a day, seven days a week, and were paid an average wage of six to twelve cents a day.[29] In the United States there was an unchristian concentration of wealth in the hands of a few. Two per cent of the people possessed over 60 per cent of the wealth.[30] Over 700,000 persons were injured in industry every year, and many of these injuries could be prevented. Some 2,000,000 were unemployed from four to six months every year and 10,000,000 were in poverty in normal times. Eddy also discussed what he called racial autocracy. Since 1885 there had

[27] Paul Blanshard, "Human Relationships and Modern Industrialism," *Christian Students and World Problems*, pp. 92-93.
[28] *Ibid.*, p. 90.
[29] Sherwood Eddy, "Present Day Social and Intellectual Unrest," *Christian Students and World Problems*, pp. 116-117.
[30] *Ibid.*, p. 120.

been approximately 4,000 lynchings, and a southern clergyman had confided that in "certain regions nearly all the lynchings had been Methodist or Baptist lynchings; that is, the majority of the mob were professing church members."[31] He closed with an appeal to follow Jesus, the greatest revolutionary of any age, and to go out and at once start building the Kingdom of God.

The opinions expressed by students in the scores of discussion groups coincided with at least the spirit of the views expressed by Blanshard and Eddy. Of the groups discussing the race question, nine were unanimously in favor of no discrimination at all, eight groups had majorities who took the same stand, four groups were unanimously in favor of no discrimination as long as it didn't involve intermarriage, three groups had majorities taking that stand, and two groups were unanimously in favor of no distinctions unless those distinctions were mutually decided upon by the races involved.[32]

On the questions of war and the social order, the students left no doubt that they shared the views of the liberal internationalists. There was general agreement "that we should do all in our power to Christianize the social order and the industrial system, realizing that predatory economic motives lie at the root of many military operations." In a vote by show of hands, all of the delegates favored the League of Nations.[33]

Sherwood Eddy contended that to follow the traditional rules of power politics could only result in another war and it was doubtful that civilization could survive another such catastrophe. Many of the speakers and apparently a great majority of the students took the position that the Kingdom of God was to be achieved in history and that anything less

[31] *Ibid.,* p. 121.

[32] Report by Erdman Harris, *Christian Students and World Problems,* p. 247.

[33] *Ibid.,* p. 261. One result of the convention was the organization by some of the student delegates of the Fellowship of Youth for Peace. See "Tomorrow's World in the Making," *The World Tomorrow,* February 1924, p. 57. Another result was the Interracial Forum at Nashville, Tennessee, carried on by the students of Vanderbilt and Fisk Universities. See "Tomorrow's World in the Making," *The World Tomorrow,* August 1924, p. 246.

than an application of the Christian principles of love and brotherhood would be impractical and disastrous.

Yet, there was no general agreement as to whether the realization of the Kingdom of God would require a fundamental reordering of contemporary institutions. Eddy was a Socialist, and there may have been some who agreed with him that capitalism must be abolished. If they did think so, they failed to say it. Some others spoke of educating employers and statesmen so that they would act in accordance with the highest Christian principles. It seems probable that most Student Volunteers had no blueprint for a new social order, believing only that it must come and that it must be built on the teachings of Jesus.

Many of the older leaders did not share in the faith that a Christian social order could be attained. Mott and Speer believed it was hazardous to say that unless Christianity offered a practical guide for the building of a new social order, it had no real meaning. The conservatives felt less strongly about the social evils that bore so heavily on the consciences of Sherwood Eddy and the young students who agreed with him. They admitted that these evils existed, but they were incapable of getting very excited about them. To them it seemed that the world was inherently evil, and that it was likely to remain so. The best they dared hope was that individuals might be led to identify their lives with the divine plan. In turn, they would provide a minority vigorous enough to save society from a complete collapse into immorality and anarchy. They held that Christianity was able to establish a Christian brotherhood in spite of a non-Christian social order.

Robert E. Speer, not without a note of resentment toward the impatient crusaders, confessed that the first generation of Student Volunteers had not understood the problems laid before this convention. They had, however, known that the world was in dire need and they had believed with "boyish confidence perhaps, with very little thinking through of all that was involved, but still clearly and surely, that Jesus Christ, and He alone, had the power to meet all the needs of the world, whatever they might be." Then he stated the very essence of the older approach:

> There is no order that does not rest on persons. We shall never build a new day in the world until we have enough new men to build it on. I do not say that we have to wait until we have made a world wholly composed of new men. There is no plenary inspiration in majorities. The minorities have determined history in the years that have gone and the minorities can make history still. But there will be no peace and justice on earth until there are enough men of good will and righteousness.[34]

The drift away from traditional theology and long-held concepts of the function of the church led to the controversy over modernism versus fundamentalism. The fundamentalists, taking the foreign missionary body as a whole, including the powerful China Inland Mission, probably constituted a majority if the term "fundamentalist" is made synonymous with "conservative." The liberals were a majority in the missions of some of the larger American denominations. While in many instances they were able to cooperate, questions of what type of Christian literature should be prepared led to a lively controversy. The more extreme of the fundamentalists organized and sought to bring pressure to bear on the boards at home to cut off the financial support of liberal missionaries. Church periodicals devoted considerable space to the controversy and the dispute was brought to the attention of the general reading public in 1924 in an article in the *Literary Digest* entitled "Ecclesiastical Frightfulness."[35]

The *Christian Century* issued frequent challenges to those charged with responsibility for the missionary program in China. Its crusade rose to a high pitch in 1930 when the editor wrote "Can Christian Missions Be Saved." China, wrote the editor, was in the midst of a social revolution. The Chinese

---

[34] Robert E. Speer, "The Relations of the Foreign Missionary Enterprise to the World Situation Today," *Christian Students and World Problems*, p. 136.

[35] "Ecclesiastical Frightfulness," *Literary Digest*, March 15, 1924, p. 33.

had surrendered their old patterns of thought and were demanding social justice and equal rights for their nation. The
editor welcomed the upheaval as a fulfillment of Christian
prayers but bemoaned the fact that now that the revolution
had come the missionary movement was wholly impotent to
provide leadership for the new forces. The fundamentalists
had an iron grip and prevented the preparation of literature
that was relevant to China's problems. What was needed was
"a new movement avowedly, even daringly, liberal, both in
administration and in approach to the peoples of these unsettled lands." The missionaries should join in the cry for revolution, but the majority of them were hopelessly enmeshed in
outworn creeds and insensitive to China's human needs.[36]

A few weeks later the *Christian Century* carried forward the
offensive for a new missionary program with an article entitled "Can a Missionary be a Christian" by F. Olin Stockwell,
a social-minded young missionary deeply aware of the fact that
China was moving towards a drastic solution. In the United
States it had been easy to take the side of the underdog, but
since his arrival in China a year before, he realized that he
was now in the camp of the privileged, and social pressure
throttled his advocacy of revolutionary reforms. Going to
church, he had seen the coolies sweating under their heavy
burdens as he prepared to sit in comfort and listen to a sermon. When he explained his agonized feelings to his fellow
missionaries, they simply replied, "Oh, you'll soon get over
that."[37]

The increasing apathy among the laity and the growing uncertainty in the realm of religious beliefs were accompanied
by a mounting hostility among intellectuals toward missionary
work. Anthropologists had now successfully diffused among
the reading public the culture concept. In the light of this
each society was considered a unit by itself and its religious

---

[36] "Can Christian Missions Be Saved," *Christian Century*, March 12,
1930, pp. 326-328.

[37] F. Olin Stockwell, "Can A Missionary Be A Christian? Haunted by
Inequalities," *Christian Century*, April 9, 1930, pp. 460-461.

expression a product of its peculiar historical experience. This not only ran counter to the notion that Christianity had a universal applicability, but it made any attempt to engraft Christianity onto an Oriental society of great antiquity seem foolish. Every native custom had some validity, and for the Western missionary to destroy these customs was to help bring about the collapse of the moral order of that society. This line of thought provided critics of missions with an intellectually respectable argument.

In an age so lacking in positive convictions as the 1920's, cynicism gained room for free play and seized the opportunity to ridicule the missionary. In 1922 appeared the first stage production lampooning the missionary, Somerset Maugham's *Rain*, a rollicking, clever satire about a missionary on a South Sea island whose Puritanism cast itself like a pall over the fun-loving foreigners who were temporarily stranded along with the missionary. Sadie Thompson, attractive and sexy, found herself the object of the poor missionary's prayers, moral exhortations, and finally of his lust.

Critical articles in popular periodicals, some by leaders within the church and even by missionaries, helped rub the gilt from the idol of a past age. Nathaniel Peffer, bringing with him to the printed page the prestige of scholarship and first-hand observation, had much to say in favor of the younger, better-educated missionary, and he praised the selfless devotion of the doctor and educator. All of this merely added to the effectiveness of the criticisms he made. A great deal of the literature on China had been written by missionaries who did not have "the equipment to understand or to judge what they saw." Through much of this literature ran "the superior, patronizing, even contemptuous note." The older missionaries were dismissed by Peffer as naïve, provincial men whose "faith was simple, their beliefs untroubled by doubt, their minds virgin of anything resembling an awareness of comparative religion, their experience in life and their knowledge of the world even more limited." The new type of missionary tried to appeal to the intellect and stressed humanitarian work, all of which was commendable except that it—even more than the old approach—raised questions of comparative creeds and comparative civilizations.[38] The net effect of the article was to raise serious doubts about the missionary movement.

Three periodicals of great influence during the 1920's, *The Atlantic Monthly, Harper's,* and *Current History,* opened their pages to critics of the missionary. Moore Bennett, in an article entitled "Christianity in China" criticized Protestant missionaries for living so comfortably that they had created an unbridgeable gulf between themselves and the people. Their annual vacations of from six to twelve weeks in China and their return to the United States every seven years separated them from the people they had chosen to serve.[39] Another contributor to the *Atlantic* called for an extensive review of the whole missionary program. He confessed that he was skeptical "not only of the basic strategy of the Protestant missionary forces, but also of the necessity for maintaining so many organizations."[40] James Norman Hall wrote an account of a visit to an island in the South Pacific where the natives had accepted Christianity, then gave up their social code, and were finally put to work on cotton plantations. At a later date opium had led to their downfall. Now the island was a scene of desolation. Surveying the scene, the writer had heard a half-dozen natives singing "Onward Christian Soldiers."[41]

Any optimism readers of *Current History* may have had as regards the future of Christianity in China was seriously challenged by Wilbur Burton's, "A Critical View of Christian Missionary Results," which appeared in June 1929 and by Hallett Abend's "The Crisis of Christian Missions in China," an article that was published in August 1930. Both of these journalists held that the day of Christian missions in China was drawing

[38] Nathaniel Peffer, "The Uniqueness of Missionaries: The Splendor and the Limitations of Those Who Challenge China with an Alien Religion," *Asia,* May 1924, p. 357.

[39] Moore Bennett, "Christianity in China," *The Atlantic Monthly,* August 1928, pp. 273-280.

[40] Mark M. Jones, "A Missionary Audit," *The Atlantic Monthly,* December 1927, pp. 750-756.

[41] James Norman Hall, "Onward, Christian Soldiers," *The Atlantic Monthly,* July 1925, pp. 19-32.

[164]

to a close. The Chinese intellectuals were agnostics who questioned Christian teachings. The Chinese, thought Abend, are "not religious-minded." Now there was the new and powerful opposition stemming from the rise of nationalism. In view of the carefully nurtured optimistic views of most Americans, this picture of the hard facts must have been especially disturbing.

The halo around the missionary was also dissipated by an article in *Harper's* by a professor of philosophy in India, who described himself as a fourth-generation Christian. The most serious of his several indictments was that missionaries were bringing about the decay of national cultures in Oriental lands. He wrote:

> The missionaries have not only despised our literature but have also condemned our music and art, because they are connected with "heathen" religions. Their intolerance of everything which in any way savored of heathenism has been so great that, in India for instance, they have not allowed their converts to retain their Hindu names.[42]

Western Christianity had also served as a tool for the imperialist governments of the West. Finally, with bitter satire, he portrayed the superiority-complex of the missionary and how he had magnified the horrors of heathen religions in order to show the superiority of Christianity. The missionary had told the Orientals only of the bright side of the West, but now the Orient had learned of Negro lynching, rotten night life, crime, and exploitation. Consequently the people of the East were asking why they should embrace the religion of such a society. When the missionary replied that Christianity had yet to be tried in the West, the Oriental critic wanted to know why it should be tried on them.[43]

In 1924 Pearl Buck began to write of the missionary. She was the daughter of a firmly orthodox missionary and had married J. Lossing Buck, outstanding authority on the agricultural economy of China, who represented the new approach.

[42] John Jesudason Cornelius, "An Oriental Looks at Christian Missions," *Harper's*, April 1927, p. 601.
[43] *Ibid.*, p. 605.

She knew the missionary compound first hand, the personal squabbles that are apt to develop among foreigners living closely together and hemmed in by a strange people; she had experienced the tyranny of a Puritan father and had witnessed the eccentrics in the missionary movement. All of these found their way into her skillfully written accounts. By 1932 her books were widely read. None of them converted any readers to the missionary cause. In January 1933 her article "Is There a Case for Foreign Missions?" appeared in *Harper's*. Miss Buck concluded that there was a case, but her readers were probably more dubious after having read her account.[44]

[44] Pearl Buck, "Is There a Case For Foreign Missions?" *Harper's*, January 1933, pp. 143-155.

CHAPTER X

THE LAYMEN'S INQUIRY
AND RECONSIDERATION OF THE ROLE OF
MISSIONS, 1931-1938

WIDESPREAD criticism of the missionary enterprise led seven major denominations to set up the Laymen's Foreign Missions Inquiry in 1930. Professor William Ernest Hocking, distinguished professor of philosophy at Harvard University, served as Chairman. The Commission of Appraisal employed a large staff, sent representatives to observe the mission work in each of the major fields, gathered the opinions of missionaries, native Christians, and non-Christian leaders. Its recommendations were presented in a book entitled *Re-Thinking Missions* and its findings of fact in a series of seven volumes known as *Fact Finders' Reports.*

Re-Thinking Missions was the high watermark of Protestant liberalism. In the dynamic world of the past one hundred years, stated the report, science, historical studies, and philosophic activity had brought progress in concepts of religious experience. Stress on future punishment had given way to a stress on beneficence. The old conflict with science was now replaced by a mature understanding of the necessity for a free religion and a free science to search for a complete world view. Christianity could no longer view itself as the sole possessor of truth; it must now accept the fact that it was only one among equals in the field of religions groping for higher concepts of the meaning of the universe. Christianity's old claim to being an especially revealed religion had led to its missionary crusade against other religions. Now it must recognize that it had no especial claim to revelation and should join hands with those same religions for the purpose of strengthening spiritual values in a world threatened by materialism.

The Commission of Appraisal found that much good work

[167]

was being done, but it denied that there was adequate ground in this fact for a renewed appeal for the further support, "much less for the enlargement, of these missions as a whole in their present form and on their present basis."[1] Every enlargement of missionary work should be conditioned upon the adoption of changed methods that would be better suited to the realization of the objectives as outlined by the commission.

Concerning the quality of missionary personnel, the Commission stated:

> Of these thousands of persons, there are many of conspicuous power, true saintliness and a sublime spirit of devotion, men and women in whose presence one feels himself at once exalted and unworthy. It is easier to say this, than to say the rest of the truth; the greater number seem to us of limited outlook and capacity; and there are not a few whose vision of the inner meaning of the mission has become obscured by the intricacies, divisions, frictions and details of a task too great for their powers and their hearts.[2]

Several recommendations were made concerning existing missionary institutions. None of these were new, having previously received some consideration by those engaged in missions. The Commission found the rural churches weak and thought more emphasis should be put upon encouraging converts to meet in groups more closely akin to native patterns.[3] In China this would mean building the Christian community around the family and experimenting with different types of worship services.[4] The Commission reported that many mission schools and hospitals had low standards, a fact they attributed to the diffusion of limited funds among a great many institutions.[5] Finally, the Commission recommended that social work should not be subordinated to evangelization.

The chief criticism of the work of missions on the home

---

[1] *Re-Thinking Missions* by the Commission of Appraisal, William Ernest Hocking, Chairman (New York: Harper & Brothers, 1932), pp. 4-5.
[2] *Ibid.*, p. 15.   [3] *Ibid.*, p. 87.   [4] *Ibid.*, pp. 87, 90.
[5] *Ibid.*, pp. 171, 201.

front was directed against the multiplicity of denominational mission boards. This situation was uneconomic and inefficient and led to the perpetuation of denominational loyalties on the mission field. The commission recommended the centralization of administration in one interdenominational board and the restricting of denominational boards to promotion and fund raising.[6]

American Protestantism, with a few exceptions, reacted violently. It was the Commission of Appraisal that found itself on trial, not the missionary enterprise. The recommendations and findings scarcely received a fair hearing. Emotion erupted into a defense of symbols long accepted. When the General Assembly of the Presbyterian Church met in Columbus, Ohio in May 1933, a committee took sharp issue with the Laymen's Inquiry, and when Robert E. Speer, already known as a sharp critic of the report, mounted the platform to attack the Commission, the audience spontaneously rose in tribute to him and to his position and burst forth in singing "Blest Be the Tie that Binds."[7]

The criticism of the Commission, on occasion, at least, was on a higher level. Speer centered the attack upon the Commission's conclusion that the permanent function of the missionary was to help strengthen native religions by sharing with them the spiritual insights of Christianity. Speer declared that Christianity was not the product of man's groping for an understanding of God; Christianity was the divinely revealed truth that is "both Jesus, the historic Son of Man and Son of God, and the Eternal Christ, the risen and ever-living Master and Lord." Man had not discovered God and spiritual truth through his own efforts; they had been revealed to him in Christ. The Commission was wrong in assuming that man was capable of progress and improvement; such faith in man's capacity was "not a true view of human nature or in accord with the reality of human experience and the chastened conviction of mankind." The grandeur of the spiritual truths of Chris-

6 *Ibid.*, pp. 314, 318-324.

7 "Presbyterian Foreign Missions: Important Action at the Assembly," *The Missionary Review of the World*, July 1933, p. 387.

tianity could never be satisfactorily explained as the product of sinful man's search for truth; man was not capable of reaching such sublime heights. Christianity could only be explained in terms of a gift of God. It was in this respect that Christianity was different from the other religions; the latter were the fruit of man's groping, and their weaknesses were a reflection of this fact. Entertaining such views, Speer quite naturally set the aim of missions as "the absolute triumph of Christ as acknowledged Lord and Saviour."[8]

A writer for the *Missionary Review of the World* denounced the appraisers. Their theological views disqualified them from making a survey of "the divinely inspired work of foreign missions." The Commission had made two grave errors in stating that the emphasis should be on humanitarian work and in recommending a compromise with "these human faiths which reach their lowest depths in the lives of the people."[9] The editor of the *Missionary Review* collected statements from missionaries, mission boards, ministers and laymen. Only the Congregational and Methodist Boards received the report favorably. Sherwood Eddy also praised it, but all the others sharply disagreed with the notion that Christianity was not the only true religion.[10] It was the so-called "modernists"—

[8] Robert E. Speer, *"Re-Thinking Missions" Examined* (New York: Fleming H. Revell Company, 1933), p. 32.

[9] Mrs. Henry W. Peabody, "A Woman's Criticism of the Laymen's Report," *The Missionary Review of the World*, January 1933, p. 39.

[10] "Reactions to the Laymen's Report," *The Missionary Review of the World*, January 1933, pp. 43-45.

There was much praise of the Laymen's Inquiry in the *Christian Century* and in the *Chinese Recorder*. The editor of the latter, Frank Rawlinson, stated that he would not publish letters which indulged in negative criticisms of the report. The editor of *The Missionary Review of the World* was critical of the report but he published articles on both sides.

The term "modernist" has no generally accepted definition. It had been applied to all those accepting the higher criticism and to exponents of the application of Christianity to social problems. Many of these undoubtedly took exception to the theology of the report. To have accepted the report would have forced them to go the full length of humanism and to have conceived of Christianity as purely a product of the social process.

The Laymen's Inquiry spelled out the full implications of the humanist position. The report stated that it would be difficult to point to any one general principle that could surely be found nowhere else. (See page 49 of

though by no means all of them—who accepted the theology of the Laymen's Inquiry.

The church-going public was scarcely prepared for such sharp criticisms. Missionary literature had been largely propaganda prepared by enthusiastic supporters for the purpose of winning public support. The leadership had been very much aware of the difficulties, but they had feared that sharing the problems with the public would weaken public support. They had never intended to give widespread publicity to the findings of the Laymen's Inquiry, but the Commission of Appraisal took the opposite course and prepared advance releases for the newspapers. The resulting news stories tended to stress the more sensational aspects of the report. The impression created was that the Commission had completely discredited the whole missionary enterprise, a reaction that can be traced in part to the failure of the missionary leaders to inform the public of the mountainous difficulties standing in the way of Christianization.

Many of the leaders on the home front and most missionaries sought to discount the validity of the Commission's fact find-

---

Re-Thinking Missions.) The humanist who rules out revelation and refuses to accept as a matter of faith any religious teaching except as it is verified by human experience must agree with the report. He may, as the Commission did, indulge in his own act of faith. Human personality and its most noble achievements along with a vision of its potential achievements may induce in him a feeling of religious ecstasy. He will also see in the highest teachings of non-Christian leaders manifestations of the best in man and will have no inclination to minimize what is noble and good in other religions. He will find the best in other religions confirming his own innermost convictions. He may admit that these beliefs are not scientifically verifiable.

The traditional Christian, who views mankind more realistically, and who is deeply conscious of the problem of evil, is unable to reconcile the grandeur of Christian teachings with man's incapacity to understand spiritual things. Seeing man's feeble efforts to live a righteous life, he is compelled to account for Christ in terms of revelation. Having done so, he is impelled by his own innermost convictions to discount the achievements of leaders of other religions. To admit that other religions have equally great truths would compel him to accept the view that these other religions are, like Christianity, the product of revelation. The great majority of missionaries belonged to this traditional school of thought, and these religious convictions were the central dynamic of the movement.

ing. The observations, it was charged, had been made in great haste and were superficial. Staff members were described as having an inadequate understanding of the problems of the mission field.[11] How could they correctly evaluate the work of a school, hospital, and mission station on the basis of a brief inspection? It was only natural that many missionaries should be resentful. They had given a lifetime to the work and had been forced to do the best possible with limited funds.

Lay critics of missions took delight in the quandary in which the missionary movement now found itself. Nathaniel Peffer praised the approach of the Inquiry but he also contended that mission work designed to cooperate with other religions could never muster financial support. The proposals were also impracticable, said Peffer, because the kind of men required for such a program did not have the psychology of missions. With a note of cheerfulness he looked forward to the death of missions, convinced that little of permanent value to men would be lost with them.[12]

The suggestion that the churches abandon missionary work was dismissed as the piffle of cynics by both sides in the intrachurch strife over the proper role of missions. The orthodox had no difficulty in stating the case for missions. Christ was the Son of God, and the Christian message of salvation was much more than the insight gained from the historical process of the West; it was universal and it represented the intervention of God in the historical process. Convinced of the truth of this approach, the orthodox had no doubts about the duty to carry on missionary work regardless of the difficulties involved. In the 1930's the conservative churches faced the problem of declining contributions due to the economic depression, but they fared much better than the liberal denominations in maintaining a missionary force in China.[13]

The liberals had to rethink the whole problem of missions.

[11] Robert E. Speer, "An Appraisal of the Appraisal," *The Missionary Review of the World*, January 1933, pp. 10-11.

[12] Nathaniel Peffer, "The Twilight of Foreign Missions," *Harper's*, March 1933, p. 408.

[13] Frank Rawlinson, "The Liberal Retreat in China," *The Christian Century*, September 25, 1935, p. 1203.

Many members of liberal churches were now indifferent, but denominational leaders insisted on missionary work being continued. To admit defeat would have been to suggest that as liberals they had nothing to offer to the rest of the world. Liberals were no less dogmatic than conservatives; they were simply dogmatic about propositions of a new variety. Whereas the orthodox had an evangelical psychology calling for an urgent effort to save individuals, the religious liberal was evangelical in saving the world from ignorance, superstition, outworn political and social creeds and institutions, and economic backwardness. Yet, liberals sensed the need for a new apologetic. Liberal missionaries were declining in number, and support at home was wavering. What was needed was a new motive in harmony with humanistic and scientific currents of thought and yet one capable of stimulating self-sacrifice and devotion. However, few mission board executives cared to face the issue; it would split their constituencies and involve them in strife. To many of them it seemed wiser to gloss over the differences and go on with the work.

Hugh Vernon White, Secretary of the American Board, and many other liberals resolved to fight out the issue. "End Mission Imperialism Now!", demanded White. The Christian church must find ways to work with other religions, its message must be something more than the expression of a national culture, and it should deliver people to whom it ministers from the dominance of the state.[14] Finally, the Christian mission should free itself from identification with capitalism. The purpose of missions, wrote White, "is not to spread institutions or dogmas" but rather to serve men.[15]

Charles Clayton Morrison, editor of the *Christian Century*, charged the mission boards with evading the issue raised by the Laymen's Inquiry and of seeking to perpetuate the conditions against which the best thought of the churches had revolted.[16]

[14] Hugh Vernon White, "End Mission Imperialism Now!", *The Christian Century*, February 14, 1934, p. 220.
[15] *Ibid.*, p. 221.
[16] "The Road to Missionary Revival," ed., *The Christian Century*, January 30, 1935, pp. 136-137; "Missions on a Wider Front," ed., *The Christian Century*, June 12, 1935, pp. 782-783.

This religious journal became the chief vehicle for the opinions of mission reformers. "I Don't Want to Christianize the World," wrote a professor at the University of Chicago Divinity School. There were other religions and other forms of government that would meet the needs of other men. "The kind of missionary enterprise which I should like to see promoted," he wrote, "is one which seeks the cooperation of all men of good will, regardless of religion, color or race, for the enrichment and liberation of human life and the building of a better world."[17] Advocates of missions arrogantly laid exclusive claim to the best in Christianity and at the same time closed their eyes to the pogroms it had organized, the inquisitions it had conducted, the human slavery it had endorsed and the bloodiest wars it had sanctified. Supporters of missions had been less than humble in judging other religions by the total culture of which they were a part while associating Christianity only with the best in Western experience.[18]

The editor of the *Christian Century* replied that he did want to Christianize the world. Seeking to reconcile the missionary motive and the sociological culture concept, Charles Clayton Morrison said that the social psychological approach led to the conclusion that religion was a product of a culture.[19] The religion of each people had been best suited to its culture. For the West with its science, the Christian concepts of God as Creator, God as Father, Grace, Revelation, Forgiveness, Redemption, Incarnation, Atonement, Providence, and others offered the best ways of communicating with God. As the scientific culture of the West moved "on its inexorable way over the whole world," it would be found that no religion "offers a comprehensive idea or set of ideas by means of which a scientific civilization may have vital commerce with the Supreme Reality except that religion whose cultural habitat has been for centuries the Western world in which this scientific culture has itself emerged."

17 Charles T. Holman, "I Don't Want to Christianize the World!", *The Christian Century*, November 20, 1935, p. 1483.

18 *Ibid.*, p. 1484.

19 Charles Clayton Morrison, "Do I Want to Christianize the World? Yes!", *The Christian Century*, November 27, 1935, p. 1516.

The Laymen's Inquiry

The most able statement of the liberal-humanistic position appeared in 1934 with the publication of Archibald G. Baker's *Christian Missions and a New World Culture*. The author was professor of missions at the University of Chicago. All religions, including Christianity, were a product of the social process, according to Professor Baker.[20] None of them could lay claim to absolute truth. Each owed much to great religious leaders but these prophets in turn reflected the society in which they lived. The truths they perceived changed in the process of being transmitted from individual to individual and from generation to generation. Each hearer of the Christian gospel must necessarily interpret it in terms of the values of his own particular culture.[21] Personality was a reaction to the culture in which an individual found himself. In seeking to influence the growth of a personality in a non-Christian culture, the missionary should put to use all that psychologists had learned about conditioning and all that the sociologists knew about the culture patterns.[22] His task was not to displace native religions but to improve society. If this could be done best by instilling new meanings into an old faith, the missionary should seek to be of assistance. Christian experience pertinent to a particular problem should be shared with natives, but the attitude of the missionary should be one of open-mindedness rather than an attitude of dogmatic insistence that his way was the best.[23]

The Secretary of the American Board of Commissioners for Foreign Missions, Hugh Vernon White, delivered a series of lectures at Andover-Newton Theological Seminary in 1935 in which he sought to develop a new theological basis for missions. The lectures were later published under the title *A Theology for Christian Missions*. White was quite willing to bury the old dogmatism. He was grateful for the contributions of psychology, the higher criticism and historical study of Christian experience. These had swept away the basis of the old

[20] Archibald G. Baker, *Christian Missions and a New World Culture* (Chicago: Willett, Clark & Co., 1934), p. 29.
[21] *Ibid.*, pp. 113, 175, 262.
[22] *Ibid.*, Chapters XIII and XIV.
[23] *Ibid.*, pp. 293-294.

dogmatism.[24] This house cleaning, said White, was necessary, but he deplored some of the developments accompanying it. Led by John Dewey, men had come to look upon religion as a purely psychological phenomena. They had denied that there was any objective truth in religion, and that any one religion might be better than any other in an absolute sense. Each, they said, was best for its own followers. This view had undermined the apologetic for missions.

White affirmed his belief in three propositions. First, it is a fallacy to say that one religion is as good or as true as another. Conversely, there is a religion that is truer because its doctrine conforms more closely to the real nature of man and spiritual reality. Secondly, it is a fallacy to say that the religion any nation already has is, for that reason, the best religion for it. Various nations had accepted a new religion, which had lifted their moral and spiritual life. Finally, he affirmed that "there is a best religion in the world" and that religion is Christianity. The truth of Christianity, said White, is to be found in the character of Christ. He it was who "discovered, experienced and exhibited the true nature of man in terms of his basic relation and attitude to God and other men." The Christian faith

> is that the life of active trust in God and love for all men is eternally right and represents the purpose of God for mankind; that such a life will be sustained by God despite all temporary defeat; and that such a life lived even in the face of enmity and through sacrifice will be a force for the fulfillment of God's purpose to win men to himself and to create a society of persons who live that life together.[25]

This was a truth, said White, that no one could know by theoretical statement alone. To know it, one must live it, experience it for himself in will and feeling and action. The role of the missionary was to live this truth and say to others, "Come,

[24] Hugh Vernon White, *A Theology for Christian Missions* (New York: Willett, Clark and Co., 1937), pp. 98-99.
[25] *Ibid.*, p. 119.

let us live it together, and think about it and try to understand it."

The charm of White's new apologetic lay in part in the author's humility, his dislike of the arrogance that had manifested itself in the use of force and polemic argument, and his openness to the fruitful findings of man's search for truth in the modern age. In his indictment of traditional missionary imperialism, with its emphasis on dogma and reckless assertion of the superiority of Western institutions, he appealed to the penitent spirit of a generation caught in the sloughs of economic depression and expecting the holocaust of war.

The new apologetic elaborated upon the basic intellectual propositions of the Laymen's Inquiry, but lofty philosophizing failed to make the logical end of Christian humanism acceptable to the church-going laity. Mission boards were also left with a cold feeling as they faced the difficulty of trying to reorient the whole vast program to fit in with the new approach. The ideas and attitudes of the Inquiry were essentially foreign to them—too philosophical, too vague to provide an adequate dynamic, too far from their faith in the superiority of Christianity. The result was a retreat of the missionary movement from liberalism toward orthodoxy.

The International Missionary Council, preparing for a meeting to be held in Madras in 1938, turned to Europe for a statement of the missionary apologetic. In Germany, Karl Barth had declared war on relativism and had affirmed his belief in the Christian gospel as the special revelation of God. Man, said Barth, was corrupt and incapable of comprehending spiritual truth except as God had revealed it to him and granted him the grace to apprehend the meaning of the revelation. Other prominent European church scholars did not go as far as Barth but they joined him in basing Christian truth on revelation. It was one of these, Hendrik Kraemer, professor of the history of religions at Leyden University, who was now invited to prepare a statement for the meeting at Madras.[26] Kraemer had reviewed the book of Hugh Vernon White, and,

[26] Review of Hendrik Kraemer's book by Paul J. Braisted, *The Christian Century*, August 3, 1938, pp. 942-943.

while expressing appreciation, had found it too humanistic for his taste. It was, he said, a book on the anthropology of missions rather than the theology of missions.[27]

In his book *The Christian Message in a Non-Christian World*, Kraemer affirmed that Christian truth was a direct revelation from God and that the role of the missionary was to make this revealed truth known.

> The only valid motive and purpose of missions is . . . to call men and peoples to confront themselves with God's acts of revelation and salvation for man and the world as presented in Biblical realism, and to build up a community of those who had surrendered themselves to faith in and loving service of Jesus Christ. . . . Other motives and purposes may, according to circumstances, be of greater or less secondary importance and value, but if they take the place of this primary motive and purpose, mission work as such is no really tenable activity.[28]

To Kraemer, Christianity was a product of divine revelation and not a tradition to be explained scientifically in terms of the social process. Few American liberals were willing to go all the way in his radical emphasis on revelation and on absolutes, but his book, nevertheless, was well received.

The discussions at the meetings in Madras in 1938 centered about the theme of a divinely inspired Christian message. Other religions, while it was admitted they had their brighter aspects, were viewed as man's efforts to comprehend the totality of existence and therefore not comparable to the God-given Christian message.[29] A delegate to the meetings noted the change in attitude that had taken place since the meetings at Jerusalem ten years before.

[27] Review of Hugh Vernon White's book by Hendrik Kraemer, *International Review of Missions*, 1937, pp. 537-540.

[28] Quoted by G. E. Phillips in his review of Hendrik Kraemer's *The Christian Message in a Non-Christian World* in the *International Review of Missions*, 1938, p. 527.

[29] H. H. Farmer, "The Faith by Which the Church Lives," *International Review of Missions*, 1939, p. 179.

It was seen that the great non-Christian religions must be judged not by incidental fine qualities and insights which may be discerned in them (this on the whole was the attitude adopted at Jerusalem), but as complex, powerful, all embracing systems or organisms of belief, proxis, culture, morality and so forth, which hold and shape the whole life of those who have part in them. Considered as such systems or organisms, considered, that is to say, as totalities—which is to consider them as they actually are in their impact upon men and women—they are in a very real sense all wrong, and must be all wrong—despite, we repeat, incidental and isolated rightnesses—for the reason that they leave (and must leave, being without Christ) the basic problem of man's existence unsolved: the problem, namely, of his alienation from God through sin.[30]

Humanism and relativism, so fashionable in the 1920's, were now in full retreat. By 1938, the report of the Laymen's Inquiry was even less acceptable to many liberals. There was an inexorable movement away from the humanistic and humanitarian views that underlay the Inquiry's report. The acceptance of an absolutist apologetic for missions was deemed so important by missionary leaders that, unlike the elaborate fact gathering made in preparation for conferences at Edinburgh in 1910 and Jerusalem in 1928, preparation for the meeting at Madras involved the preparation of a book on principles and the theory of missions. There was no fact gathering in 1938. Missions and theology, together with many secular agencies, were now involved in a hectic search for first principles. American liberals were uneasy about Kraemer's theism but they were also uncertain that the answer lay in a humanistic approach.

[30] *Ibid.*

CHAPTER XI

MISSIONARIES AND THE STORM OF CHINESE
NATIONALISM, 1920-1927

By the 1920's a hundred years of inferior status had given the Chinese a paranoic sense of both real and imaginary grievances against the West. The unequal treaties and foreign control of economic enterprises, especially mining, were not the real causes of China's troubles but they were the readily observable marks of bondage on which the blame could be placed.

Beyond these hated reminders of foreign influence was a miasma of pitiful economic conditions. The average monthly wage of $9 for a twelve-hour day and seven-day week in the cotton industry in Shanghai, the miserable sheds where industrial workers slept, the women and children who constituted 80 per cent of the working force in textile mills, the absence of the simplest precautions for health and safety in factories, and the exorbitant rents, taxes, and interest rates extorted from the peasants generated the hate that turned the wheels of Dr. Sun Yat-sen's Nationalist revolution.

Sweeping across the Chinese landscape in pursuit of the diabolical Western imperialists it held responsible for China's misery, the revolution hit the missionaries. Unequal to the task of unifying the country under a strong central government and quite incapable of satisfying their thirst for glory by effectively asserting themselves against the nations infringing on China's sovereignty, the Nationalists found vent for their patriotism in attacks on missions. Neither a strong government nor a strong army was required for this objective.

Missions, moreover, were deeply offensive to ardent Nationalists. The chapel, school and hospital of the missionary were foreign in every respect, managed by foreigners, patterned after Western institutions, flying foreign flags and obviously aimed at Westernizing the country's religious life. Chinese who fell under their influence might become better people in the eyes of the missionary, but they became a kind of hyphenated Chinese. Mission schools were especially humiliating to a patriotic Chinese. A primary function of education as viewed by a Nationalist was to inculcate patriotism, and mission schools directed by foreigners could scarcely be trusted to do this. Hospitals, however much they might minister to physical needs, were scarcely less humiliating. The very fact that many of them offered the best medical service made them all the more dangerous, for they were all the more likely to stimulate respect and kindly feelings toward foreigners and Western nations. It is not surprising that schools and hospitals suffered more frequent attacks than did mission chapels.

Only the slightest spark was needed to convert these nationalistic and anti-Christian sentiments into an organized crusade. In 1922 two happenings helped set fire to the smouldering resentment against the missionaries, the meeting in Peking of the World Christian Student Federation and the publication of a book by the China Continuation Committee with the unhappy title *The Christian Occupation of China*. Both of these events struck Chinese students as bold ultimatums of defiance from the West, and they eagerly seized upon them. They now organized the Anti-Christian Alliance, a short-lived instrument devised to combat the missionaries.[1] The main burden of attack was carried by the already influential Young China Society. It sponsored lectures and devoted a large part of its periodical to promoting a defense against Western Christianity.[2] The new crusade benefited by the leadership of Dr. Hu Shih, the highly respected father of China's intellectual renaissance. Christianity, said this influential leader, was essentially foreign and inconsistent with the national spirit of China. Hu Shih made much of Christian superstition and its conflict with science. The crude teachings of Billy Sunday and Aimee Semple McPherson provided him with illustrations of the vulgari-

[1] H. C. Tsao, "The Nationalist Movement and Christian Education," *China Christian Yearbook*, ed. Frank Rawlinson (Shanghai: Christian Literature Society, 1928), p. 174.
[2] *Ibid.*

ties and lack of intellectual content of American Christianity.[3] China's heritage of humanism with its dignity and openness to scientific teaching obviously had nothing to gain from association with Christianity, which was now fighting its last desperate battle for survival in the West.

The nationalistic anti-Christian crusade had already attained widespread support among intellectuals and students when the Communists began to make significant headway in China. They joined the crusade and provided it with new slogans. According to their ideology religion was, of course, an opiate and a servant of the *status quo* capitalism, and missionaries were nothing more than the "running dogs of imperialism."[4] With the entry of the Communists into the movement, some diplomatic officers blamed them for everything unpalatable to Westerners. Most American consuls, however, and the American Minister in Peking recognized that the rise of nationalism was responsible for anti-Christian outbreaks rather than the Communists, who merely supported the movement in the hope of strengthening their own position.[5] The President of Shantung

[3] Hu Shih, "China and Christianity," *The Forum*, July 1927, p. 2.

[4] A circular distributed by the Anti-Christian League described Christians as the vanguards of the imperialists, capitalists, and militarists. "In short," the circular closed, "we cannot do any thing to the coming generations, to emancipate China and to get rid of our chains, unless we can strike down the vanguards and runners of the imperialists, capitalists and militarists." A copy of this circular was forwarded to the Department of State by the Consul-General at Canton on January 7, 1925. Department of State Archives.

[5] Jacob Gould Schurman, American Minister, considered the following factors most important:

"(1) The ever-present Chinese aversion to foreigners and a new sense of the danger of foreign control of education,

(2) the rising consciousness of nationality and the aspiration for a system of national education,

(3) Bolshevik propaganda against other nations in China, which has been especially successful in winning over and utilizing educators and students, and

(4) a Bolshevik and Chinese drive against the so-called "Anglo-Saxon nations" who support most of the foreign missions and schools in China. France and Italy are scarcely mentioned in this connection and of course Japan not at all."

Schurman to the Secretary of State, January 12, 1925, Department of State Archives.

Christian University, Doctor Balme, an Englishman, in a careful analysis, which eventually reached the American Department of State, observed:

There is an unfortunate tendency at the present time to ascribe all nationalistic or anti-foreign movements to Bolshevistic propaganda, and thus to lose sight of the important fact that all through China today thére is a strong undercurrent of feeling with regard to the motivation of Christian educational work which is capable of being easily roused into active opposition.[6]

Beginning in December 1924 the missionary school masters in central and southern China faced almost complete anarchy. The first outbreak came at Yale-in-China at Changsha in the middle of December. Students announced plans for an anti-Christian demonstration and parade on Christmas day. Next they held an unauthorized meeting. On their return to the campus they were told that they must either sign a statement that they would abide by the rules in the future or they would be expelled. Nearly four-fifths of the students refused to return and, with aid from the Educational Rights Maintenance Society, embarked on a publicity campaign. The students asked for certificates transferring them to government schools but they were refused by the provincial authorities.[7] By the close of the month about 200 of the 320 had returned to classes. At the same time that these disturbances were taking place at Yale-in-China, a number of other mission schools in the same province of Hunan were having strikes. The American Vice-Consul at Changsha, in explaining the causes, said:

In all this agitation there is to be seen a spirit of anti-foreignism, but it is not the old anti-foreignism which was blind, unreasoning, and sometimes terror-stricken, hatred for that which had for centuries been called despicable and dangerous. The present spirit is more one of awakening

[6] A. L. Warnshuis to M. F. Perkins, Department of State, March 13, 1925, Inclosure Doctor Balme to A. L. Warnshuis, Department of State Archives.
[7] C. D. Meinhardt, Vice Consul at Changsha, to Minister Jacob Gould Schurman, January 23, 1925, Department of State Archives.

to a fear of future aggression and increased control from outside, producing resentment, whether rightly or wrongly, directed at the foreigner in China and at home. Jealousy of foreign success, a realization of the country's own weakness, and the characteristic habit of refusing to face the facts squarely can not be left out of consideration in seeking to understand this agitation.[8]

The student outbreaks in Hunan were paralleled by a large-scale three-day demonstration at Canton during the Christmas holidays. Unlike the student insurrection at Changsha, which had no support from officials, a number of political leaders took part in the movement at Canton. The President of the University spoke at a meeting in the assembly hall at Canton University and the Chief of the Bureau of Labor in the Kuomintang party helped sponsor demonstrations in which the cadets at the Whampoa Military School participated.[9] As at Changsha, the Communists played a part.

The demonstrations at Canton led the American Consul-General in that city, Douglas Jenkins, to write a long and informative report on the history of the anti-Christian movement, pointing out that many conservative intellectuals had sponsored it in 1922. It was his opinion that the fresh outbreaks at Canton were traceable in part to Sun Yat-sen's failure to get Western loans for various railroad and other internal improvement projects. As a result he had turned to Russia where he received both money and ideas.[10] Jenkins outlined many other sources from which the movement had stemmed. He cited a letter reflecting the views of the merchant class that had appeared in a local guild paper. In it the writer said that while foreign schools had some virtues, their defects, if continued, would destroy Chinese nationality. These schools always induced students to become Christians. The Chinese writer had closed by saying: "The chief object of these schools is to teach America. In a word, they regard America as everything in the

[8] *Ibid.*

[9] Douglas Jenkins, Consul General at Canton, to Minister Jacob Gould Schurman, January 7, 1925, Department of State Archives.

[10] Jenkins to Schurman, January 29, 1925, Department of State Archives.

world. We, citizens of the Republic of China, are utterly filthy, unworthy of mention."[11]

Consular officers in southern China and in the province of Hunan encountered a violent antiforeignism in 1924 and 1925. At Foochow, in January 1925, young Nationalists sought to shut off the business of American fish merchants, forced the closing of Anglo-Chinese College, and put up posters urging action: "Be Angry! Hate! Kill!" Confronted by this situation the American Consul in that city warned Minister Jacob Gould Schurman:

> Whither are we drifting? Unless this thing is checked, right now, we are drifting into a general anti-American, and very possibly, anti-foreign boycott. From here the movement may easily spread to other parts of China. Then, it is only one more step to a Pan-Asiatic alliance of yellow and near-yellow-Bolshevik Russia, Bolshevik China, and an imperialist Japan, which to save herself from the Bolshevik menace has already laid the foundation of such an alliance. I believe this to be no idle fantasy, but a real danger. The ties of blood, the sympathy of color, are stronger than any political or theoretical alliance.[12]

Schurman agreed that there had been an "outrageous infraction of treaty rights" and that it might be necessary to send some naval vessels close enough so that they could be seen by the entire population of Foochow.[13]

In April 1925, Consul-General Jenkins at Canton was equally appalled by the antiforeign activities in that city. Placards had

[11] *Ibid.*

[12] Ernest B. Price, Consul at Foochow, to Jacob Gould Schurman, January 12, 1925, Department of State Archives.

[13] Schurman wrote: "I hope this may lead to a cessation of the outrageous infraction of our treaty rights. [He had sent a member of the legation staff to Foochow to protest.] In the contrary case, however, the next step would seem to be the sending of one or more vessels. These, however, would produce little or no effect if they cannot go above Pagoda anchorage and penetrate into the heart of the city, preferably I should say up to the bridge of Ten Thousand Ages where they would be seen by the entire population." Schurman to the Secretary of State, March 1, 1925, Department of State Archives.

been posted with such inscriptions as "Strike the Imperialistic Countries Down," "Demand Cancellation of all Unequal Treaties," "Demand the Return of the Foreign Concessions," "Demand Control of the Maritime Customs" and "Demand a Division of Property Ownership so as to bring the Capitalists under Control."[14]

Infinitely more serious violence commenced with the Shanghai Incident of May 30, 1925. A strike had paralyzed the Japanese textile mills in Shanghai since December 1924. There was considerable violence and on May 15 one of the participants in a riot was killed. After a memorial service on May 30 a crowd led by students and laborers entered the International Settlement carrying banners with slogans charging the Japanese with killing Chinese and demanding cancellation of the unequal treaties. The police of the International Settlement arrested several and sought to push the crowd back from the police station. For a time they encountered no serious opposition but at one point the crowd excitedly refused to retreat further and began to move forward. The British officer in charge warned that unless the crowd stopped he would shoot. A few moments later, as the crowd continued to move toward the police station, he gave orders to fire. Twelve Chinese were killed and seventeen were injured.[15]

All of China was set aflame. Everywhere there were meetings and strikes. The antiforeign movement, sporadic and scattered until now, became general as a result of the drama in Shanghai. Soon the Shanghai Incident was referred to as the Boston Tea Party of the Chinese revolution. Strikes, boycotts and riots ensued. Christians joined in protesting the killing of Chinese youth by foreigners. A Chinese reviewing the effect on literature wrote:

[14] Douglas Jenkins, Consul General at Canton, to the Secretary of State, April 25, 1925, Department of State Archives.

[15] The Shanghai Incident, the Shameen Incident, and the violence accompanying the occupation of Nanking received a great deal of attention in American newspapers and periodicals. A reliable account is to be found in Dorothy Borg's *American Policy and the Chinese Revolution, 1925-1928* (New York: American Institute of Pacific Relations and the MacMillan Company, 1947), pp. 20-30, 41-42.

The Storm of Chinese Nationalism

The Shanghai incident of May 30th had the effect of an active volcano; hardly a single person who could write did not write or try to. If much of the literary lava was more heated than solid, the heat was indicative of the latent energy that has been encased within.[16]

The editor of the *China Christian Year Book* observed that a wave of nationalism "surged around and through the Church."[17] The argument that the church must win respect by severing foreign ties and by becoming indigenous now gained widespread support among Chinese Christians.

The Shanghai Incident, in turn, led to the Shameen Incident at Canton. A strike in protest against the happenings in Shanghai had led to a paralysis of the entire area in and around Canton, including the British and French concessions on the island of Shameen. Consternation developed among British and French officials when they learned that students scheduled to march in a parade on June 23 were planning to cross the bridges leading to the concessions. Warnings were issued that such an attempt would be repelled by force. On the appointed day the parade took place. Someone fired—which side fired first was never determined. For fifteen minutes a battle raged. One Frenchman was killed and four British were wounded, but it was the Chinese who suffered the heaviest casualties, fifty killed and a hundred wounded.

Southern China presented a chaotic scene during the winter and spring of 1926. Nominal control was already in the hands of the Kuomintang in that area, but officials soon learned that they were powerless to control labor unions and student groups who embarked on strikes, boycotts, and riots and made mobs their political instruments. In the twilight of the old order and before the dawn of a new one, disorder was inevitable, simply because it served the interests of some groups. These same groups, bitterly antiforeign and often anti-Christian, found vent for their resentment in attacks on missionaries.

[16] William Hung, "Main Tendencies in Literary Circles," *China Christian Year Book, 1926*, p. 365.

[17] Frank Rawlinson, "Present Characteristics of the China Christian Movement," *China Christian Year Book, 1926*, p. XVI.

The revolutionary upheaval in the winter of 1926 centered in the Canton area. Reports told of missionaries and Chinese Christians facing the full fury of the widespread hatred of all that was foreign. The American mission compound at Kuchek, on the island of Hainan, was invaded on January 21 by a mob of students and Cantonese troops. The hospital was broken into and the Chinese attendants were beaten. Several chapels in the area were occupied. In a final gesture of defiance the crowd tore down the American flag and trampled upon it.[18]

On March 9 a mission hospital at Canton became the center of a heated labor dispute. When the missionary staff refused the demands of the union, pickets surrounded the hospital, refused to permit any Chinese to enter and cut off the food supply of the foreigners.[19] A month later, soldiers took over the American Baptist hospital at Wuchow and held it until the following September.[20]

The Baptist compound at Kweilin fell victim to a mob on March 12. A native Christian, known for his helpfulness to foreigners, was beaten, stoned, and then tied to a scaffold where fireworks were to be set off. Two missionaries intervened at the risk of their own lives. When a Chinese official came to his rescue and placed him in the yamen for protection, the mob demanded his release and the following day was dissuaded from entering the mission compound only after soldiers fired over their heads.[21]

Not since the Boxer Revolt had the missionaries faced such a critical situation as they did in the following year of 1927. Hankow was the scene of violence as the year opened. On January 3 a Chinese mob took possession of the British Concession at Hankow after the British troops retreated to ships on the

[18] J. V. A. MacMurray to the Secretary of State, February 26, 1926, *Foreign Relations of the United States, 1926* (Washington: Government Printing Office, 1926), Vol. I, pp. 695-696.

[19] J. V. A. MacMurray to the Secretary of State, March 13, 1926, *Foreign Relations of the United States, 1926*, Vol. I, pp. 698-699.

[20] J. V. A. MacMurray to the Secretary of State, July 19, 1926, *Foreign Relations of the United States, 1926*, Vol. I, p. 712.

[21] Douglas Jenkins to the Secretary of State, April 15, 1926, Inclosure, Robert L. Bausum to Doctor Leavell, March 16, 1926, Department of State Archives.

Yangtze amid a hail of bricks and stones. A few days later the British surrendered their concession at Kiukiang under similar circumstances. Conditions in southern China had seemed to improve as the more extremist leaders had gone north, but on January 14 Foochow was the scene of a wild outburst against a group of Spanish missionaries who were accused of murdering two infants whose corpses had been discovered. Three days later soldiers and civilians joined in a general looting of mission property. Two residences of the American Board lost three to four thousand dollars worth of clothes, bedding, typewriters, watches, etc. The YMCA, a large Methodist church, an Anglican church, and two hospitals were swept clean and some other churches suffered heavy losses. Two British ladies were driven through the streets by a mob.[22]

The foreign women and children had scarcely been evacuated from Foochow when the Methodist mission at Yenping was attacked by a mob led by a certain Ku Ch'ien-li who was attached to the Nationalist army. During March the local mission hosptial, a parsonage, two foreign residences, and a church were occupied and looted.[23] In October the American Consul reported that these missionary buildings were still occupied by the Chinese.[24]

These attacks on missionaries culminated in the sack of Nanking by Nationalist troops on March 24. Many women and children had boarded the foreign warships before the entry of the Nationalists into the city, but many had remained, guided by a feeling that scares were frequent in China and

[22] Samuel H. Leger, "What Happened at Foochow," *Chinese Recorder,* April 1927, pp. 288-290.

[23] Ernest B. Price, Consul at Foochow, to the Secretary of State, June 15, 1927, Department of State Archives. The Consul expressed his surprise at the courage of the Chinese Christians who were attacked. He wrote: "Although a believer in Christian missionary enterprise in China, I had not thought I should ever witness the time when a body of Chinese Christians would stubbornly insist on holding religious services, boldly present petitions to a hostile officialdom, parade as Christians through the streets of a Chinese city and suffer beatings, imprisonment and threat of death for their cause."

[24] Samuel Sokobin, Consul at Foochow, to the Secretary of State, October 4, 1927, Department of State Archives.

that this emergency would blow over, like many others, without any serious consequences. In this they were mistaken. Within an hour of their arrival, bands of soldiers accompanied by officers systematically looted all foreign buildings, smashed windows and furniture with the butts of their guns, stripped many foreigners of their clothes, threatened women with rape, and sought to frighten captives with threats to kill.[25] The Vice-President of the University of Nanking, Dr. John E. Williams, was killed when he asked permission to retain a gold watch that had been given to him. A group of forty-nine foreigners, who at first gathered at the American consulate, fled to the Standard Oil headquarters. There they were surrounded by snipers. They finally escaped under the cover of a barrage from American and British warships. Five residences at the University of Nanking were burned; University buildings and equipment were damaged to the extent of $30,500 and staff members suffered personal property losses of $124,000.

The harried missionaries emerged from the holocaust with two conclusions: that the attack was ordered by high officers of the extremist wing of the Kuomintang who were intent on driving all foreigners out of Nanking, and, secondly, that the Chinese were still generally friendly. Servants, students, and local officials had risked their lives to help protect them. Missionaries had been hidden in Chinese homes and one, at least, had been concealed in the police station.

The Nanking Incident was a severe blow to the missionary enterprise, but actually it was only the most dramatic event in the series of setbacks. A typical situation was the one that existed in the missionary middle school connected with Boone College. In May 1927, the students refused to take examina-

[25] For firsthand accounts of the happenings at Nanking on March 24, 1927, see File "Conditions in China, 1927," Missionary Research Library, Union Theological Seminary. Missionaries and missionary administrators feared that the highly graphic accounts in the American press would have a harmful effect on the missionary cause and an effort was made to have returning missionaries subordinate their experiences of violence. For a good illustration of a friendly missionary account of the happenings at Nanking see M. Searle Bates, "The Ordeal of Nanking," *The Missionary Review of the World*, August 1927, p. 587.

tions, called off classes to attend political mass meetings, and sponsored parades. The school assemblies were taken over for the delivery of political harangues. On May 8 the students staged a demonstration against the Divinity School and its students. A procession on a Sunday morning carried banners "Down with Religion" and "Theological Students Are Social Parasites."[26]

By June 1927, many school administrators undoubtedly shared the sentiments of the President of Hangchow College, who gloomily admitted that "it is almost impractical, either to close or to open our College this fall. . . . If we announce that we shall not open for at least another year, we shall probably suffer confiscation." And if they did open, he felt certain that there would be student agitation forcing them to close. "We are," said the intimidated president, "between the devil and the deep Black Sea,—nothing blue to it except in our feelings."[27]

In hundreds of cases, when Nationalist troops occupied an area, they took over mission schools and hospitals for their headquarters or for barracks. In December 1927, Frank P. Lockhart, Consul-General at Hankow, presented a lengthy report of forty-five pages citing fifty-one cases in his area where missionary property had been taken over by Nationalists. Lockhart observed:

The plan of occupation was so systematized and so widespread that one cannot escape the conclusion that it was a fixed policy of the Nationalist Government, inspired no doubt by Bolshevik influence, to make use of foreign missionary property as occasion might require. It might even safely be said that the radical faction of the Government had pursued this policy with the double purpose of utilizing the property for military purposes, and at the same

[26] Statement by Arthur M. Sherman, Principal of Boone College, File "China Christian Education Association," The Missionary Research Library.
[27] Statement by Robert F. Fitch, President of Hangchow College, June 1, 1927, Department of State Archives.

time permanently driving the missionary from the field, or at least curbing his influence, if such could be done.[28]

The Communists were undoubtedly hostile to the missionary, but the Kuomintang continued to occupy mission schools and hospitals long after Chiang Kai-shek had thrown out the Communists. When property was occupied, it was usually badly damaged and no rent was paid. Both schools and hospitals ceased to function in many areas.

Amidst the engulfing waves of hostility there were shining examples of heroism and profound Christian loyalty that bolstered the faith of missionaries. I Fang, a Quaker school for girls at Changsha, was under the direction of the grandson of the great general Tseng Kwo-fan, the military leader who had saved the Manchu dynasty from destruction by the Taipings. In the spring of 1927 the Communist troops who came to Changsha were determined to wreck this school with its eighty young girls, ten of whom were professing Christians. At a conference of the staff it was decided that the Chinese superintendent and his wife must go into hiding and that it would be wiser to have a foreigner in charge when the hostile troops arrived.

Accordingly a young Norwegian girl of the YWCA in Changsha was invited to take over. The students rallied to her support. Whereas previously the majority of them had been indifferent or hostile to religious instruction, all eighty of them now insisted on morning devotions and the holding of classes in religion in order to show their spite for the crude and fanatical soldiers. Faced with this defiance, the Communist officers decided to undermine the school by having four soldiers move into the girls' dormitory. For the girls to stay on was to invite slanderous charges against their morals. They decided to remain. During classes in religion taught by the Norwegian YWCA worker, the soldiers made so much noise that she could not be heard. "Shall we quit?" she asked. "No," came the unanimous response, "we can write out our lessons." Finally,

28 F. P. Lockhart to the Secretary of State, December 5, 1927, Department of State Archives.

the troops announced that they were going to burn the school and the girls should get out. The students quietly told them to stand aside for they would leave in an orderly way. They marched from the school with hymn books in hand, formed a circle in front of the building which was now being ignited, and then announced that the spirit of I Fang must never be allowed to die.

The young Norwegian girl now advised her Chinese land-lady, who was not a professing Christian, that in view of the antiforeignism it would be better if she did not accompany her on the streets. The Chinese woman gathered her robes about her and as she left her home with her foreign friend re-marked: "You told me the story of Peter."[29]

[29] Interview with Mrs. Emil Schieche, December 18, 1955.

CHAPTER XII

MISSIONARY ADJUSTMENTS TO CHINESE
NATIONALISM, 1920-1931

A HARDY OLD VETERAN defended the unequal treaties as "God's way of opening up the country to his servants." Without the treaties, imposed by force, missionary work in China would have been impossible. And thus the missionaries had found justification for the use of force.

Their position did not change until 1924 when Chinese violence and the arguments of their Chinese colleagues convinced them that the association of the missionary enterprise with the treaties had become a major obstacle to their work. To the casual observer the change added up to expediency: force had been justifiable when necessary to the carrying on of Christian work, and now that the old instruments of force stood in the way of evangelization, force itself was condemned as inconsistent with Christianity.

Not until 1924 did the missionaries perceive the danger of their reliance on the treaties. Their failure to recognize the strength of Chinese nationalism until so late seems strange. At the peace conference at Versailles in 1919 and again at the Washington conference in 1921 Chinese delegates had made a determined stand for China's rights as a sovereign nation and many an outburst of patriotic sentiment among Chinese students should have indicated to them the emergence of a Chinese national spirit. Recognition of this fact by the missionaries was delayed by their myopic concern with the daily routine of their mission stations, by their failure to look beyond the civil strife created by war lords and bandits, and by their theological bent, which taught them to accept Saint Paul's dictum that the wisdom of this world is foolishness with God. Local conditions, in many cases not yet submerged under the new wave of nationalism, also blinded many to the true nature of the national situation. Thus, more than half of the missionaries questioned in 1924 replied that they had not detected any anti-Christian or antiforeign feeling.[1]

When Chinese nationalism was finally accepted as a fact, recognition was hastened by the more liberal spirit of younger missionaries who had been won over to the humanistic views so widely prevalent in theological seminaries in the United States. They were bent on Christianizing all of society, and force was to them unchristian. It was this conviction that led them to conclude that the treaties were inconsistent with the very code of Christian ethics they, as missionaries, were seeking to implant.

This quite sudden discovery of evil in the treaties that earlier missionaries had actually written caught the old China hands in the Department of State by surprise. J. V. A. MacMurray, Chief of the Far Eastern Division, met with representatives of the Foreign Missions Conference of North America on February 21, 1924. He had assigned himself the supposedly unpleasant task of explaining that the situation in China now made it impossible to extend protection in many areas. Instead of the arguments he expected to hear in favor of effective protection no matter what the cost, the mission administrators sounded a completely new note. "Curiously enough," he wrote, "the only hint of any lack of mutual understanding between their viewpoint and ours was indicated by a report from one of them that there was a strong and growing movement among the missionaries against reliance upon special privileges (such as extraterritorial rights) or upon any form of force—they did not think it consistent with missionary ideals to ask indemnities for depredations, or even to let themselves be forcibly rescued or be ransomed in case of capture by brigands."[2]

In August 1924 two missionaries informed Minister Jacob Gould Schurman in Peking that, as missionaries, they must

[1] Harley F. MacNair, "The Protestant Christian Movement and Political Events," *China Christian Year Book, 1926*, ed. Frank Rawlinson (Shanghai: Christian Literary Society), p. 4.

[2] J. V. A. MacMurray to the Secretary of State, February 23, 1924, Department of State Archives.

oppose the treaties because of the unchristian nature of the agreements. The missionaries went on to say that "the connection of Chinese Christians with missionaries, and with the foreign military force behind them, has nourished a servile dependence, and has given justification to the stigma of 'foreign church' and 'foreign religion'—even a 'religion of force.' "[3] By December 1924 the discovery of the sinful nature of the treaty system had proceeded far enough so that the new view was endorsed by the Tientsin Missionary Society. The Consul-General at Tientsin, Clarence E. Gauss, found the new views quixotic, but Tyler Dennett in the Department of State advised J. V. A. MacMurray that he did not like to see the statement of the missionaries "dismissed as merely idealistic." Their position impressed Dennett as legally wrong but ethically correct, and sooner or later, he warned, the Department of State would have to reconcile itself to the rise of Chinese nationalism.[4]

During 1925, to the consternation of MacMurray and many consular officials, scores of missionary groups in China and boards at home rushed forth with resolutions of repentance for their part in the unchristian treaty structure.[5] In all of these

[3] Jacob Gould Schurman to the Secretary of State, January 6, 1925, Department of State Archives.

[4] Tyler Dennett to J. V. A. MacMurray, February 13, 1925, Department of State Archives.

[5] J. V. A. MacMurray later reported that 109 of the 134 missionaries of the American Board, North China Mission, had signed statements that they did not desire to receive any protection from their government in any way. MacMurray to the Secretary of State, July 22, 1927, Department of State Archives.

The missionaries who favored treaty revision usually went on record as being opposed to receiving protection. The Department of State consistently took the position that a citizen could not surrender his rights.

China Christian Year Book, 1926, Appendix III "Actions of Mission Organizations in re Extraterritoriality and Toleration Clauses," pp. 510-512.

Ibid., Appendix II "American Societies Statement By American Mission Board Secretaries," pp. 449-502. Copies were sent to the Secretary of State and these are available in the Department of State Archives.

Estimates of the proportion of missionaries favoring the yielding of rights and the revision of treaties vary according to the point of view of the observer. A former professor at the University of Nanking told the author that almost every missionary in that area favored revision while very few in the vicinity of Peking took this stand. Minister MacMurray advised the Secretary of State that only a minority were revisionists. He thought that.

repentances there was a subordinate note, namely, that the extraterritoriality and toleration clauses were prejudicial to the progress of the Christian movement in China. What had for so long appeared as God's way of opening up the country suddenly seemed unchristian as it dawned on the missionaries that it impeded their work. It was no wonder that MacMurray found in the endless flood of resolutions evidence of expediency.

By January 1926 eighteen missionary societies and a strong majority of the larger denominations had taken action in support of treaty revision. The outbreaks of violence at Shanghai, Canton, and other cities during the previous year had put the missionaries in a highly precarious position. Some of the missionaries who had favored treaty revision now concluded that they had been wrong, but most of them continued to call for an end to the treaties. On the other hand, those who had never been won over to treaty revision were quick to cite the violence that had taken place as proof of the idealistic naïveté of the revisionists.

The time for insistence on the old treaty rights, of course, had passed. Any attempt to enforce them would only add to the fuel of the Nationalists. Unable to wage war on equal

---

in general, the so-called modernists and teachers in the universities were revisionists while the conservatives opposed treaty revision. Evidence is not available for making any accurate estimate of the percentage of American missionaries who favored a change but there is little question about their constituting a strong and especially vocal minority.

Some of the missionaries who favored retention of treaty rights wrote letters to the *North China Herald*. Others confided to American consuls that they were opposed to any surrender of treaty rights. A Baptist missionary told the American Consul at Chungking that he had no sympathy with the missionaries in Shanghai and Peking who prated about revision. He said: "One gets so weary about the platitudes on 'National Aspirations.' Who of us are not interested in the genuine article? I fail to see how the foreign governments are preventing the aspirations from budding. I resent the phrase 'Special Privileges.' We don't want any except the ordinary rights that are due any civilized person in this day and age. . . . I don't see much exploiting being done on the Yangtze, other than what the Chinese officials are doing." Walter A. Adams to the Secretary of State, October 30, 1926, enclosing a letter from W. Robert Taylor, a Baptist missionary at Suifu.

terms with her real or supposed enemies, China's people took matters into their own hands. In the power of the mob lay China's only instrument for redress. The most remarkable fact, observed one missionary in 1927, was not the violence that had occurred but "the large measure of restraint with which China has prosecuted her war against 'foreign imperialism.' "[6]

The willingness of the missionaries to surrender their treaty rights in the hope of rescuing their enterprise from the on-rushing holocaust of nationalism was met with ridicule and disgust by the business interests and old China hands in the diplomatic service. Shortly after the Shanghai Incident of May 30, 1925, the Hankow Chamber of Commerce cabled the Department of State protesting against Senator Borah's advocacy of treaty revision and warned that it was the Moscow Third International that was responsible for the trouble in China and not the unequal treaties.[7] On June 25 the executive committee of the American Association of China cabled the Secretary of State urging the adoption "of the strongest attitude and representation to the Chinese Government to suppress the present state of lawlessness directed against foreigners, which in our opinion is due primarily to the long-existing unsettled political conditions and aggravated by Soviet propaganda."[8] The American Chamber of Commerce in China delayed taking any position until the Commission on Extraterritoriality, headed by Silas Strawn, prominent Chicago attorney, had filed its report. It then endorsed Strawn's opinion that it would be unwise to make any changes with regard to extraterritoriality.[9]

The resentment of business men against those missionaries who sought treaty revision was further displayed in an article in the *Far Eastern Review*. The writer, George Bronson Rea,

[6] See report written by C. W. Shoop, the Superintendent of the mission of the Church of the United Brethren in Christ. A copy of the report is available in the File "Conditions in China in 1927" in the Missionary Research Library, Union Theological Seminary.

[7] Dorothy Borg, *American Policy and the Chinese Revolution, 1925-1928* (New York: American Institute of Pacific Relations and the Macmillan Co., 1947), p. 27.

[8] "American Association of China," *The North China Herald*, June 27, 1925, p. 485.

[9] Borg, *op. cit.*, p. 191.

charged the missionaries with having dictated appointments of American ministers to China and of having forced the Department of State to sacrifice commercial interest. Those charged with the carrying on of relations with China, said Rea, had to be constantly mindful of the political power of the churches. Friendly relations with China had to be maintained at all costs simply because any friction would undermine support of the missionaries.[10]

The business point of view was most strongly expressed by the British-owned *North China Herald*. This newspaper lashed out at the National Christian Council for its stand on political questions. The editor questioned the NCC's authority to speak for Christians in China. In July, after the NCC attributed part of the trouble to "foreign aggression and domination; unequal treaties; racial pride," the British-owned newspaper commented sarcastically on the impertinence of the religious group interfering in political affairs.[11] On August 1 *The North China Herald* expressed regret because reports from Washington stated that there was to be an investigation concerning the question of extraterritoriality. The talk of holding an investigation, said the writer of the news story, "is not only absurd but dangerous, because bitter experience teaches that such investigations are prone to be influenced by imaginary expediency, not by fact."[12] During 1926 and 1927 this newspaper also urged intervention on the ground that China could never work out her own salvation. The editor likewise condemned the missionaries for misrepresenting the situation in China to the American people.

The missionaries favoring revision also found themselves at odds with the American Minister in Peking, J. V. A. MacMurray, a career diplomat with long experience in China. He had served as Chief of the Far Eastern division in the Department of State from 1919 until 1924 when the Coolidge administration appointed him Minister to China. The appointment had

10 *Ibid.*, pp. 90-91.
11 "The N.C.C. Again," *The North China Herald*, July 25, 1925, p. 45.
12 "The Powers' Attitude Toward China," *The North China Herald*, August 1925, p. 71.

the approval of the missionaries. In his position as Chief of the Far Eastern division he had met frequently with representatives of missionary interests and his sympathetic point of view made a favorable impression.

A gulf between the revisionist missionaries and MacMurray developed immediately upon his appointment as Minister. MacMurray, an eminent authority on the treaties between China and the West, took a legalistic view and was firmly opposed to China's unilateral abrogation of the treaties. He was also a firm believer in the policy of cooperation with other powers worked out at the Washington Conference and he saw in any change worked out between China and the United States alone, the ruination of that policy. Above all there was no lack of chaos and confusion, lawlessness and military despotism in China, all of which supported his view that to yield the treaty rights would make foreign residence in China impossible.[13]

MacMurray's reports to Washington charged the missionaries with expediency. Missionaries, he wrote, now felt compelled to make concessions to the Chinese and they made these concessions in the political and economic area while they continued to adhere to the assumption that Christianity was superior to any other religion. They were anxious to protect the Christian movement in China and were willing to do so at the expense of other Western interests.

MacMurray thought the missionaries "optimistic, to say the least" in believing that abrogation of the treaties would be followed shortly by the granting of general privileges of travel and residence to all foreigners.[14] The arguments against treaty revision were all of secondary importance, as MacMurray saw it, to the primary consideration of the untimeliness of immediate relinquishment. He wrote:

> I must, however, enter my decided dissent from the wisdom
> of their general stand. Chinese opinion, nationalistic or

[13] The views of J. V. A. MacMurray presented in this paragraph are based on a letter he wrote to the Secretary of State, September 10, 1926, Department of State Archives.

[14] *Ibid.*

otherwise, is never conciliated by a policy of sweeping and unconsidered concession. Concession is here regarded as a policy of weakness and engenders a belief in further concessions to be obtained by continued pressure.[15]

What were these further concessions? MacMurray never explained what he had in mind, so we are left to make our surmises. By 1928 he was convinced "that the heyday of Christian missionary endeavor in China is seemingly past never to come again, and the extent to which it can even survive depends upon a number of factors, many of which cannot be accurately determined in advance." The future missionary, he thought, would "almost literally have to be as wise as a serpent and as harmless as a dove." His work would "have to pass the hypercritical Chinese intellectuals and be such as to escape the ire of the extreme chauvinists." At best the volume and prestige of American missionary work were bound to steadily decrease.[16]

Nothing could be done to save the missionary enterprise as MacMurray saw it. He never said what he considered to be the prospects of the other side of American activity in China, namely, the commercial interests, but presumably he was less gloomy in his view of their future. To surrender all the special treaty privileges would have made it difficult for American business interests to continue functioning in China. Moreover, it seems safe to say MacMurray believed that to have yielded these privileges would lead not only to the loss of these rights, but to further restrictions. If the treaty rights were to be given up, the United States should at least receive some concessions in return. In brief, the treaties gave the United States some bargaining power.[17]

Missionaries of the revisionist point of view had no patience with the MacMurray approach. Sometime in early October

[15] *Ibid.*

[16] J. V. A. MacMurray to the Secretary of State, March 3, 1928, Department of State Archives.

[17] Nelson T. Johnson, who played a major role in negotiating with the Chinese representatives in Washington, in an interview with the author, stated that the value of the treaties as a bargaining point was a consideration in refusing to revise them.

1926, some twenty missionaries met with him in an informal conference. Frank Rawlinson, editor of the *Chinese Recorder*, who was present, wrote a highly critical account. He had gained the impression that MacMurray's ideals were not very high and that he was "just simply whirling around the old vicious circle, with no idea of how to get out of it." When asked what was being done to formulate new treaties, the minister replied that there was no government in China with whom the United States could come to terms. This struck Rawlinson as pure sophistry; when it came to making concessions, the diplomats talked "about the *fiction* of the government, but when it [came] to holding on to the present treaties they [talked] in terms of a government that [had] a shred of reality." Rawlinson was inclined "to think the real fact is the diplomats are out to hold on to the economic advantages embodied in the treaties as long as they can, and that they feel that if the worse comes to the worst they can use military force to back them up." Rawlinson summed up the missionary view of the situation:

> I and many others look at it differently. If the situation is such that the treaties are practically abrogated and that any treaty satisfactory to the Chinese has a better chance of being carried out than one that is not, it would seem to me that the diplomats ought to capitalize goodwill rather than their traditional economic position. But I did not get the least hint of this in the interview with Mr. MacMurray that he has any such ideals. In fact I feel that you fellows who supported him rather lost out.[18]

Rawlinson and the revisionist missionaries were more imaginative and more hopeful for the future than the American Minister. Their confidence in the future of China sprang in part from their close acquaintance with and admiration for many Chinese Christian leaders. These leaders were ardent advocates of treaty revision and of the nationalist aims of the Kuomintang. Secretary of State Kellogg and the American people shared the missionary point of view on treaty revision. In

[18] Frank Rawlinson to A. L. Warnshuis, October 20, 1926, Rawlinson Letters, Missionary Research Library.

the United States years of missionary propaganda had created a tremendous reservoir of good will toward China. This now helped to make Chinese demands appear reasonable and just.

The United States led the way in granting China tariff autonomy. A draft for a new treaty had been prepared by the Department of State in October 1927. By July of 1928 Secretary Kellogg was ready to proceed with the negotiations. The new treaty was negotiated within the space of a few days with T. V. Soong, the Minister of Finance, representing China, and J. V. A. MacMurray, the United States.

The question of yielding extraterritorial rights proved more difficult. Shortly after the negotiation of the new treaty granting China tariff autonomy, Secretary Kellogg and Nelson T. Johnson, Chief of the Far Eastern Division of the Department of State, entered into discussions with Chinese representatives on the question of extraterritoriality. Two obstacles soon appeared. China had not yet enacted the code of laws recommended by the Commission on Extraterritoriality in 1925. Secondly, while willing to make changes, Secretary of State Kellogg did not wish to place Americans in China in a less favorable position than citizens of other nations. This meant that any concessions granted to China would go into effect only when other nations took similar action. The Chinese, anxious to make immediate progress, asked that the United States make an outright surrender of extraterritorial rights. Negotiations dragged on until the Japanese invasion of Manchuria in September 1931. From then until the United States and China became allies in the war against Japan, there was no further progress. Finally, in 1943, the United States surrendered its extraterritorial rights in China, exactly one hundred years after the Cushing treaty, which had provided for them.

The unequal treaties provided a subtle device for Western control over questions that the same Western nations, in their own case, jealously regarded as falling within their own domestic jurisdiction. Western intrusion was maintained because of a lack of confidence in the ability and good faith of the Chinese.

This same lack of confidence caused a majority of the missionaries to cling tenaciously to their control of all Christian institutions in China. The suspicion of the native, bred of arrogance, was the very essence of the imperialism so hated by the Chinese, whether it appeared in the smugness of the diplomat or the pious expressions of concern of the missionary. The Western Christian seldom recognized his own arrogance for it was buried under a thick cover of argument in behalf of preserving the purity of the Christian faith. Fortunately, a considerable number of missionaries were able to rise to the occasion and joined the Chinese in the movement for Chinese church autonomy.

Chinese Christians bluntly denounced the imperialism of the missionary. T. Z. Koo told a conference in 1926 that missionaries discouraged new lines of development when suggested by Chinese and imposed their own views. "I have yet to find in the Christian missions that desire and ability to work under Chinese control."[19]

A year later Koo was even more outspoken. The Chinese failed to take any initiative, he said, simply because they did not feel that it was their church and consequently the problems were not their problems. Secondly, the missionaries had established large institutions beyond the ability of the Chinese to finance. Thirdly, the attitude of missionaries was an obstacle. They took pride in a particular institution to the point where they were afraid to entrust it to the Chinese. Koo also charged them with a love of position and power. Finally, he expressed fear that Chinese Christians under the tutelage of missionaries were "subject to a certain insidious satisfaction connected with a sense of giving."[20]

The Chinese Christians had an able but small group of liberal missionaries who supported them in their fight for control. Frank Rawlinson was one of these. Few missionaries were more colorful or had a broader background of experience.

[19] *Report of Conference on the Church in China Today* (Shanghai: National Christian Council, 1926), p. 41.
[20] See File on "China: Church and Mission Relations," Missionary Research Library.

Born in England in 1871, he had immigrated to the United States at the age of eighteen with only five dollars in his pocket. After working at a variety of menial jobs, he enrolled at Bucknell University where he graduated *summa cum laude*. He went to China under the Southern Baptists, but the theology of this denomination did not harmonize with his liberal views, and in 1921 he transferred to the American Board. As editor of the *Chinese Recorder* he had pursued a bold course, arguing for an indigenous church, sharply criticizing missionaries for retaining control of Chinese Christian institutions, and championing the Social Gospel. When the more conservative missionaries sent letters bristling with criticisms of the Laymen's Inquiry, he simply announced that he would not publish them. Flourishing his inevitable cigarette, he could dispose of the arguments of his opponents with a formidable array of facts and sharp analysis.

Another ardent supporter of the Chinese Christians was Dr. James Yard, missionary teacher and later editor of the *Christian Advocate* in China. In 1926 Dr. Yard returned to the United States on a special mission to protest to the Methodist Board and its Secretary, Dr. Ralph Diffendorfer, against the failure to let Chinese Methodists run their own activities. Neither the board nor its secretary would listen and Yard was dismissed.

The rise of an angry Chinese nationalism gave the advocates of a change their opportunity to press forward, and much progress was made. By 1926 the Chinese constituted 75 per cent of the National Christian Council and they gave most of the speeches, dominated the discussions and held the most important offices. Frank Rawlinson wrote jubilantly that finally it seemed "the future of the Chinese Church is really in the hands of Chinese Christians."

In 1928 the National Christian Council overhauled its own system and provided that it should be made up only of representatives of the Chinese churches.[21] This went into effect in 1929. The Council spoke for approximately 70 per cent of the membership of the Protestant churches. The more conservative

[21] T. C. Bau, "National Christian Council in 1928," *China Christian Yearbook, 1929*, p. 225.

missionary organizations, such as the China Inland Mission, had withdrawn in protest against the liberal pronouncements the Council had issued. Although the Council had no authority over its members, it came closer than any other agency to speaking for Chinese Protestantism.

The second major development in the rise of the Chinese to control was the establishment of the Church of Christ in China. The first steps were taken in 1918 at a meeting of the Federal Council of the Presbyterian Churches in China. Representatives of the London Missionary Society and the American Board participated and, together with the Presbyterians, drew up a proposal for a federation of churches of various denominations. When the committee charged with drawing up further plans met in 1919, Chinese led the way in arguing for an organic rather than a federal type of union and they won their point.[22] In 1922 a provisional general assembly adopted a constitution and a statement of doctrine. The plan called for the organization of church government along Presbyterian lines. In the next few years a number of synods came into being, one in Kwangtung, one in South Fukien, one in Hunan, and still another in Hupeh. Nineteen denominations indicated a willingness to join the new Chinese Church. In late September, 1927, the first General Assembly met at Shanghai and organized the Church of Christ in China. About one-third of the Chinese Protestants were members of the new church, 70,000 of them from American-founded churches and 50,000 from churches of British background. Presbyterians and Congregationalists constituted the largest number. The Baptists generally refrained from joining.[23] The Methodists joined later.

The Chinese were now in a position to dislodge the missionaries from control in the national church. The Church of Christ almost at once demanded that they should appoint missionaries of their own choosing and that they should have the

[22] See File "China: Church Union," Missionary Research Library; see also Kenneth Scott Latourette, *A History of Christian Missions in China* (New York: The Macmillan Co., 1929), p. 800.

[23] "The Church of Christ in China," *International Review of Missions*, April 1928, pp. ii-iii.

right to deal directly with the mission boards in the West and not have to negotiate through the missions.[24]

The transfer of more authority from missionaries in denominational missions to the Chinese churches proved more difficult. Many Chinese churches enjoyed a high degree of autonomy, but they wished to extend their control to mission policy and to the appointment of missionaries. They also called for a voice in the administration of schools and hospitals.

The Chinese made some headway in all denominations, but their advance was uneven. The Congregationalists went further than any other denomination. Their North China mission had established the North China Council in 1914. Its members were elected by the churches, but half of those elected had to be missionaries. Missionaries who were heads of institutions could also be co-opted. In 1927 this was revised so as to permit the churches to elect only Chinese if they wished. Since 1914 the North China Council had determined policy; it was now also granted control over funds and the appointment of missionaries.[25] The Foochow mission of the Congregationalists moved more slowly. The local Congregational churches did control their own affairs and determined the policy for the elementary schools but Chinese were not permitted any voice in the formulation of policy for the mission. At a meeting on January 27, 1927, all this was changed. All affairs of the mission, including the control of schools and hospitals, Foochow College, and all evangelistic activities, were now transferred to committees and a Board of Managers appointed by the Chinese association of Congregational churches.[26]

In other denominations, missionaries were less willing to subordinate themselves completely to Chinese control but most

24 *Laymen's Foreign Mission Inquiry, Fact-Finders' Reports: China*, Vol. V, ed. Orville A. Petty (New York: Harper & Brothers, 1933), pp. 68-69.

25 "North China Meeting of 1927," *Records of the North China Mission*, Vol. 37, in the archives of the American Board of Commissioners for Foreign Missions, Houghton Library, Harvard University. Hereafter cited as ABC archives.

26 W. E. Strong to Paul G. Hayes, March 29, 1927, *General Letters*, ABC archives.

of them yielded some ground. The Baptists devised a system of concurrent action whereby the appointment of missionaries required action by the mission and by the convention of Baptist churches.[27] In most denominations the mission retained final authority over schools, hospitals, and new fields of evangelistic work.

The loss of legal authority did not always result in any sharp diminution of the missionary's influence. Sometimes it meant no more than that he found it necessary to "educate" the Chinese along the lines that he thought should be followed. Moreover, his long experience and intense interest gave him an advantage over the Chinese, who were unaccustomed to responsibilities in the church and who, while sensitive on the question of foreign control, had little interest in exercising it once it had been transferred to their hands.

The Nationalist revolution, as already seen, hit out against the foreignizing influence of mission schools. It was charged that graduates of mission schools turned out to be compradores for foreign firms, that they had no adequate grasp of Chinese culture, and that they acquired a Western attitude toward China.[28] Some graduates of mission schools confessed that they were ashamed of their school association and that they would never permit their children to attend a foreign school. Foreign curricula and foreign teachers were viewed as proof of the imperialist aims of Christianity.

The most difficult period for mission schools came to an end in April, 1928, after the expulsion of the Communists from the Kuomintang. The students who had presented a set of demands to the government calling for student participation in school administration, the abolition of examinations, and the right

[27] *Laymen's Foreign Missions Inquiry, Fact-Finders' Reports: China*, Vol. V, p. 71.

[28] One Chinese author has written: "The tradition of dogma and the restriction of freedom of thought through compulsory Bible classes and chapel attendances, have generally resulted in the production of servile minds. Missionary products are, as a rule, therefore, only suitable as recruits, as compradores of the foreign trading houses, or, at most, as would-be drawing-room diplomatists." T'ang Leang-Li, *China in Revolt: How a Civilization Became a Nation* (London: Noel Douglas, 1927), p. 67.

to dismiss teachers were now rebuked and told to refrain from political activity.

But the anti-mission-school movement had crippled the foreign schools for a time. Several colleges were closed, temporarily enrollment declined sharply, and scores of primary schools closed permanently. The number of students in the middle schools fell from 11,000 in 1922 to 5,500 in 1927.[29] In the 1930's the middle schools and particularly the universities made a substantial recovery.

The student revolt against Christian schools was only one aspect of the problem that grew out of the rise of nationalism. The sometimes irrational and irresponsible action taken by students helped dramatize the serious and genuine concern over the foreignizing influence of mission schools felt by every element in Chinese life. This concern had led to demands that all foreign schools be compelled to abide by a number of regulations and that they register with the government.

Registration first became an issue in 1918 after the promulgation of rules the previous year requiring that the name of the mission or the church should not be attached to the school, that no religious teaching or ceremony should be compulsory, that non-Christians should be admitted, and that no distinction should be made between them and Christians.[30] Two factors tended to postpone any strong controversy: registration was not compulsory and there was little prospect of the government actually enforcing the regulations. Again, in 1921, the government at Peking announced a new set of regulations, which centered about the stipulation that "the content of the curriculum and the methods of teaching shall include nothing in the nature of propagation of religion." The broad interpretation of this by the government left the schools free to pursue a course in harmony with their own views. Moreover, registration was not required and schools that did not register were not subject to the regulations.

[29] Earl Herbert Cressy, "Christian Education in 1928," *China Christian Yearbook, 1929*, p. 273.

[30] H. C. Tsao, "The Nationalist Movement and Christian Education," *China Christian Yearbook, 1928*, p. 176.

This state of things did not satisfy the professional educators and the new burst of energy of the anti-Christian movement in 1922 prompted them to campaign for more effective action by the government. In July, 1922, the National Association for the Advancement of Education recommended that no religious education should be allowed in elementary schools.[31] Two years later the National Conference of Educational Associations called for a prohibition of religious teaching in all grades of schools and for cancellation of registration or closing of any school violating the order.[32] Again, in September, 1924, the problem was the center of discussion at a conference of the National Federation of Provincial Educational Associations, and a whole series of resolutions was passed.[33] Among the evil effects of foreign education cited were the inculcation of a loyalty and admiration for a foreign country that destroyed the students' spirit of national independence and a primary emphasis on the propagation of religion rather than on education. The Chinese educators proposed that all schools applying for registration must desist from teaching religion, must have Chinese administrators, and that teachers should have the qualifications specified by Chinese law. They also recommended that all schools failing to register should be closed.

From 1925 to 1927 each of the several governments, the Peking government, the Canton government, and the Kuomintang, after it assumed power in the north, issued regulations for registration and required that all schools register. There was no significant difference among the various sets of rules laid down. Of chief importance was the provision that courses in religion must not be compulsory and that attendance at chapel services should be on a voluntary basis. Each of the governments also specified that administrators must be Chinese and that half of the board of trustees must be Chinese.[34]

[31] *Ibid.*, p. 175. [32] *Ibid.*

[33] *Ibid.*, p. 176. In his letter to A. L. Warnshuis, Doctor Balme, President of Shantung Christian University, traced the history of the movement to regulate Christian schools. It is the most complete statement known to the author. Warnshuis to Perkins, March 13, 1925, Department of State Archives.

[34] For a discussion of these regulations see Chester S. Miao and Frank

The question of registration and regulation provoked a long debate among missionary educators as to whether, under these circumstances, schools could remain true to the purpose for which they had been founded. A majority of the leaders agreed with Professor W. F. Hummel of Nanking University, eminent scholar in the field of Chinese history, who argued that required courses in religion and compulsory attendance at religious services aroused anti-Christian attitudes and defeated the very end for which they were established.[35] As early as April, 1925, the China Christian Educational Association voted that Christian schools should register.[36] By 1929, seventy per cent of the schools had registered or had applied for registration.[37] Missionary groups who failed to cooperate with the Chinese were subjected to criticism, but after 1929 the question provoked very little discussion, a fact to be explained in terms of the willingness of many missionary educators to face realistically a new situation.

The more cooperative attitude of the Kuomintang government after 1928 manifested itself in a willingness to permit religious services and courses in religion as long as they were not required, which in turn made it easier for the missionaries to cooperate. The Christian schools, in a large majority of cases, were now placed in the hands of Chinese.[38] For the most part missionaries also accepted without serious protest the government policy requiring a memorial ceremony to Sun Yat-sen every Monday morning and a requirement that students receive instruction in the principles of the Kuomintang.

W. Price, *Religion and Character in Christian Middle Schools*, pp. 6-20, and H. C. Tsao, "The Nationalist Movement and Christian Education," *China Christian Yearbook, 1928.*

[35] Miao and Price, *op. cit.*, p. 38.

[36] *Ibid.*, p. 40.

[37] *Ibid.*, p. 17.

[38] Earl Herbert Cressy, "Christian Education in 1928," *China Christian Yearbook, 1928*, p. 270.

CHAPTER XIII

THE RISE OF THE CHRISTIAN SOCIALIZATION
WING OF MISSIONARIES, 1920-1931

AFTER World War I there were three groups of missionaries, the fundamentalists, the conservatives, and the liberals. The two former shared a common theology and held to the traditional view that it was the role of the missionary to lead individual heathen to salvation. They differed only in their attitude toward liberals. While conservatives regretted the rise of the new heterodoxy, they did not expend energy combatting liberalism. The fundamentalists, in contrast, were belligerent in their opposition and in their campaign against the liberals, made a fetish of loyalty to what they considered vital statements of doctrine.

In the summer of 1919 the editor of the interdenominational *Missionary Review of the World* cited the testimony of the Rev. Charles Inwood, a Bible teacher and evangelist, that "the greatest menace to the efficiency of Christian missions is found in the lack of conviction as to the inspiration of the Bible as the authoritative content of the Christian Message." The editor joined in warning that the modernists, in a praiseworthy effort to "save the world" collectively, were neglecting the prime necessity of saving the soul of the individual.[1] In the following year, 1920, the fundamentalist missionaries, to be found in almost every denomination, organized the China Bible Union with the expressed purpose of rooting out the new heresy. The constitution of this organization called for a defense of the "saving truths revealed in the Bible, especially those now being assailed, such as, the Deity of our Lord and Saviour Jesus Christ, His Virgin Birth, His Atoning Sacrifice for Sin, and His Bodily Resurrection from the Dead; the

[1] "The Missionary and His Message," ed., *The Missionary Review of the World*, August 1919, pp. 567-568.

Miracles both of the Old and New Testament; the Personality and Work of the Holy Spirit; the New Birth of the Individual and the necessity of this as an essential prerequisite to Christian Social Service, . . ."[2] This statement of what the fundamentalists deemed vital truths was accompanied by a declaration of war on all those who differed. The Bible Union announced that it would present to the mission boards and supporters at home the importance of sending only missionaries who ascribed to its particular articles of Faith. Before long its leaders aroused the wrath of the liberals by launching a campaign to have everyone who did not accept its program denied financial support. By 1921 the Bible Union had 1,700 members among the missionaries.[3]

In 1928 a new group, the Christian Fundamentals League for China, began the publication of *The China Fundamentalist*. In belligerent tones it fought for the doctrines of the virgin birth and the physical resurrection of Christ and denounced the theory of evolution.[4]

The most influential vantage point retained by the fundamentalists was the China Sunday School Union. This organization published much of the literature used by missionaries, and it promoted the more conservative doctrinal views. Its president was the Rev. E. G. Tewksbury, a Congregationalist. The liberals, exasperated by this situation, sought to use their influence in the World Sunday School Association, from whom the China Sunday School Union obtained a considerable part of its funds, to relax the hold of the fundamentalists. In 1929 Dr. Robert M. Hopkins, General Secretary of the Association, went to China and suggested that the constitution of the Union be amended so as to make it more representative of church

---

[2] *China Mission Year Book, 1923*, ed. Frank Rawlinson (Shanghai: Christian Literature Society, 1923). See Chapter XIII, "The Bible Union of China." A copy of the constitution of the Bible Union is available in the Laymen's Inquiry papers in the file entitled "Major Problems of the Christian Evangelization of China," Missionary Research Library, Union Theological Seminary.

[3] Kenneth Scott Latourette, *A History of Christian Missions in China* (New York: The Macmillan Co., 1929), p. 796.

[4] See Laymen's Inquiry papers, File on "Major Problems of the Christian Evangelization of China," Missionary Research Library.

opinion. He immediately met strong opposition led by the China Inland Mission which threatened to withdraw if there were any change. When the conservatives rejected the proposal, the World Sunday School Association withdrew its financial support.[5]

Bitter recriminations by both sides seem to have been reserved to a handful of fundamentalists led by Edgar E. Strother on the one hand and some of the more liberal church periodicals in the United States representing the other side. Charles Clayton Morrison, editor of the *Christian Century*, for instance, was dogmatic in proclaiming that the entire missionary enterprise depended upon Christianity identifying itself with revolutionary social forces and that the fundamentalists were the chief block to bringing this about.[6] Many missionaries from both schools of thought, on the other hand, maintained mutual respect and a spirit of cooperation, choosing to avoid discussion of doctrinal differences.[7]

Both the fundamentalists and the conservatives were essentially nonpolitical. In the years after World War I they devoted almost all their energies to the traditional program of evangelization and continued to look upon their task as one of bringing salvation to the heathen. The economic problems besetting the peasant and the industrial worker were far beyond their ken. When asked about the rents and taxes paid by his parishioners in a remote area of western China, a member of the China Inland Mission expressed complete surprise at the question and said he had never inquired into such matters. While he was able to give a graphic description of the poverty, he attributed it to the fact that too much land was given over to the raising of opium and much money was wasted on gambling. On the other hand, members of the China Inland Mis-

[5] See letter of June 22, 1929, in collection of Frank Rawlinson circular letters in the Missionary Research Library. See also Laymen's Inquiry papers, memorandum entitled "China Sunday School Union."

[6] "Can Christian Missions Be Saved," ed., *Christian Century*, March 12, 1930, pp. 326-328.

[7] This statement is based on interviews with former missionaries Plummer Mills of the Y.M.C.A., and the Rev. and Mrs. Nathan Sikes of the Methodist Episcopal Church.

sion lived in extremely modest circumstances when compared with those who enjoyed a regular salary from a denominational mission board, and consequently they were able to get closer to the people.

The Christian socialization wing constituted the third group. Most of them had come to China just prior to the war or immediately afterwards. Theology had never seemed of primary importance to this group. They had drunk deep of Christian idealism and the contemporary belief in progress. Humanitarianism was to them the heart of the Christian gospel. And China had been a profoundly constructive experience to them. In the language schools they studied Confucius and found in his writings those same principles of the Christian gospels that seemed most important to them. They could no longer speak of the Chinese as "heathen" and they were less driven by the desire to convert than they were by a passionate desire to help the Chinese acquire modern medicine, education, and an understanding of Western society. Its members affirmed their belief in religion as an individual experience but placed greatest stress on the social aspects of Christian teaching and spoke continuously of Christianizing society.

These social gospelers owed much to the rise of Christian humanism in the United States but some of their most able leaders were sons of missionaries. Lucius Porter—who in his later years of retirement at Beloit College ran the high hurdles with the college boys at the age of seventy-five and who boldly opposed Senator Joseph McCarthy when to oppose him was to risk execution of one's reputation by his Senate investigating committee—was one of these sons of missionaries who crusaded for missions with a social point of view. He was a pietist in his personal religious life but he was likewise a passionate believer in Christianizing and humanizing Chinese industry and an enthusiastic advocate of a social approach to the Chinese peasants.

Porter attributed this to the influence of his father, a country physician, pastor, and educator, and to the fact that as a boy in China he had known and loved Chinese peasants and wanted to see a richer life opened to them. As Dean at Yenching he introduced courses in sociology, employing for this purpose Stewart Burgess and Sidney Gamble who had been engaged in YMCA work in China. Yenching became a center for the training of social service workers, and its students made significant social surveys in Peking.

Numerous missionaries and Chinese leaders felt strongly that Christianity must somehow be geared into the new movement for economic and social rehabilitation and the spiritual values of Christianity must be realized in working for a new and better economic order. What this school of missionaries hoped for was a mass movement of Christians in favor of reconstruction along lines compatible with the ethical teachings of Christianity. Just as the Communists sought to capitalize on the rise of Chinese nationalism and social unrest for the purpose of fixing on China the soviet system, so did these Christian leaders hope to link up the social-ethical teachings of Christianity with the aspirations of the Chinese people so that Christianity might become an integral part of the new nation that was emerging.

The liberal wing held a dominant position in the educational sector of the missionary enterprise. By the 1920's missionary schools were a central feature of the missionary effort with almost as much personnel and as great an investment as the more direct evangelical missionary work. In 1927 there were sixteen universities and colleges; ten Christian professional schools of collegiate rank; four schools of theology and six schools of medicine—some 4,000 students enrolled. These schools represented a total property investment of $19,000,000. Their current expenses amounted to $3,250,000 annually.[8]

The mission boards had also established a system of middle and primary schools. In 1919 there were 265 Christian middle schools with an enrollment of 15,213.[9] No accurate statistics

[8] B. A. Garside to Members of the Permanent Committee for the Coordination and Promotion of Christian Higher Education in China, November 29, 1927, *General Letters*, archives of the American Board of Commissioners for Foreign Missions, Houghton Library, Harvard University.

[9] Chester S. Miao and Frank W. Price, *Religion and Character in Christian Middle Schools* (Shanghai: China Christian Educational Association, 1929), p. 7.

on the number of primary schools is available but they numbered in the thousands before 1927. In 1930 the Methodists had 551 primary schools, and about 29,000 students. The Presbyterians had 383 primary schools with about 15,000 pupils.[10]

This vast educational enterprise, launched with much enthusiasm and experiencing a rapid expansion during the first two decades of the century, became a dead weight around the necks of the missionary leaders in the 1920's. It was tremendously costly and expenditures increased rapidly after the war, but this was only a minor aspect of a more serious problem. At home more and more questions were being asked about the efficiency of the schools in meeting Chinese needs. In 1921 the China Continuation Committee set up the China Educational Commission, better known by the name of its chairman as the Burton Commission. This Commission included several prominent leaders in American education including Mary E. Wooley, President of Mount Holyoke College, William F. Russell, dean of the College of Education at the University of Iowa, and Kenyon Butterfield, President of Massachusetts Agricultural College. Its function was defined as proposing a general program for Christian schools in the light of the rapidly expanding public school system in China.

On its return to the United States, the Burton Commission criticized the lack of a well-defined policy as to the purpose of the education and the failure to make a scientific adaptation to the needs of either the China of today or the China of tomorrow. Most schools offered the same program of courses given in the United States, England, or Canada. No attention was given to the needs of China. The Commission also deplored the lack of professional training among elementary school teachers and the too great dependence on men with only a theological training.[11]

As we have seen, the Laymen's Inquiry of 1932 went far be-

[10] *Laymen's Foreign Missions Inquiry, Fact-Finders' Reports: China*, Vol. V, ed. Orville A. Petty (New York: Harpers and Brothers, 1933), p. 421.

[11] *Christian Education in China: The Report of the China Educational Commission* (New York: Committee of Reference and Counsel of the Foreign Missions Conference of North America, 1922), pp. 86-87.

yond the Burton Commission in severely criticizing the mission schools. It focused its attention on the tendency to emphasize courses in religion and adherence to the traditional classical curricula of the West. One of the better colleges offered one-third as many courses in religion as were offered in economics, history, political science, and sociology. Another institution offered twenty courses in religion and only eight in economics.[12] The emphasis on religion and on classical studies led the author of the Laymen's report on education to ask why mission schools seemed so intent on preparing students for Harvard and for heaven rather than for life in China.

A majority of the missionaries continued to judge schools in terms of their efficacy as evangelizing agencies and they were increasingly inclined to doubt their effectiveness. In response to the Laymen's Inquiry, only 24 per cent thought there should be an increase of emphasis on elementary schools while 44 per cent favored decreasing the emphasis. Only 19 per cent thought secondary schools should be given greater emphasis and only 13 per cent expressed themselves in favor of a greater stress on universities and colleges.[13] In short, many missionaries criticized the schools for their failure to win converts for Christianity, and Christian educators from the West felt they did not measure up to minimum educational standards.

Missionary teachers and school administrators, as we have seen, accepted the government requirements of registration and the placing of courses in religion on a voluntary basis. However, they feared that with the removal of religious requirements the mission schools might become wholly secular. The problem was made more difficult by the fact that an ever declining percentage of students were Christians: in 1933-1934 only 27 per cent of the students at Nanking, 23 per cent at Soochow and 36 per cent at Yenching.[14] During the 1930's this

[12] *Laymen's Foreign Missions Inquiry, Fact-Finders' Reports: China*, Vol. V, p. 405. For the Inquiry's evaluation of Christian colleges in China, read pp. 404-409.

[13] Laymen's Inquiry papers, File on "Major Problems of the Christian Evangelization of China," Missionary Research Library.

[14] Minutes of the Committee on Christian Character, Staffing, and Cur-

problem was the central topic of discussion. The voluntary system resulted in a sharp decline of registration in religious courses and a falling off of attendance at worship services.[15] In 1929 a study of seventeen schools showed 29.8 per cent attending chapel exercises and 18.8 per cent Sunday services in boys' schools.[16] The girls proved more amenable to religious appeals, 72.7 per cent attending chapel and 54.9 per cent attending Sunday worship.[17] The same was true of registration for courses in religion, only 36.6 per cent of the boys elected courses in religion while 64.5 per cent of the girls did so.[18]

The Associated Boards for Christian Colleges in China, representing thirteen colleges, set up a special committee known as the Committee on Christian Character, Staffing, and Curriculum. In 1934 several of the universities presented detailed reports on methods employed in developing Christian character. There was uniform complaint of small attendance at chapel services and of the low percentage of students electing courses in religion. Many experiments had been made in the way of developing courses in religion, courses such as "The Bible as Literature" and "What May We Believe," but the feeling prevailed that these had been unsatisfactory.

In the face of the breakdown of traditional methods, schools now sought to justify themselves by placing great value on the religious environment they provided. J. Leighton Stuart of Yenching University, later American Ambassador to China, although profoundly disturbed, concluded that Yenching was a Christian influence in many ways. It was, first of all, a university dedicated to a search for truth, and he had no fear that the commitment to Christianity interfered with this search. Secondly, wrote Stuart, "whatever else it may be, a Christian university is at least an exhibition of the way in which a group of Christians conduct an institution of higher learning." The maintenance of high academic standards, the attitude of the

---

riculum, April 20, 1934, Associated Boards of Christian Colleges in China, Missionary Research Library.

[15] Chester S. Miao and Frank W. Price, *op.cit.*, pp. 91 and 193.

[16] *Ibid.*, p. 91.   [17] *Ibid.*, p. 91.   [18] *Ibid.*, p. 193.

teaching staff toward economic and social problems, the harmonious relationships among faculty members and between faculty and students, the integrity of all financial accounting, and the moral discipline pervading the community, were all lessons in Christian living. Stuart regretted the lack of interest in formal worship but he thought this was in part a reaction to "the highly stimulated activities of the earlier days of missionary domination." It was due also, thought Stuart, to absorption in national problems and to the common disinclination among intellectuals in China to engage in public worship.[19] An extensive program of religious meetings was sponsored by student groups at Yenching and while attendance was not what might be desired, at any rate students came not because of compulsion or dead habit. Stuart's attitude toward the problem was representative of most Christian colleges in China.

Awareness of the failure to reach down to the masses of the Chinese people lay heavily on many missionary educators and led to an interest in the Mass Education Movement. At the close of the first World War, nine out of every ten people in China were still illiterate. Government schools and mission schools, while greatly expanded, offered little hope that this problem could be met. It was, moreover, a problem that was made more difficult by the intricacies of China's written language, which required close acquaintance with thousands of written characters in many cases scarcely distinguishable from one another to any but the most highly trained eye. Real proficiency required a lifetime of study.

The difficulty of the language and some of its other inadequacies had received considerable attention in the years immediately following the revolution. The Literary Revolution, a movement that had as its slogan "to write as one speaks," promoted the use of Pei Hua (the spoken language) in writing. This made the problem of learning to read and write much easier. At the same time the government was interested in de-

---

[19] Minutes of the Committee on Christian Character, Staffing, and Curriculum, April 20, 1934, Associated Boards of Christian Colleges in China, Missionary Research Library.

veloping a uniform language for the entire country. In 1913 the Ministry of Education had sponsored a conference to work on a uniform system of pronunciation. The conference decided on the pronunciation of some 7,000 characters.[20] During World War I, when thousands of Chinese coolies were sent to France, James Yen, a Chinese YMCA worker, determined to teach them to read. He selected a thousand characters of common usage and set to work. The results were gratifying and on his return to China, Yen, working with the education section of the YMCA, and Professor H. C. Chen, a recent graduate of Columbia University, made a scientific study to determine which thousand characters would prove most useful.[21]

In 1922 the popular education movement was launched by Jimmie Yen and the YMCA in the city of Changsha. A textbook with twenty-six lessons designed to teach the thousand characters within a period of a month with only an hour and a half a day of study had been prepared as well as a series of readers that the graduate could master. Yen had unlimited energy, enthusiasm, and imagination. He had everyone of importance in the city help in promoting the campaign, prepared thousands of posters, and started the enterprise with a parade. From March to July, 1,200 illiterates from all walks of life were taught and 967 completed the work satisfactorily. In September another campaign was begun at Changsha.[22] So encouraging was the response that a similar campaign was begun at Chefoo in Shantung in the spring of 1923. More than 1,600 completed the course in the first three months. Another was conducted at Kashing in Chekiang and here the leaders experimented with the use of a stereopticon, which became standard equipment in all future efforts.[23] The success of Yen and his associates gained the attention of leading educators and in

[20] Y. C. James Yen, "The Campaign Against Illiteracy," *China Mission Year Book, 1923*, p. 207.

[21] *Ibid.*, p. 208.

[22] *Ibid.*, pp. 209-214.

[23] Y. C. Yen, "The Popular Education Movement," *China Mission Year Book, 1924*, p. 313.

August 1923 the National Popular Education Association was organized.[24]

In 1924 the North China Mission of the American Board launched an experimental campaign in mass education. Jimmy Yen and his assistant came to the mission and instructed the evangelists who, in turn, organized classes in the local churches. At the close of the year there were one hundred classes and 3,000 enrolled. By the end of 1925, 5,600 students had been taught. Elmer Galt, missionary at the Paotingfu station, reported that the movement was so cordially received that "we are fully persuaded it is much the most hopeful movement of the sort yet to appear. . . ." Aside from justifying the undertaking as a service to the Chinese, Galt pointed out that there was some religious instruction in the textbooks and that literacy was "one of the biggest steps we can now take towards making possible effective evangelism and nurture in the next few years."[25]

The Christian churches and missionaries confronted a more formidable problem in seeking to improve the working conditions in factories. Direct action was scarcely within the scope of the church, especially so in view of the widespread indifference and ignorance concerning labor conditions. The vested interests present in this sphere made the problem more difficult than in the case of the literacy campaign where no one had anything to lose.

The effort to do something for labor commenced in Shanghai where the social conscious YWCA had been seeking ways to help factory girls. In 1920 the world conference of the YWCA had taken a determined stand committing the organization to helping women in industry, encouraging them to organize unions, and to acquaint all members with the principles of labor organization.[26] Miss Grace Coppack, American-born Gen-

[24] *Ibid.*, pp. 315-316.

[25] Elmer Galt, "General Work Report for the Year 1924. The Paotingfu Station," Archives of the American Board of Commissioners for Foreign Missions, Vol. 38, North China Mission, Houghton Library, Harvard University.

[26] Anna V. Rice, *A History of the World's Young Women's Christian Association* (New York: The Woman's Press, 1947), p. 174.

eral Secretary of the Shanghai YWCA, knew that no place in the world was there a greater need, particularly to rescue the children in the textile factories. Chinese children accompanied their mothers to the factories when only infants and by five years of age were regularly employed. In 1920, due to the efforts of Miss Coppack, the National Committee of the China YWCA requested the help of an industrial specialist.[27] Agatha Harrison, a leader in the welfare movement in England, was appointed. Only a few weeks after she took up her new tasks, the National Committee resolved to put aside palliative work among factory girls and make a thorough study that could be used to create public opinion favorable to remedial legislation.

When the National Christian Conference convened in 1922, Grace Coppack had succeeded in getting the industrial problem included in the agenda. Among those ready to support the cause at the Conference was Henry Hodgkin, former Secretary of the Friends Foreign Missionary Association in Great Britain, a handsome man who had shared in the establishment of the Fellowship of Reconciliation, had met with a mob attack during the war, and had lent a hand to a great many social causes. Hodgkin had emerged from the war with passionate convictions as to the necessity for a Christian revolution. His complete sincerity, engaging oratory, and deep conviction that Christ was the answer to the appalling human needs won him large audiences in both England and America. In 1920 he went to China where he delivered 420 lectures and addresses during a little over a year, arousing Chinese Christian leaders and missionaries alike to the social implications of Christianity.[28] At the National Christian Conference he rallied support for the YWCA proposal that something be done to alleviate the condition of the working class. The goals set by the League of Nations were approved and the conference resolved that the following standards be promoted by the church at once: (a) No employment of children under twelve years of age. (b) One day's rest in seven. (c) The safeguarding

[27] *Ibid.*, p. 190.
[28] H. G. Wood, *Henry F. Hodgkin: A Memoir* (London: Student Christian Movement Press, 1937), p. 185.

of the health of the workers, e.g., limitation of working hours, improvement of sanitary conditions, and installation of safety devices.[29] When the conference established the National Christian Council, Hodgkin was instrumental in getting the latter to establish an industrial committee. Within the next year industrial committees were organized in seventeen of the larger cities.

The YWCA cooperated with this committee in gathering information and preparing literature. The committee members plunged into the new work and were soon so busy that they had to set up a cabinet of five members, which met three times a week to handle the administrative jobs.[30]

The most dramatic fight took place in Shanghai where the YWCA had already aroused the interest of women's clubs and with them had established a joint committee with May-Ling Soong, the future Madame Chiang, as Secretary. In 1922 this joint committee appealed to the Municipal Council of the International Settlement of Shanghai and the latter responded, in 1923, by appointing the Commission on Child Labor.

This Commission had as one of its members Agatha Harrison, who remained in China until February 1924. Her place was taken by Mary Dingman from the United States, a woman of drive, energy, and a spirit of adventure in the realm of economic and social problems. In the same year Adelaide Anderson, an experienced leader in the British movement to improve labor conditions, came to China upon the invitation of the joint committee and helped the Commission in its work. In July 1924 the Commission reported to the Municipal Council. In the summary the Commission stated:

> In many mills the conditions during the night-shift are, according to Western ideas, most unusual. Rows of baskets containing babies and children, sleeping or awake as the case may be, lie placed between the rapidly moving and

[29] Helen Thoburn, "The Church and Modern Industry," *China Mission Year Book, 1923,* pp. 390-391.

[30] Adelaide Mary Anderson, *Humanity and Labor in China: An Industrial Visit and Its Sequel* (London: Student Christian Movement, 1928), p. 106.

noisy machinery. Young children who are supposed to be working, but who have been overcome by fatigue or who have taken advantage of the absence of adequate supervision, lie asleep in every corner, some in the open, others hidden in baskets under a covering of raw cotton.[31]

The Municipal Council now drafted a bylaw to submit to the rate payers. The proposal was moderate, if not timid, prohibiting the employment of children under ten years of age. Those who had worked for reform were satisfied that this was all that could be hoped for at the time. In the course of the investigation Adelaide Anderson became aware of the unusual difficulties standing in the way of creating minimum labor standards—the lack of an effective Chinese government, the conviction of Chinese peasants that they could not survive without their children's earnings, the difficulty due to the fact that many competing factories lay outside the jurisdiction of the International Settlement, and the lack of schools that raised the question of how children would be cared for when their mothers were at work.

There was good reason to believe that the work so energetically pursued by the YWCA would bear fruit, but the effort failed. Strong Chinese opposition to two other proposed by-laws caused many rate payers to stay away from the meeting where the vote was to be taken, thereby preventing a quorum. Another meeting was then arranged for June 2 and the YWCA workers, led by Mary Dingman, carried on an effective campaign to have the rate payers attend. Then on May 30 occurred the clash between the British police and the Chinese students, the famous Shanghai Incident. The city was still a scene of rioting on the day of the scheduled meeting. It was necessary to advise people to remain indoors, and once again the proposed legislation failed for lack of a quorum.

31 *Ibid.*, p. 143.

CHAPTER XIV

THE PROBLEM IN RURAL CHINA,

1920-1937

In 1922 only 6 per cent of China's population lived in cities of over 50,000. Yet, 66 per cent of the missionaries, 34 per cent of the Chinese Christian workers, and 24 per cent of the church members resided in these urban centers. Only a third of China's 10,000 villages had some Christian work.[1]

The more important fact is that wherever Christian work was started in the rural villages it tended to wither away. The reason is obvious. Christianity had very little meaning to the Chinese villagers. They were bogged down in dire poverty, calamitous infancy mortality rates, widespread disease, and when disaster threatened they knew no better means of relief than magical rites and superstitions. In the absence of any real solution to their vast social problems, lethargy prevailed. China needed a social spirit, leadership, and ideas. A few isolated Christian Chinese, such as Jimmie Yen, provided some constructive programs but they did not have the support of the majority of missionaries.

As China floundered so did the Christian church in China. The only vision Christianity held out was a timid beckoning to individuals to desert their old gods, give up harmful practices, and walk a straight and narrow path, a path by-passing the jungle of China's social degradation. Christianity made itself irrelevant by failing to include the community, and, in turn, the community never embraced the esoteric Christian enterprise. The Christian convert, left to pursue his own meaningless existence in a brutal society, with no sustenance for his Christian life aside from hymn singing and literal interpretations of Bible texts, drifted away from the church. Christianity

[1] *The Christian Occupation of China*, ed. M. F. Stauffer (Shanghai: China Continuation Committee, 1922), p. 385.

might, under more imaginative leadership, have helped the convert to realize the deeper meanings of its teachings by illustrating its relevance to the social situation.

Everywhere in the rural parishes during the early 1930's a disheartening futility took command. In 1930 a Methodist missionary was so discouraged that he thought the best thing to do in his province was to close up all the churches and start over again.[2] Another Methodist missionary in central China divided the Chinese rural pastors in his conference into four groups, unreliable radicals with no real interest in the church, lazy rice Christians who hung on as long as they could eke out a living, opportunists who were simply waiting to see who would win the struggle that was going on, and finally, the smallest group of all, "those who loved the church and would suffer for it if necessary."[3]

Not a few Chinese pastors worked in the spirit of their colleague who, in a sermon on "Feed my sheep," held that it was his duty not only to feed his sheep but to sheer them, since it was bad for his parishioners to have too many worldly goods.[4] Others jostled missionaries aside so as to make way for themselves. A Chinese district superintendent, wishing to get rid of missionary leadership, sent scrolls to the funeral of a boy who had died while under the care of a foreign doctor on which were inscribed: "Foreign quack doctor killed this boy." In another case a Chinese Methodist district superintendent rented out his church for a brothel. Especially galling to the missionaries was the fact that when he was brought to trial, his Chinese colleagues defended him.[5]

Equally uninspiring were the crudities and distortions that inevitably crept into the worship service. These were not necessarily indicative of a lack of a sincere religious spirit. A particularly tolerant missionary of the American Board was amused but not offended when he saw the rural pastor who

[2] See reply of a Mrs. Libby, Methodist missionary at Nanchang, dated November 25, 1930, to questionnaire sent by Laymen's Inquiry, Laymen's Inquiry Papers, Missionary Research Library, Union Theological Seminary.
[3] See File on "Rural Work in China," Laymen's Inquiry Papers, Missionary Research Library.
[4] *Ibid.*   [5] *Ibid.*

had introduced him paring his toe nails during the sermon. Others found the unconventional behavior more disturbing— people eating sugar cane, feeding their babies, and children urinating on the floor during the church service.[6]

While these situations were trying to foreigners with a Western-conditioned sense of propriety, the really fundamental question that stumped more thoughtful Westerners was whether the embodiment of Christianity in the institution of the church, as in Western lands, was feasible in rural China. Oriental religions had never expressed themselves in organized churches holding regular worship services and led by a pastor dependent on the contributions of his parishioners for a livelihood. The average rural church had only thirty-five members. Less than a third of these churches were self-supporting. In some instances buildings constructed with Western funds were wholly deserted, in part because their constituency could not afford to maintain them.

The other fundamental difficulty was how to make Christianity an integral part of the life of a Chinese, relevant to his everyday economic and social problems. There were those Chinese who viewed religion as a purely personal matter, a way of attaining inner peace and solace, or a way of achieving the aid of the good spirits and warding off the evil ones that were almost uniformly held to determine man's fate in this world. Of a group of 149 who were asked to write an explanation of their decisions to become Christians, only forty could write an intelligible explanation.[7]

Rural pastors, with a narrow conception of their function, did not know how to use their time to raise the level of their parishioners. W. C. Lin, president of Fukien Christian College, said of them:

Now their chief activity is to sit around and complain about their salaries, the people they work with, and gen-

[6] *Ibid.*

[7] See Appendix D. Stories on "How I Became a Christian," in File on "Major Problems of Christian Evangelization of China," Laymen's Inquiry Papers, Missionary Research Library.

eral conditions. They do not see the opportunity to serve the community.

In their work they preach sermons that emphasize only saving their souls, going to heaven, belief in a foreign God, no practical applications of preaching. The people do not understand these ideas and care little. This emphasis needs to be changed.[8]

In this respect, the sheep were not far from their rural missionary shepherds. An overwhelming majority of the rural missionaries saw no need for relating the Christian message to China's economic and social problems. These problems, as they saw it, would be solved when more converts were won, who would in turn introduce higher moral standards.[9] Many of the rural missionaries had lost their zest and were bogged down in routine matters. A Presbyterian missionary said that much of their time was

consumed in tasks that appear trivial, like settling disputes, punishing wayward pastors, renting houses for workers.

This makes them discouraged; they accomplish little; think things are hopeless; and give up in despair. A defeatist psychology develops. They do what they can and accept this as the thing to do.[10]

During the 1930's, when the liberals were desperately trying to summon the church to meet the challenge of a bankrupt social order, almost the only sign of vitality in the rural areas was the rise of a revivalistic pentecostal movement. Nontheological, emotional, and unrestrained by any knowledge of the role of the Christian church historically, the movement prospered and rural churches, many of them practically deserted, came to life. A Chinese evangelist, John Sung, won popularity by denouncing a paid ministry, denominational differences,

8 See File on "Rural Work in China," Laymen's Inquiry Papers, Missionary Research Library.

9 See File on "Social Welfare Work," Laymen's Inquiry Papers, Missionary Research Library.

10 See File on "Rural Work in China," Laymen's Inquiry Papers, Missionary Research Library.

and by stressing the second coming of Christ, the Resurrection, and the Judgment. In a trying period of war and of economic catastrophe, concentration on the future life provided an attractive escape from reality. At the meetings emotional orgies occurred in which both the preacher and members of the congregation, delivering themselves from all conventional restraints, went into trances in which they claimed that the Holy Spirit was speaking through them. Another prominent feature of the revivals was faith healing. Stories circulated of remarkable cures. Sung's attacks on education were popular and he also pandered to lower tastes by reviling the regular clergy and particularly prominent liberal leaders. On one occasion he committed his entire audience to boycotting the meetings then being held by Sherwood Eddy.

The response to Sung's techniques was tremendous. He preached to spellbound audiences for hours at a time. In some areas young Chinese suddenly became fanatical preachers who went about in both the cities and the countryside beseeching people to repent. One missionary, cautiously sympathetic, reported that where Sung had preached "there were many who responded to the invitation, and there is a record throughout the southern cities of many changed lives, of restitution for past dishonesty, of families reunited, and a general quickening of the spiritual life of the churches."[11] Liberals were often disillusioned, but perhaps this was the indigenous Christianity that they had so long advocated in theory or at least a necessary stage before the sophisticated and more intellectual version for which they stood could make any progress among the masses.

Among a handful of missionaries a new vision of a reconstructed rural China permeated by Christian ideals had gradually emerged. One of these was John H. Reisner, a man with a tremendous faith in the possibility of improving the condition of the peasants. Reisner was a professor in the College of Agriculture and Forestry at the University of Nanking. One of his

[11] C. Stanley Smith, "Modern Religious Movements," *China Christian Year Book, 1934*, pp. 104-109.

colleagues was J. Lossing Buck who had earlier been in charge of the agricultural work at a Presbyterian mission. Buck became the outstanding authority on Chinese agricultural economics. By 1919 these two men were leading an agitation for a greater emphasis on training Chinese teachers of agriculture and extension workers.[12] It was at this time, too, that the American Board established the Shao-wu Agricultural Experiment Station and appointed Charles H. Riggs to supervise the work.

A tragic famine in 1921 added to the interest in the economic condition of the peasant. Missionaries carried a large share of the burden of distributing relief, and mission boards cooperated with the China Famine Relief Committee, appointed by President Woodrow Wilson, in raising funds. After the emergency was over, the committee had an unexpended balance of $900,000. These funds were set aside for the study of the causes of famine, the best methods of relief, and the education of Chinese in agriculture and forestry. The University of Nanking and Yenching University were allotted the larger part of the funds to undertake these studies.[13]

The interest of social-minded missionaries in cooperatives was indicative of their concern with the economic problems facing the Chinese. In 1917 an Anglican missionary, the Rev. Fred Hughes, organized a credit society among his parishioners in northern China who were victims of flood. This society disbanded after the emergency, but it had made a favorable impression in the area. It was in the same locality that the first union of credit cooperatives was later organized. In 1921 the China International Famine Relief Commission, with a number of missionaries on its staff, began an experiment with rural

12 John H. Reisner, "Recent Developments in Agricultural Education under Missionary Auspices," *China Mission Year Book, 1919*, pp. 158-166; J. Lossing Buck first worked as an agricultural missionary at the Presbyterian station at Nanksuchow in the province of Anhwei. He introduced agricultural courses for the farmers in the vicinity in 1919, probably the first experiment along this line. For an account of his experience, see J. Lossing Buck, "Agricultural Work of the American Presbyterian Mission at Nanksuchow, Anhwei, China, 1919," *Chinese Recorder*, June 1920.

13 John H. Reisner, "China Famine Fund Balance Committee," *China Christian Year Book, 1926*, pp. 315-325.

cooperative credit societies. The first one was organized near Nanking by a Chinese professor.

After 1928 the Kuomintang took the lead in establishing co-operatives. The 722 societies in existence in that year grew to 37,318 by the end of 1936 and to 90,738 in February 1940.[14] The role of the missionaries was relatively minor although they played an active part in setting up many of the earlier credit societies. In 1939 the National Christian Council organized a standing committee to study cooperatives and to serve as a clearing house for cooperatives connected with the churches.[15] It sought to convey to the churches the idea that cooperatives were in accord with the Christian ideal of human brotherhood.

When the Japanese occupation of eastern China forced a large-scale withdrawal of Chinese to the Western provinces, and the war led to demands by the government for army supplies, industrial cooperatives were organized under the auspices of the Kuomintang government. By September 1940 there were 1,810 industrial cooperatives and their production was estimated at $7,000,000 per month.[16] Missionaries held important positions, especially Lewis Smythe and Charles H. Riggs of the University of Nanking.

Long before the cooperatives had come into full bloom thanks to the demands of the war, a new vista of possibilities had been opened up in the 1920's by the work of Samuel Higginbottom at the Allahabad Agricultural Institute in India. To the highly practical-minded American church-going public, now less and less interested in theology, the proposals for sending missionaries of technology seemed eminently sensible, and therefore mission boards had reason to lend a friendly ear.

[14] Lewis S. C. Smythe, "Cooperatives and Christian Missions," *Chinese Recorder*, August 1940, pp. 481-491. This is a brief but authoritative article on the relation of the church to the cooperative movement by one who was active in founding cooperatives.

[15] T. H. Sun, "The Church in China's Rural Reconstruction," *Chinese Recorder*, August 1940, p. 500.

[16] Minutes of the Committee on East Asia, September, 1940. The author was kindly permitted to use the minutes of this Committee and to study the files of the Committee's bulletin. They are located in the Far Eastern Joint Office, Division of Foreign Missions, National Council of the Churches of Christ in the United States of America at 156 Fifth Avenue, New York, N.Y.

The Problem in Rural China

When the International Missionary Council, a body representing Protestants all over the world, met at Jerusalem in 1928, sufficient interest in the possibilities of agricultural missions had developed so that it was arranged to have a series of four papers presented on the subject of missions and rural problems. Kenyon Butterfield, the leading American proponent of agricultural missions and Vice-President of the American Board of Commissioners for Foreign Missions, had by this time evolved a whole ideology in which rural missions were integrated into a large program of building a Christian society. He ably presented his conclusions in the first of the papers. The central thought of Butterfield's paper was that the moral, spiritual, and mental growth of a Christian depended not only on meditation and worship but also on his daily activities. Unless these activities of everyday life were conducive to a broader outlook and a wish to cooperate for the achievement of a better life for all mankind, then spiritual growth would be stunted. Race prejudice, class prejudice, and exaggerated nationalism must be replaced by a recognition of the intrinsic worth of the individual. Society, in order to be Christian, he believed, must be so constituted that it would encourage individuals to live an abundant life and one dedicated to service to human brotherhood.[17]

Butterfield listed seven goals for an enlightened rural missionary program:

1. That the farmer shall have access to the land he works, on such terms as will insure him personal freedom and economic encouragement, while society is amply protected by efficient production and conservation of fertility.
2. That the cost of market distribution from farmer to consumer shall be cut to the lowest possible terms, both farmers and consumers sharing in these economies.
3. That there shall be every encouragement to the or-

---

17 *The Jerusalem Meeting of the International Missionary Council, 1928*, Vol. VI, "The Christian Mission in Relation to Rural Problems" (New York: International Missionary Council, 1928), p. 14.

ganization of farmers for economic ends, particularly for cooperative sales and purchases.

4. That there shall be available an efficient system of both vocational and general education of youths and adults living on farms.

5. That special efforts shall be made to insure the farmer adequate social institutions, including the church, the school, the library, means of recreation, good local government, and particularly the best possible farm home.

6. That there shall be a widespread development of organized rural communities, thoroughly democratic, completely cooperative, and possessed with the spirit of common welfare.

7. That there shall be the fullest measure of friendly reciprocal cooperation between the rural and city workers.[18]

The advocates of rural reconstruction in China found these proposals helpful and made plans for developing selected communities in which the church would become the center not only of religious life but of training in scientific agriculture, credit cooperatives, and health and sanitation. Appealing as was this vision of a Christian rural community, implementation of the ideal was difficult and the number of experimental centers launched was limited. The University of Nanking led the way. This University had conducted extensive experimental work and had on its staff three of the most able and enthusiastic advocates of rural reconstruction, Reisner, Buck, and Frank W. Price, head of its Theological Seminary.

In 1931 it started work on a rural demonstration center at Shunwachen, a market town fifteen miles southeast of Nanking. The first step taken was a careful survey of the town and some sixty villages in the vicinity. A program for training church members in voluntary Christian work, in religious education for boys and girls, and in evangelism and community service was begun. The objective, said Frank Price, was to study "what one rural church can do for its members and the

[18] *Ibid.*, p. 15.

community, how the church can help in introducing better seeds, in bringing better health, in combatting superstitious customs, in organizing its members for mutual aid and for betterment of the life around them." Elaborate sociological studies of the area were undertaken. A People's School offered the Thousand Character Course of the Mass Education Movement. Some work was done in health education, and a playground program was carried out.[19]

The work done at Nanking also included an extension service. This branch of the University ran the experiment station at Nanking and assisted some fourteen cooperating agencies. Through its extension service the University cooperated with at least 600 rural pastors.[20]

The Department of Sociology of Yenching University operated the Ching Ho Rural Service Center where students received practical training in rural social service.[21] The project was active in promoting cooperatives. Cheeloo University in Shantung established a Village Service Center at Lungshan, which sponsored an educational program for farmers, a credit society and egg-marketing association, and a health center and schools for boys and girls.[22]

In the 1930's the idea of instilling a new spirit of cooperative living in rural villages made rapid headway. James Yen and the Mass Education Movement broadened its program, setting up departments of health, livelihood, and citizenship. The Mass Education Movement organized credit and marketing cooperatives, making money available to the farmers at low rates of interest and cutting the profits of the money lenders and privately owned enterprises. In so doing the Mass Education Movement aroused the wrath of money lenders and local merchants, who were also in many instances hsien officials. In these skirmishes with vested interests, the Mass Education

[19] See letter from Frank W. Price to friends, September 9, 1931, File on "China Conditions in 1931," Missionary Research Library.
[20] J. H. Reisner, "Agricultural Missions Foundation Report," Laymen's Inquiry Papers, Missionary Research Library.
[21] P. C. Hou, "Christian Rural Reconstruction in China," *China Christian Year Book, 1936*, p. 322.
[22] "Cheeloo Rural Institute," *Chinese Recorder*, May 1933.

Movement, with the backing of Chiang Kai-shek and his government, took over the political administration of the county.[23] Non-Christian leaders shared the vision of a higher level of village life, and "Go to the People" became a slogan in schools and colleges. In Shantung a noted Buddhist scholar and philosopher took the lead in setting up rural experiments and received government cooperation. These developments coincided with Kenyon Butterfield's trip to China where he traveled extensively, talking to missionaries about ways of organizing rural work.[24]

In 1934 a number of Christian leaders in the government asked the Christian churches to aid in a program of reconstruction in Kiangsi, an area devastated by the Communists, and the National Christian Council immediately urged the churches to accept. A group of Christians organized the Kiangsi Rural Service Union, and this organization became the agency through which the churches cooperated with the government. The National Economic Council, the government agency, set up ten rural centers; the one at Kuo-tsai-chou was assigned to the Christians and the Rev. G. W. Shepherd of the American Board served as Acting General Secretary. In addition to schools for children and an adult education program, the Rural Service Union established a health clinic, cooperatives, a project for the development of home industries, and a research program aimed at improvement of the local paper industry.[25] Generalissimo and Madame Chiang contributed $5,000 in Chinese currency for five years. A government bulletin boasted that the cooperatives in the area had 304,590 members in 1935. Frank Rawlinson, editor of the *Chinese Recorder*, had reservations concerning the Kiangsi project and scolded the government for failure to undertake land reform and for permitting money lenders to operate.[26]

[23] Letter from the Rev. Hugh Hubbard to author, November 4, 1956.
[24] *Ibid.*
[25] "Christian Rural Project in Kiangsi," *Chinese Recorder*, January 1934, p. 61; G. W. Shepherd, "Reconstruction in Kiangsi," *International Review of Missions*, April 1937, pp. 167-176. The latter is the firsthand account of the Director of the project during its early years.
[26] "Rural Reconstruction in Kiangsi," *Chinese Recorder*, September 1933, p. 574.

The Problem in Rural China

The most significant illustration of the possibilities at hand took place in Hopei. Hugh Hubbard of the American Board became one of the leading exponents of the new approach. He had long been moved by the condition of the Chinese peasantry, hungry, illiterate, subject to disease, famine, floods, and the sufferings of war. In 1931 Hubbard accompanied Butterfield on a tour, through China and caught the latter's vision of "the larger rural parish." Among Hubbard's closest friends was Jimmie Yen, who urged him to start an experiment in rural reconstruction. In 1933 Hubbard, his wife, and a Chinese Christian determined to make the experiment in an ancient village of some 1,400 inhabitants, about three miles from Paoting, where the station of the American Board was located.

No mission had embarked on its work in the manner of this Christian group. They moved to Fan village only after being extended an invitation to come and help find solutions to the problems of the community. They were resolved not to undertake any project until the people asked for it. No religious instruction would be given unless the people requested it. Any posters or other signs carrying Christian propaganda were barred. This was to be an interfaith venture in meeting practical life situations with Buddhists, Confucianists, and Christians seeking to bring something to the solution of problems. Christians and non-Christians entered upon the experiment in the spirit of the devout Buddhist in the village who said: "You teach me Christianity and I will teach you Buddhism; and hand in hand we will travel the road to Heaven."[27]

The insulating compound would have been a highly unsuitable headquarters for such a heterodox adventure. The Westerners and Chinese Christians moved into a simple Chinese house, and the Chinese occupied the most honorable apartment on the west. All American supplies were left behind, and the Westerners lived on the local Chinese diet and adopted Chinese wadded clothes to counter the cold. Only one certainty

[27] A highly interesting account of this venture was written by Mabel E. Hubbard in partial fulfillment of the master of arts degree granted her by Oberlin College in 1938. It is entitled "An Experiment in Teaching the Christian Religion by Life Situations in Fan Village, China."

stood forth: Fan village abounded in needs, some of them recognizable by the villagers, others obscured from their view by a thick crust of superstition. Eighty per cent of the men were illiterate and only one girl in the entire village of 1,400 had received a primary education. Ninety-two per cent of the school boys had trachoma. Smallpox took a heavy annual toll, and tuberculosis haunted every family. A majority of children died in infancy because of a lack of elementary sanitation.

Droughts withered the cotton plants before they reached maturity with a discouraging frequency, in spite of elaborate rituals at the temples and shrines. Family ties served as fences shutting off the individual from community obligations. The leaven of identification of oneself with a larger cause was absent.

In the spirit of co-workers the Christians discussed these problems with their neighbors, suggesting ways in which the community could meet them. They accepted no posts of authority and quietly let the newly formed Reconstruction Committee take the lead in arranging projects.

It was the native villagers who, guided by the suggestions of their newly made Western friends, wrought a transformation. They established a school for women and girls with the help of the Mass Education Movement. With the assistance of a missionary doctor they learned how to take elementary precautions against the diseases that had plagued them, and by instructing midwives in the importance of cleanliness they sharply reduced infant mortality. They dug a hundred wells and watered their cotton until yields reached record proportions in spite of drought. They increased their economic returns through a cooperative marketing association. They introduced a constructive recreational program of theatricals and sports. Tree planting changed the appearance of previously drab landscape and new roads made the transportation of goods much easier. To the gratification of the missionaries, without their ever uttering a proselyting word, the new adventure was linked up with Christianity and the villagers asked for religious instruction. A visitor to the Fan Village Experiment after the work had been underway for three years noted the intangible results: "real changes in lives, a new sense of the value of personality, an appreciation of nature and of nature's God, a technique by which problems can be actually solved, new motivation and a gradual development of Christian character."

These attempts to socialize Christianity had the support of the National Christian Council. The Committee on Christianizing Economic Relations recommended (1) the promotion of rural and small-scale industries in connection with rural churches, (2) cooperatives, and (3) a share in management for labor. In 1933 it sponsored a conference on rural reconstruction at which the discussion centered about the ways in which churches could help in mass education. After 1937, when thousands fled to the western part of the country, the National Christian Council did its best to encourage churches to set up rural projects in the area and it helped with the refugee problem.

A scientific survey was undertaken in 1936 to gather a wide range of factual material about rural life and the contributions of the church.[28] Statistics were gathered from seventy-three churches of twenty-five mission or denominational groups in thirteen provinces. One purpose of the survey was to provide the rural clergy with vital facts of importance in the development of a church program fitted to the needs of the populace. The methodology employed conformed to the highest standards of sociological research and the findings constituted a rich and reliable source of information on economic and social conditions.

The statistics indicated that the rural church, in most cases, had made little significant progress toward the stated objective of becoming a driving force and shaping influence in the reconstruction of rural China. Yet, two-thirds of the churches studied sponsored some kind of community service project. Twenty-two churches had literacy classes, nine were developing supplementary industries, six had begun farmers' cooperative societies and fourteen of the seventy-three were seeking to extend the use of improved seeds. The rural church, present

[28] Frank W. Price, *The Rural Church in China: A Survey* ("Studies in The World Mission of Christianity," No. IX [New York: Agricultural Missions, Inc., 1948]).

in only one-third of China's villages and in most cases weak in respect to leadership, numbers, and finances, was scarcely in a position to play a vital role in China's economic and social reconstruction.

The Christian missionary understood better than anyone else the Biblical precept "unto the Greeks foolishness." Without his faith his program appeared foolish when measured against the facts. As it developed, his dream was overtaken by the rise of a rival faith.

Almost all of the community experiments that had been launched in the early 1930's fell victim to the Japanese invasion. Some of them had won friends for Christianity and had enriched the lives of the relatively few they reached, but they had never won the full support of either missionaries or Chinese Christians. Like so many other missionary enterprises they were subject to criticism because the cost of maintaining the many services was beyond the resources of the small groups of rural Christians.

The Nationalist revolution of the 1920's wrought significant changes in the missionary enterprise: the movement toward Chinese control of Christian institutions, a new concern with the problems accompanying industrialization, and an effort on the part of a few to improve the lot of the peasants. Always these attempts to move in new directions suffered because the triumph of Chiang Kai-shek and the Nationalist wing of the Kuomintang failed to usher in a period of order and stability in which the missionaries might have devoted all of their attention to the carrying out of their now varied program. Instead they had to contend with a chaotic situation in many areas produced by the failure of the central government to exercise effective control. The old warlords, nominal allies of Chiang, carried on almost constant warfare until 1931. The new regime was scarcely more than a loose federation of regional militarists, and fragmentation of political power continued to be the essential characteristic of Chinese politics behind the Kuomintang façade. As late as 1935 Chiang exercised effective control of only eleven of the twenty-three provinces.

The Problem in Rural China

Missionary work met with its greatest difficulties in the provinces dominated by the Communists. From 1928 to 1934 they controlled large sections of Kiangsi, Fukien, and Honan. After the northern march of 1934 they established themselves in the northwestern provinces of Shensi, Kansu, and Ninghsia with their capital at Yenan. Communist power did not stop there. In many other sections, and particularly among laborers and peasants, the party was well-organized. A small but fanatical group in the larger cities firmly believed that the solution to their country's ills lay in Communism. The prominent British missionary leader, Dr. Henry T. Hodgkin, after a trip through Honan and Hupeh in the early fall of 1927 observed:

> The party is kept alive by the intense enthusiasm of a small group whose convictions are very hard to shake. They are deeply convinced that communism is the solution of China's troubles and are prepared to sacrifice anything for it. The conduct of some communists who have been executed has inspired the witnesses with the feeling that these men and women have found something that was capable of filling them with courage even in the hour of their deaths.

The Communists gained much strength by the very fact that they knew exactly the direction they wished to take, while the leadership of the Kuomintang was uncertain which way to move.

Estimates of the China situation varied from missionary to missionary and as the fortunes of the Kuomintang improved or declined, but there can be no doubt that by the mid-thirties the Communists had recouped the losses they had suffered in 1927. In the summer of 1935 Nelson T. Johnson, the American Minister, noted that "there continued to be communist forces scattered in various provinces under General Chiang's control, these forces in themselves presenting minor problems but, because of the increasingly serious economic situation of the country, constituting a potential menace."[29] In 1937 a truce

---

[29] Nelson T. Johnson to the Secretary of State, July 12, 1935, *Foreign Relations of the United States, 1935*, III, (Washington: Government Printing Office, 1935), p. 307.

was reached temporarily in the face of the Japanese invasion, but real unity was never achieved.

The Kuomintang faced another serious difficulty. Local officials, though members of the party, frequently flaunted its orders and all too frequently proved themselves poor and dishonest administrators. The American Vice-Consul at Foochow, in December 1931, voiced a not infrequent complaint that the provincial party bureau was made up of "job-hunters, selfish rather than patriotic," who "give no support but rather opposition to the government which in various departments under trained and qualified heads, is trying to build up the country."[30]

Under these circumstances the fate of missionaries depended upon the area in which they were working. In Shantung, after 1929, they experienced quiet and enjoyed the cooperation of the civil and military officials of the regime headed by General Liu Chen-nien.[31] The area in the vicinity of Peking and Tientsin was likewise free from interference with missionary work.[32] To the north, in Manchuria, Chang Hsueh-liang provided protection and there were no reports of interference.[33] Missionaries in Chekiang likewise enjoyed peace although they complained of pressure on mission schools to register and to comply with government regulations.[34]

In sharp contrast the missionaries in the provinces to the south and in central China faced frequent and, in many cases, constant hostility on the part, not only of Communists and bandits, but of civil and military officials of the Kuomintang. The northern part of Fukien was the scene of endless dif-

[30] Gordon L. Burke to Nelson T. Johnson, December 24, 1931, Department of State Files, General Services Building, Washington, D.C. Department of State correspondence cited in this chapter is from this collection.

[31] Leroy Webber, Consul at Chefoo, to Nelson T. Johnson, December 2, 1930, Department of State Files.

[32] C. E. Gauss, Consul General at Tientsin, to Nelson T. Johnson, April 21, 1931, Department of State Files.

[33] E. B. Thomas, Consul at Harbin, to Nelson T. Johnson, May 14, 1931, Department of State Files.

[34] Edwin S. Cunningham, Consul-General at Shanghai, to Nelson T. Johnson, May 18, 1931, Department of State Files.

ficulty. A missionary of the American Board complained that the local Kuomintang headquarters called meetings at mission schools without notice and then required all students to listen to "usually unprofitable tirades" by party speakers. School work also suffered because students were called upon for party propaganda work. Party leaders also did their best to dictate the appointment of teachers. This same missionary of the American Board reported that soldiers, under orders from the highest military and civil authorities, had occupied mission property in a great many places in his district. The Shao-wu mission of the American Board was the victim of strong anti-foreign feeling whipped up by nationalist propaganda against "cultural imperialism." Communists and bandits added to the woes of the mission. The Kienning station of the Shao-wu mission, once the scene of flourishing schools for boys and girls, a well-equipped hospital, and a church was reduced "to a mere shadow of its former glory" by 1931. A Methodist hospital at Kutien, occupied by troops in 1929, still remained in their possession two years later.[35]

In 1930 the South China Alliance Mission in Kwangsi reported that many of its stations had been forced to close because of military hostilities in their neighborhood. Communists had also interfered. At one station the Communists had moved in and had forbidden the holding of religious services. No sooner had they left than a group of non-Communists looted the station. At another station an angry mob invaded the compound and the preacher and his family fled over the back wall. At another post the Communists had set the place on fire and then shot down the occupants as they sought to escape from the flames.[36]

In no province did the missionaries experience greater tribulations than in Kiangsi, where Communists and Nationalists were in a struggle for control. The most bitter complaints came from an American Catholic missionary who described the

[35] Gordon L. Burke, Vice-Consul at Foochow, to Nelson T. Johnson, December 24, 1931, Department of State Files.
[36] J. W. Ballantine, Consul-General at Canton, to Nelson T. Johnson, April 1, 1931, Department of State Files.

situation as one of "unutterable and illimitable chaos." He wrote:

As I forecasted in previous letters, Kiangsi, owing to the culpable negligence of the provincial government, has become a Red inferno. It is a state of affairs that could be condoned and consequently tolerated, if the provincial authorities, using what means they had in hand, had failed to prevent this fiasco. But present conditions have been brought about by crass and seemingly wilfull negligence on the part of those in authority in this province. And what makes the crime more dastardly, is that these conditions have been deliberately misrepresented in Nanking, thereby preventing the intervention of the National Government.[37]

The indifference of the Nationalists concerning the safeguarding of foreign property contrasted with the pronouncements from Nanking that it was willing and able to protect foreigners, caused the Catholic missionary to accuse the government of "gigantic sham" and of recklessly engaging in "the traditional 'make-face' business."[38]

Protestant missionaries in Kiangsi gave equally grim accounts of looting and burning by Communists and of the in-

[37] F. P. Lockhart, Consul-General at Hankow, to the Secretary of State, December 30, 1930, Inclosure from the Right Rev. J. A. O'Shea to Nelson T. Johnson. The Right Rev. O'Shea wrote a great many letters protesting against the Nationalists. An American diplomat prepared an estimate of the number of words in telegrams received and sent during 1929 and 1930 "regarding the safety and whereabouts of Bishop O'Shea and members of the American Catholic Mission at Kanchow, Kiangsi." His purpose was to indicate the time required by consuls in their efforts to gain protection for missionaries. The total number of words in telegrams during 1929 was 2,483 and 6,744 in 1930. In addition there had been a "bulky" mail correspondence. The writer thinks this was an extreme case but the time given to missionary cases was tremendous as indicated by the literally hundreds of letters on file. More than one consul had complained of the time consumed in handling such matters. If all missionaries had reported the attacks they suffered, the correspondence would have been a great deal heavier. The church or denomination to which a missionary belonged had no bearing on the willingness to protest; it seems to have been a question of the individual missionary's attitude rather than of his connection.

[38] *Ibid.*

effectiveness of the Nationalist troops. When Nationalist troops did move in, they wrecked mission work by occupying mission facilities. A Presbyterian mission at Sutsien, Kiangsi, was occupied nineteen times by various groups of soldiers within a year's time.[39] Repeated protests to the Ministry of Foreign Affairs, complained Mahlon Perkins, Counselor of Legation, brought only "*purely pro forma*" replies.[40] In fact, more property was being occupied continuously. Perkins, on April 2, 1931, advised the Secretary of State that the legation was "reluctantly inclined to the opinion" that the national government was "deliberately working toward the conscious end of rendering impossible the carrying on in China of all foreign missionary activities with the possible exception of medical work." In fact, observed Perkins, the missionaries had fared best in the three eastern provinces where the influence of the national government was merely nominal.[41]

In the neighboring province of Honan, conditions were also unfavorable. The presence of Communists, bandits, and at other times the battles being fought had forced many missionaries to vacate their properties. These were then readily taken over by troops and left in a condition that made them veritably useless. In many cases missionaries were driven out of their buildings. During 1929 and 1930 the seventeen stations of the Lutheran United Mission in southern Honan suffered from repeated military occupation. One station was taken over nine times in 1929 and three times in 1930. Two stations were held by soldiers for the full two years. Two other stations were completely destroyed. Not a single station had escaped occupation at some time or other.[42]

A Methodist missionary in Hupeh told of the suffering endured at the hands of the Communists and how, once they had

[39] Mahlon Perkins, Counselor of Legation, to the Secretary of State, April 2, 1931, Inclosure Paul W. Meyer to Nelson T. Johnson, March 4, 1931, Department of State Files.

[40] Mahlon Perkins to the Secretary of State, April 2, 1931, Department of State Files.

[41] *Ibid*.

[42] F. P. Lockhart, Consul at Hankow, to Nelson T. Johnson, January 27, 1931, Department of State Files.

left, the regular soldiery and militia played havoc. Missions in a large part of the province faced the usual difficulty of having soldiers take over their physical plants. The same was true in parts of Honan. The American Consul at Hankow, within whose district these provinces lay, said that the reports of the illegal occupation of mission property had been legion. The Consul stated that with the exception of the provinces of Kweichow, Szechuan, and Shensi, there was "not a single piece of mission property in the interior sections of the Hankow consular district, where foreigners are not in residence, that has not been occupied by troops of some sort or other during the past five years."[43] Even those that were occupied in part, were "constantly subjected to the forceful entry upon and occupation of all vacant space by such troops as may be passing through that place." He might have added that many stations had been taken over when fully occupied. According to the Consul the practice had become so common that there was a tendency on the part of missionaries in the Hankow consular district to refrain from reporting.[44]

The defiance of civil authorities by the military occurred repeatedly. The Secretary of the American legation told of strict orders being issued by the Minister of Military Administration, forbidding under pain of severe punishment all troops to occupy mission properties. When such orders were posted on mission stations, they were sometimes treated as invitations to defiance. The Secretary of the American legation informed the Department of State that in "many cases military units even deliberately" occupied mission property that posted a copy of the proclamation ordering troops to leave the mission alone. He cited one instance when a group of soldiers of the Wireless

[43] *Ibid.*

[44] The Consul wrote: "There has been noticed an increased tendency on the part of the missionaries resident at interior points to refrain from reporting such illegal occupations unless unbearably inconvenienced thereby, as the action that it is possible for the consular officer to take in the circumstances is no longer as effective as formerly, and there is an increased atmosphere of resignation on the part of the missionary, silently to bear the burden of illegal occupations as they occur, and to strive to carry on in spite of the difficulties." Lockhart to Johnson, January 27, 1931.

Corps, on having their attention called to an order issued by Chiang Kai-shek forbidding trespassing, replied that Chiang was not in direct command of them and therefore they were not subject to his orders.[45] But it was not only the military that took over mission property, although this branch of the government was chiefly guilty. In some places both local civil officials and local representatives of the Kuomintang party demonstrated a contempt for foreign property rights. After 1933 there was a considerable improvement in the situation, but missions continued to make occasional complaints against the Kuomintang or against agents of the party. In 1934 Nationalist forces operating against the rebellious Nineteenth Route Army in Fukien occupied American mission property in six places. Minister Nelson T. Johnson protested to the Chinese Minister of Foreign Affairs that the occupation was characterized "by much wanton and uncalled-for destruction of property." The Minister expressed "surprise at the continued disregard of American property rights by armed forces under the direct control of the National Government." "The frequency with which the occupation of American mission property in Fukien was, and, I am inclined to believe is still being undertaken by undisciplined troops of presumably responsible units of the armies now in occupation of that Province indicates that it is deliberately done," said Minister Johnson. He added that when the Nineteenth Route Army had been in control of the province, it had almost always respected property rights and had thereby won for itself an enviable reputation among Chinese and foreigners alike.[46]

[45] C. Van H. Engert, First Secretary of Legation, to the Secretary of State, July 31, 1931, Department of State Files. Mr. Engert wrote that "the financial loss and damage sustained amounts to a considerable figure in each instance, and the sum representing the total loss and damages incurred by American missionary organizations during the past three years through theft, looting, and pilferage, and wanton damage and destruction on the part of the armed forces of the Republic of China, is surprisingly large. In addition to tearing out wooden fixtures, including even door and window frames, and fouling and blocking up wells, Chinese troops carry away in daylight, under the eyes of the missionaries, benches, tables, and chairs, and other movable property."

[46] N. T. Johnson to Chinese Acting Minister for Foreign Affairs, March 3, 1934, *Foreign Relations of the United States, 1934*, III, p. 467.

These happenings were not widely publicized in the United States. Neither missionary administrators nor the missionaries themselves cared to make the American people aware of the true situation. They knew that newspaper publicity concerning the violence of 1927 had dampened missionary enthusiasm and had led to a decline in the amount of contributions. Those missionaries who had placed their confidence in the Kuomintang's ability to provide security for foreigners and who had argued for revision of the extraterritoriality features of the treaties had added reason for not advertising the weakness of the new government.

The missionaries, however exasperated by the obstacles placed in their path by the powers of darkness, thought they saw signs of the coming of a better day. In 1931 came the conversion of Chiang Kai-shek. "When the devil's ill, the devil a monk would be," commented a Washington official. But among the missionaries any scepticism was set aside by stories of Bible reading and prayer meetings in the Chiang household. Time and again missionaries spoke with reverence of the sincerity of the Generalissimo, and from this time on many of them came to regard his regime with blind adulation. A few quietly expressed the opinion that the Generalissimo was perhaps limited in his understanding of the Christian message although he was probably sincere. A few, at least, were eventually to express disgust with him as a political leader.

There were other signs by 1932 of a recovery of the Christian movement. Reviewing the difficulties that the missionaries had faced from 1926 to 1931, the American Minister to China, Nelson T. Johnson, expressed the opinion that they had not constituted a severe setback. He observed that while in some fields the work "may have registered a halt," in other fields there was a distinct advance. By 1933 work was resumed at most places where it had been carried on before the troubles, which began in 1925. The number of Protestant missionaries, Johnson estimated, was back to 80 per cent of what it had been in 1926. Most schools and churches were open again.[47]

[47] N. T. Johnson to the Secretary of State, March 28, 1933, Department of State Files.

The Problem in Rural China

The American Minister then gave his evaluation of the contributions of the missionary to the life of China:

It may be safely claimed on behalf of Protestant Christian missionary effort in China that it has given to Chinese leaders a higher conception of the status of women, a new conception of the responsibility of political leaders toward the welfare—both physical and mental—of the masses, and, last but not least, the spirit of nationalism which is now acting like a ferment throughout the country.[48]

This was the positive note sounded by the best friend of the missionaries in the diplomatic corps and by one inclined to take a long view and an optimistic one.

The measure of recovery after the years of trial between 1926 and 1931 was reflected in the growth of church membership. In a survey of rural churches Frank Price cited some twenty-five rural churches that had a net gain of 42.6 per cent from 1932 to 1936.[49] The total number of Chinese communicants, as reported in the *Handbook* on the Christian movement in China, increased from 446,631 in 1928 to 512,873 in 1935.[50] Whereas the number of Protestant missionaries had declined from 8,325 in 1926 to 4,375 in 1928, by 1936 the number had risen to 6,059.[51] These gains were accompanied by a new determination on the part of many missionaries to make the churches count for more as agencies of social welfare, a phase that we have already examined. The rapid increases in mission school enrollments likewise injected a new spirit into the enterprise. After 1926 the number of students had sharply declined but by 1935 Christian colleges had an enrollment of 6,475, approximately twice as many as ten years before.[52] Missionary leaders expressed concern over the danger that these schools, particu-

48 *Ibid.*
49 Frank W. Price, *The Rural Church in China* (New York: Agricultural Missions Inc., 1948), p. 106.
50 *Handbook of the Christian Movement in China Under Protestant Offices*, eds. Charles Luther Boynton and Charles Dozier Boynton (Shanghai: National Christian Council of China, 1936), p. IX.
51 *Ibid.*
52 *Ibid.*, p. 150.

larly those on the college level, might become purely secular institutions, but this was a problem of a different nature from the one they had faced a few years before.

Yet, China continued to be a sea of crosscurrents. Evidence of a more receptive attitude toward Christianity was paralleled by ever present manifestations of hostility. In 1931 Sherwood Eddy conducted meetings in north China and in Manchuria. Everywhere he was greeted by capacity audiences. At the Imperial University in Peking three thousand students came to hear him. In Tientsin the largest church was filled to overflowing night after night. Four hundred inquirers signed up to join Bible classes, and more than one hundred declared themselves Christians. But there was a jarring note. Communist students attended every meeting and on one occasion a hundred of them "sprang up in all parts of the hall at an agreed signal and began to shout, 'Down with this running dog of Imperialism! Down with Capitalism! Down with Christianity!'" Two thousand other students leaped up and shouted, "Down with the Communists." Eddy described the ensuing scene as one of pandemonium, and, in his own effervescent way, wrote: "My heart leaped for joy as we seemed to be getting back to apostolic days."[53] In much the same fashion, in most areas of China, the same blend of friendliness and enmity to Christianity existed.

[53] Report from Sherwood Eddy, File on "Conditions in China in 1931," Missionary Research Library, Union Theological Seminary.

CHAPTER XV

MISSIONARIES AND THE SINO-
JAPANESE WAR, 1931-1941

THE maelstrom of revolutionary forces sweeping across China in the 1920's could scarcely be harnessed by the missionaries and made to serve their own aim of Christianization. The forces they had helped unleash threatened to engulf them, but the missionaries worked on with a grim sense that they must do their duty. Possessed by an inner drive they continued to preach, teach, and to heal, finding in the hostility they met evidence of the real meaning of the Christian cross.

Their inner drive did not exclude a deep concern for the welfare of the people they had come to serve although few of them thought in terms of political and social reform. They had learned to love the people and had come to identify themselves with China. The interests of that nation became their own interests and they were prepared to be their advocates before the world. That they should have acquired a genuine sense of affection for the country is not difficult to understand. China had provided them with their chosen life task. It was China that had given meaning to their lives, and amid all the hostility they encountered they could also remember that there had been faithful converts. And most others had been polite even when they were indifferent.

Many had manifested the understanding revealed by the Chinese woman who attended a service conducted by the father of Pearl Buck. The congregation was growing restless in the face of an unusually long sermon and many were leaving. Seeing that the earnest missionary was disturbed, the woman turned to the people and admonished them thus: "Do not offend this good foreigner! He is making a pilgrimage in our country so that he may acquire merit in heaven. Let us help him to save his soul!"

[251]

Others could recount when they had been hunted by an angry mob and how Chinese, at the risk of their own lives, had provided a place of hiding. Missionaries had learned that they could feel contempt for Chinese politicians but they could never feel contempt for a great people. It was inevitable that when a foreign invader struck, the missionary would become a defender of these people.

When the Japanese invaded Manchuria in 1931 the missionaries in China inevitably took the side of their adopted land. Long before 1931 they had helped create a set of mind favorable to China. When hostilities began in Manchuria they could send their reports to scores of church periodicals, could present their views directly to church audiences while home on furlough, and if it chose, the Committee on Reference and Counsel of the Interdenominational Foreign Missions Conference of North America could utilize its connections with Washington to present their views to those who determined policy. Missionary opinion, however, could be an important force only if it could mold the opinions of the vast church constituency. As it turned out, other forces counteracted the flow of missionary opinion.

From the time of the Manchurian Incident of 1931 to Pearl Harbor the American Protestant missionaries in China dedicated themselves to enlightening the home constituency. Japan was portrayed as a militaristic nation, callous to all humanitarian considerations, bent on reducing China to a servile status. Sherwood Eddy, who was in Mukden the very night that Japan unleashed her forces to take over Manchuria, in September 1931 sought to set in motion all the forces of righteousness against the evil doer. He immediately cabled to leading American and British statesmen, informing them that his on-the-spot information pointed "to a premeditated and carefully prepared offensive of the Japanese Army without the provocation of any Chinese attack." Later he forwarded a sworn statement of interviews with Chinese leaders "who testify to repeated pressure of the Japanese to induce them to head independence governments." He added that should the League and the signatories of the Kellogg Pact fail, the Nanking government would probably fall. Already there was a "notable turning toward Soviet Russia as an ally."[1]

During the autumn of 1931 missionaries in the lower Yangtze valley were torn between their own inclinations toward pacifism and their sympathetic reaction to China in her hour of plight. They deplored war and their first impulse was to be "Christian" about it: that is, to work for peace and refrain from hatred. But when the war moved to Shanghai, they saw awful scenes of bombed-out homes, of refugees, and the thousands of wounded or killed. Their deepest feelings of sympathy went out to the Chinese. No Japanese pleas of self-defense could erase the horror they felt at Japan's callous disregard for the safety of civilians.

Scores of letters to mission boards and to friends in the United States told of the Japanese attack on Shanghai in tones of righteous indignation.[2] Missionaries volunteered for relief work, and in the first-aid stations there was no neutrality. Chinese friends told them that "peace will not work now." Early in February 1932, 128 missionaries, American and British, joined in denouncing Japan's actions.[3] They urged "immediate positive moral judgment" under the Nine Power Treaty and the Kellogg Pact. The threat of internal disaster, they said, could only be avoided if the responsible elements in China received help to stabilize the economic and social order.[4]

The Manchurian Incident awakened serious concern in the United States. Japan was identified as the aggressor and subjected to sharp moral condemnation. Criticism of Japan, however, was tempered by a determination not to become involved in the war, and President Herbert Hoover and the public shied

[1] Report from Sherwood Eddy, File on "Conditions in China in 1931," Missionary Research Library, Union Theological Seminary.

[2] See letters on file in Missionary Research Library.

[3] File on "Conditions in China in 1932," Missionary Research Library; A. L. Warnshuis to Stanley K. Hornbeck, Department of State, February 13, 1932, Department of State Files, General Services Building, Washington, D.C.

[4] Warnshuis to Hornbeck, February 13, 1932, Department of State Files. The fear was expressed by many missionaries that failure of the League of Nations and the United States to come to China's aid would cause the Chinese to turn to Soviet Russia.

away from both military and economic measures to halt Japan. Secretary of State Henry L. Stimson, although much more inclined toward economic sanctions, finally contented himself by announcing the nonrecognition doctrine, stating that the United States would not recognize territorial changes resulting from use of force and violation of treaty agreements.

The influence of the missionary enterprise on American thinking was clearly revealed in Secretary Stimson's later explanation of why he had issued the nonrecognition doctrine. It was, he said, aimed more at China than Japan. He explained that he had been moved by a knowledge of the

> incalculable harm which would be done immediately to American prestige in China and ultimately to the material interests of America and her people in that region, if after having for many years assisted by public and private effort in the education and development of China towards the ideals of modern Christian civilization, and having taken the lead in the movement which secured the covenant of all the great powers, including ourselves, "to respect her sovereignty, her independence and her territorial and administrative integrity," we should now cynically abandon her to her fate when this same covenant was violated.[5]

A more practical demonstration of American sympathy would have suited the Chinese better, and in the years of trial that lay ahead they were to develop a rather cynical attitude toward the words of good cheer that emanated from the United States. Here again American diplomacy was being guided in part by the belief that missionaries had created a tremendous reservoir of good will for the United States in China, that missionaries were leading China into the new age of Christian humanitarian ideals and technological progress, and that the United States must not let China down because that nation looked to America as a disinterested friend. Granted that this approach was in some part a sublimation of less altruistic economic and stra-

[5] Henry L. Stimson and McGeorge Bundy, *On Active Service in Peace and War* (New York: Harper and Brothers, 1947), p. 90.

tegic considerations, nevertheless it was also a force in itself, one of the dynamics of America's China policy.

Missionary antagonism to Japan continued during the interlude of peace between May 1933 and July 1937. When war broke out again, missionaries took up China's cause with renewed vigor. Their first response to the crisis was to praise General Chiang Kai-shek. The editor of the *Missionary Review of the World* testified that "China has now the most enlightened patriotic and able rulers in her history."[6] Long articles on the New Life Movement told how the Chinese, led by the wife of the Generalissimo, were engaged in a great crusade to eliminate old evils from Chinese life and replace them with the "Christian" virtues of cleanliness, patriotism, and self-sacrifice.

During this crucial period even Communists won the acclaim of missionaries, a reversal of opinion brought about in part by the Communists who now catered to the missionary. Not many years before Chinese Soviet leaders had labeled the missionary the "running dog of imperialism." The crisis China now faced required a favorable opinion in the West and the Communists were wholly willing to make the necessary concessions. A Protestant missionary explained that the Communists in China had abandoned many Russian ideological concepts and much of their violence; "they are now Chinese first and foremost; their aim now is to institute a movement for socialized reform compatible with the aspirations of all progressive people."[7] Two missionaries in Chengtu wrote of the change among Communists, and they explained that there "is no more compulsion about it than there is in a church school."[8] The Rev. Donald D. Rees of Hankow, after a trip through a Communist-controlled area, told of the friendly reception he had received, how he had preached, and that the highest authorities had professed friendly feelings for missionaries. Gen-

[6] "Japan's Losing Battle," ed., *Missionary Review of the World*, September, 1938, p. 391.

[7] "What About the Communists?" *Missionary Review of the World*, July 1939, p. 378.

[8] Dr. and Mrs. Wallace Crawford, "A Missionary Epistle from China," *Missionary Review of the World*, April 1939, p. 172.

eral Chu Teh, Commander-in-Chief of the Red army, had given him a letter expressing the appreciation of the Eighth Route Army "for the kindness and help rendered to China by the foreign missionaries."[9] By 1939 some missionaries in China were denying Japan's claim that she was fighting because she wished to deliver China from the Communist threat. There was no such threat.

Missionaries in North China, frankly sympathetic to the Communists during the early years of the United Front, caught a glimpse of "things to come" by 1939 and early 1940. The Japanese were never able to occupy more than the main centers. In the neighborhood of Paotingfu they returned to the city every night, going out into the countryside in the daytime to collect taxes, fodder, and to commandeer animals and men of military age. "At night the guerrilla forces which were organized by the communists and incorporated into their Eight [sic] Route Army," observed Hugh Hubbard, "came into this same territory after taxes, fodder, animals and men. Most villagers had to organize two governments, one by day to negotiate with the Japanese and another to deal at night with the guerrillas." He found his Chinese friends speaking of being "under the saw" —meaning that they were being sawed to pieces by the opposing armies.

According to Hubbard, during 1937 and 1938 most rural missionaries felt that the Communists were giving the villages a better government than had ever been known before. By 1939 their observations alerted them to the fact that the Communists were using the war for party aims. Hubbard came to the conclusion that they were more eager to fight the Nationalists than to repel the Japanese, that the leaders were primarily Communist and secondarily Chinese, and "that they were successfully using the war, and even ready to prolong it, for the purpose of strengthening their influence, building up their organization and army, in preparation for taking over North China after the Japanese had been defeated."[10]

[9] "Can Communists Be Christian?" *Missionary Review of the World*, January 1939, p. 57.

[10] Letter from the Rev. Hugh Hubbard to author, November 4, 1956.

The Sino-Japanese War

Upon the reopening of hostilities in 1937 the United States government advised missionaries to leave the battle zone areas, but the missionaries announced it was their duty to stand firmly by their friends in time of trial. Scores of them sought to help in camps for refugees and virtually all of them encouraged the Chinese to resist the invader. In turn they received the praise of Chinese government officials. One of the finest contributions missionaries could make, wrote Frank Price, President of the Theological Seminary at the University of Nanking, was to help maintain the morale of the people.[11] By remaining at their posts in the face of attack, when they might have left, they undoubtedly did contribute to Chinese morale.

The dominant note of missionary reports was criticism of Japan. Before many months of fighting had passed, a group of twenty-three missionaries in Shanghai issued a statement that was directed to the American people.

With the resounding explosions of bombs and shells, the hum of airplanes, and the rat-tat-tat of machine guns in our ears, constantly reminding us of the struggle to the death in which this beloved country of our adoption is engaged, we a company of twenty-three of your missionaries temporarily in Shanghai, amid all the confusion and misery around us, would fain send a message that would be heard above the din of battle strife and reach every member of our home church.

We are witnesses of the heroic sacrifices and sufferings of the people to whom we have been sent, in their determined oneness of purpose to preserve at all costs their national existence and freedom against a powerful and inhuman military machine. The bravery of the Chinese soldiers commands our admiration, and the patient endurance of the ordinary people stirs our sympathy and desire to help. But more than this, we are touched by the

11 Frank W. Price, "Christian Morale in War-Torn China," *Missionary Review of the World*, January 1938, p. 30.

turning of the people to us for comfort and encouragement in this darkest hour of their national history.[12]

In December 1937 the Japanese captured Nanking. There were heavy losses among both Chinese soldiers and civilians. Missionaries and newspaper correspondents placed part of the blame on General Chiang who had blundered in engaging the superior Japanese forces from a fixed position. The city could not be defended and to do so was to invite the massacre of civilians and to sacrifice thousands of soldiers uselessly. Several missionaries led by M. Searl Bates and Lewis S. C. Smythe took the lead in trying to set up an inviolate safety zone.[13] They also sought to arrange a truce but General Chiang gave only a most perfunctory reply to the proposal and the Japanese gave no response. An Episcopalian missionary, the Rev. John Magee, served as Chairman of a committee of foreigners that undertook to provide some care for the thousands of wounded soldiers.[14] In fact, the Chinese military commanders had committed such errors of judgment that there was some feeling of relief when the Japanese entered the city and "scattered bands of civilians actually cheered Japanese columns as they marched in from the South Gate and West Gate." But then Japanese barbarities began, relief and welcome soon gave up to terror. Soldiers looted, committed rape, attacked civilians, and indulged in "unspeakable" brutalities.[15] In their letters home the missionaries wrote chiefly of the latter, and religious periodicals made no mention of the callousness of Chinese leadership.

Letters presenting the Chinese point of view met with a friendly hearing and the missionaries in China were energetic in giving their side. A letter to the *Christian Advocate* from Nanking described the Japanese actions in Nanking as "the depredations of a horde of degraded criminals of incredible bestiality, who have been and are now working their will, un-

[12] *Ibid.*
[13] F. Tillman Durdin, "Japanese Atrocities Marked Fall of Nanking after Chinese Command Fled," *New York Times*, January 9, 1938, p. 38.
[14] *Ibid.*
[15] *Ibid.*

restrained, on a peaceful, kindly, law-abiding people."[16] Bishop
Ralph A. Ward contributed an account of Japanese atrocities
entitled "Hell in Nanking." Over 10,000 unarmed persons had
been killed. The bishop told the grim story of how they had
been tied together in gangs, lined up along the river bank,
mowed down with machine guns and their bodies thrown into
the river. Other hundreds were shot and their bodies piled and
burned. Some 8,000 women and girls had been raped.[17]

The Committee on the Far East of the Foreign Missions Conference received scores of letters from missionaries in Nanking
telling of Chinese suffering and of Japanese atrocities. Its members gave careful consideration to the problem of whether any
of these firsthand accounts should be released. Any group representing missionary work in Japan as well as elsewhere in Asia
had to take into account the adverse effect the anti-Japanese
opinion of American missionaries in China would have on the
Christian movement in Japan. They were also well aware that
American public opinion was determined in its opposition to
American involvement in the war. Therefore there was the
danger that any large-scale publicity given to missionary reactions to the Japanese atrocities would lead to criticism of the
missionaries and possibly to demands that they be withdrawn
from danger zones. Nevertheless the Committee on the Far
East, shortly after the Nanking tragedy decided that "it is our
responsibility to use these documents for the information of the
American people, and particularly our church constituencies,
in ways which will forward definitely Christian ends."[18] The
Committee thereupon sent copies to a limited number of ministers and others.

The decision to release the letters led to their publication
in *Reader's Digest*. The editor wrote an introduction explain-

[16] "Missionaries Write Home," *The Christian Advocate*, January 6, 1938,
p. 7.
[17] Bishop Ralph A. Ward, "Hell in Nanking," *The Christian Advocate*,
April 21, 1938, p. 376.
[18] Minutes of the meeting of February 25, 1938, of the Committee on
the Far East. Both the minutes of the Committee and files of the bulletin
it issued were made available to the author in the offices of the Foreign
Missions Conference of North America at 156 Fifth Avenue, New York City.

ing that they were from Americans who had stayed in Nanking. A missionary surgeon had described the Japanese occupation as "this modern 'Dante's Inferno,' written in huge letters with blood and rape." He had written in his diary:

> Two patients were admitted this afternoon whose condition represents about the last word in fiendish, unmitigated, atavistic brutality. One is the sole survivor of 140 led from one of the refugee camps to the hills where they were first sprayed with a few shot and then soaked with gasoline and set afire. His head is burned to a hideous fixed stare minus the eyes, which are burned out.[19]

A small group of missionaries led by Frank Price of the Theological Seminary at the University of Nanking established the China Information Service in September 1938. From their headquarters in Washington, D. C., they sent out a small mimeographed bulletin. The articles and news stories came largely from missionaries in China who had seen the Japanese in action. Every item in the pages of the bulletin aimed at arousing the people in the United States to the justice of China's cause. The writers told of indiscriminate Japanese bombing, criticized the United States for selling war material to Japan, and took issue with the neutrality legislation of 1937, which if applied to the "China incident," would deprive China of badly needed supplies at the same time that it denied these to the aggressor.[20]

The Department of State likewise received firsthand accounts of the methods of terrorism and appalling suffering of the Chinese. Searle Bates, professor at the University of Nanking, wrote to the American Consul in January 1938, that the University was sheltering 30,000 refugees. This service, he said, had been "tenaciously maintained amid dishonor by soldiers, murdering, wounding, wholesale raping, resulting in violent ter-

[19] "We Were in Nanking," *The Reader's Digest*, October 1938, p. 41.
[20] Complete files of this mimeographed bulletin are available in the Day Library of Missions at the Yale Divinity School and were very kindly made available to the author.

ror."[24] This letter was forwarded to Washington. Another forty-five page document giving excerpts from letters of missionaries narrating their war experiences was prepared by Wynn C. Fairfield of the American Board and sent to the Department of State.[22] No document could have offered a more severe indictment of Japanese methods.

In the fall of 1938 a missionary wrote of the dangers that lay in a Japanese victory. If Japan should win, "the door of missionary opportunity in the Orient . . . will gradually be closed." A victory for China, on the other hand, would "be a great victory for democracy, for human freedom, and for religious liberty." It would be a "triumph of right over might." It would "mean the liberation of the Japanese people themselves from the inhuman tyranny of their own wicked military leaders." "Surely," he wrote, "Christian hearts all over the world should daily join in prayer for China and her brave Christian leaders."[23]

Missionaries were among the most ardent advocates of an embargo against Japan—an embargo that would seriously hurt Japan. The neutrality legislation enacted by Congress in 1937 was written with the intent of keeping America out of war, not to give the President a weapon against aggressors. Therefore Congress had provided that wherever the President found a state of war to exist he must cut off both belligerents from American supplies. As neither China nor Japan officially declared war the President was free to treat the war as an "incident," and he did not invoke the law. Had he done so, it would have hurt China more than Japan.

The missionaries in China voiced dismay as they witnessed the bombings of the Chinese made possible by the sale of scrap iron and oil to Japan. The members of the Fellowship of Reconciliation at West China Union University in Chengtu cabled the American branch: "We believe it is a moral duty to dis-

---

[21] Clarence Gauss to the Secretary of State, January 15, 1938, Inclosure Searle Bates to Gauss, Department of State Files.

[22] Wynn C. Fairfield to the Secretary of State, January 21, 1938, Department of State Files.

[23] *China Information Service Bulletin*, November 3, 1938.

tinguish between the aggressor and his victim, and to take appropriate measures regardless of consequences."[24] In February 1939 the Secretary of the Baptist Foreign Missions Board, J. W. Decker, a former missionary in China, told of a trip through the war-stricken country. Everywhere he had been asked why the United States sold war material to Japan.[25] A Baptist missionary, in the spring of 1939, told her denominational brethren in the United States that all over China the cry was, "When will America stop assisting Japan by sending them equipment, and thus bring this terrible slaughter and destruction to an end?"[26]

The feeling that it was morally imperative that the United States lower the boom on exports to Japan mounted after the outbreak of the war in Europe in September 1939. Missionaries did not retreat from this position as the question of an embargo led to an earnest consideration at home of the possibility that taking such a step would cause Japan to declare war on the United States. In November 1940 a prominent Baptist missionary in China, who was a member of the National Christian Council, the Rev. Charles L. Boynton, wrote to A. L. Warnshuis giving him a picture of missionary opinion. He observed that missionaries in China abhorred war and earnestly desired peace, "but only a peace with justice." He wrote:

> They believe that a critical stage has come in Far Eastern affairs where a strong embargo resolutely backed up by naval force, if necessary, will bring the kind of a settlement of the Far Eastern situation, which they consider essential in the cause of righteousness. They believe that, like a surgical operation, this will be very painful not only to the Japanese but also to themselves, but that the interests at stake are so great that they should not count the personal cost.[27]

[24] "War, But Not For Me," *The Christian Century*, March 8, 1939, pp. 309-310.

[25] J. W. Decker, "No Trace of Defeatism in China," *Missions*, February 1939, p. 75.

[26] Ada Nelson, "It Was a Long Journey from Minneapolis to West China," *Missions*, May 1939, p. 274.

[27] Charles L. Boynton to A. L. Warnshuis, November 6, 1940, Committee on East Asia Bulletin, November 28, 1940.

The Sino-Japanese War

At its meeting on January 25, 1941, the Committee on East Asia listened to a letter "from an unusually well-informed missionary, with many years of experience in China," which the secretary read. The missionary gave his opinion that American policy ought to include an unequivocal declaration of American intentions, "reinforced by further economic restrictions and other unmistakable proofs." He closed his letter by warning that conciliatory gestures would be of no avail, that worse still, they would be misleading and "increase the likelihood of more disastrous hostilities later."[28]

The effect of the spirited defense of China's cause by missionaries in that unhappy land was partially offset by the defense of Japan by missionaries working there. Deeply influenced by their Japanese friends they could never believe that Japan was quite as satanic as the friends of China would have the American people believe. They were likewise deeply influenced by the knowledge that every indication of American opposition to Japanese aims increased the hostility toward themselves in Japan. One such spokesman charged the editor of the *Christian Advocate* with going beyond the truth in condemning the island empire. China, he said, was a difficult and exasperating neighbor, and Japan had many legitimate grievances against her. Moreover, he said, "The stories of the Japanese military forces deliberately destroying hospitals and schools in China, and deliberately slaughtering innocent Chinese people, are slanderous lies."[29]

William Axling, one of the best known missionaries in Japan, sought to justify Japan. The West was responsible for Japanese expansionism. They had closed the doors to Japanese immigration and set up trade barriers against her goods. For long years Japan had patiently sought a peaceful solution to her population and economic problems but the West had blocked all her efforts. The West also wished to dominate China and exclude Japan from that area. He wrote:

[28] Minutes of the meeting of the Committee on East Asia, offices of the Foreign Missions Conference of North America, 156 Fifth Avenue, New York City, January 25, 1941.

[29] "Missionaries Write Home," letter from Arthur D. Berry, *The Christian Advocate*, January 6, 1938, p. 7.

China today has become the battleground of a titanic economic struggle in which all the major nations are participating. In the background of this Sino-Japanese crisis the great powers are maneuvering for the upper hand in China's vast and expanding market. In this economic rivalry Japan is not only a participant but the target of the contending forces.[30]

Another American missionary in Japan, T. T. Brumbaugh, head of the Wesley Foundation for student work, was equally cynical about the aims of the United States. The real policy of the United States, he said, was to sell to both countries. Japan's needs were real and it was sheer hypocrisy to condemn her for aggressiveness. China, he concluded, must be saved but not at the expense of Japan.[31]

Many missionaries in Japan not only staunchly opposed war between the United States and Japan but they sought to warn the United States against taking economic measures. Six leading missionaries cabled the Foreign Missions Conference in October 1940:

Bear witness to substantial Japanese sentiment for American friendship. We are convinced continued economic and other pressures will cause open break. Urge Federal Council make every effort to preserve peace.[32]

On October 24, 1940, William Axling wrote to A. L. Warnshuis that exactly what he had feared had now happened: increasing American pressure had driven Japan into the arms of the Axis powers. Then he warned:

If the United States attempts to shut off Japan's oil supply in the Dutch East Indies it is a foregone conclusion here that Japan will fight. And she will have the entire nation back of her. Not because Japan wants war with the United

30 William Axling, "Behind the Far Eastern Crisis," *The Christian Century*, February 9, 1938, pp. 171-172.

31 T. T. Brumbaugh, "Toward a New Far Eastern Policy," *The Christian Century*, October 12, 1938, pp. 1229-1231.

32 Six missionaries in Japan to Foreign Missions Conference of North America, October 16, 1940, Minutes of the Committee on East Asia.

States. She does not want war with the United States. But she must have oil. No industrial nation can live today without oil, and Japan can only live in the future as she industrializes her national life.[33]

The foreign missionary in Japan became increasingly suspect as nationalistic feelings were whipped up by the government in the summer and fall of 1940. To escape the stigma of foreign connections Japanese Christians met in the early autumn of 1940, withdrew from all connections with missions, and organized their own national church.[34] A missionary who had returned from Japan complained that they were constantly being spied upon.[35] He cited the increased emphasis on State Shinto and the compromises Christians had to make. The same writer told how missionaries had to give silent assent to Japan's war aims and that Japanese Christians had to applaud them. The pressure led one lady missionary who had spent thirty years in Japan, after boarding a boat for the United States, to say: "I feel as if an iron jacket had been taken off of my soul."[36]

The reservations of the missionaries in Japan concerning the totalitarian government increased their sympathy for Japanese Christians who were under severe pressure to give their first loyalty to Shinto and the state. It is impossible to determine how many of them became apologists for Japan but they constituted a considerably smaller percentage of the total missionary body than did defenders of the Chinese cause among their brethren on the continent of Asia. Nevertheless, the views they presented to the American public constituted one of the few presentations of the Japanese viewpoint in the

[33] William Axling to A. L. Warnshuis, Minutes of the meeting of the Committee on East Asia, October 24, 1940.

[34] Three-page letter from an unnamed missionary who had recently returned from Japan, quoted in the Minutes of the meeting of the Committee on East Asia, April 21, 1941.

[35] *Ibid.*

[36] *Ibid.* The missionaries in Japan did not support the invasion of China, but they could not speak out against it and expect to remain in Japan. Some did take the position that Japan was doing nothing more than Western nations had already done. By the summer of 1941 there were only 131 American missionaries still in Japan.

United States. There is no reason to believe that they had any significant influence on the general public's conception of the struggle. But there is evidence to the fact that they helped neutralize the position taken by mission boards, who were anxious not to weaken their work in Nippon.

The efforts of the missionary spokesmen for China met infinitely stronger resistance from isolationism and pacifist inclinations among the clergy and church-going public than from the neutralizing effect of the missionary propaganda emanating from Japan. Probably at no time in American history have so many of the clergy identified war as an absolute evil to be avoided at all costs, including the cost of seeing a pagan totalitarianism dominate the world. Many of those who were not ideological pacifists shared in the isolationist spirit that frowned on American involvement in world affairs. Even the internationalists were in most cases opposed to traditional military alliances and balance of power diplomacy, placing their faith in collective security.

Everywhere in the Protestant churches there was a determination not to repeat the mistakes of 1917. On the last day of January 1938 the executive committee of the National Council of Methodist Youth notified President Roosevelt that they would not support the government in a Far Eastern war. Ministers in the New York city area held a peace meeting in March 1938.[37] Led by Harry Emerson Fosdick and John Haynes Holmes, 216 of them pledged themselves to renounce war and never to support another conflict.[38] When President Roosevelt called for a naval building program early in 1938, the executive committee of the Federal Council of Churches said that it was "unwarranted by any evidence thus far presented and is calculated in the present world situation to stimulate the spirit of fear and unrest which is the parent of war."[39] When the Baptists met at Los Angeles in 1939, some of the delegates accepted an invitation from the Navy to inspect some of the bat-

[37] *New York Times*, February 1, 1938, p. 3.
[38] *Ibid.*, March 2, 1938, p. 7.
[39] "The President Calls for a Bigger Navy," *The Christian Century*, February 9, 1938, p. 164.

tleships in the harbor. The editor of *Missions* was outraged: "Are Baptist protests against America's mounting naval and military budget merely platitudes?"[40] The editor of the *Christian Century* reflected a large proportion of Protestant opinion when he wrote:

> Either we must scrap the idea of neutrality and be prepared again to fight to make the world safe for democracy whenever democracy is endangered—and the surest thing about the mind of America is that it does not want to do that—or else we must make the best of being neutral even when the side we favor is getting the worst of it. That is precisely where we stand now with reference to the war in China.[41]

On May 5, 1940, a group of Protestant ministers pledged themselves to take no part in any way in the Sino-Japanese conflict. The list of signers included the most illustrious names in the Protestant pulpit: Harry Emerson Fosdick, John Haynes Holmes, Paul Scherer, Ralph W. Sockman, Ernest Fremont Tittle, and Halford E. Luccock.[42] Such an attitude rendered the appeal of the missionaries in China ineffective in so far as creating any feeling capable of demanding a commitment to the Chinese cause. The rather widespread condemnation in church circles of sales of war equipment to Japan rested in considerable part on a feeling of guilt as the suffering of the Chinese was contemplated, but it was also based on the conviction that the United States could avoid war if it refused to sell munitions to either of the belligerents. The desire for peace nullified the missionaries' appeal for an embargo against Japan and aid to China.

Agitation for an embargo against Japan in the United States came largely from secular groups and, while some churchmen supported it, the churches as a whole opposed it. A. L. Warnshuis, for many years an executive of the Foreign Missions Con-

---

[40] "Convention Glory and Humiliation," ed., *Missions*, June 1939, p. 325.
[41] "Sympathy Puts a Strain on Neutrality," ed., *The Christian Century*, October 6, 1937, p. 1220.
[42] *New York Times*, May 6, 1940, p. 7.

ference of North America and prior to that a missionary in China, as late as January 1940 opposed an embargo against Japan because he believed it would lead to war.[43] Kenneth Scott Latourette, eminent historian of missions and a leader in the missionary movement at home, asked if the church was to make war on Japan. He deplored the fact that

> Many of our most active church leaders, with the most sensitive consciences, among them numbers of missionaries and men and women prominent in missionary circles, are advocating measures which, if taken by our government, will very possibly bring us to that issue.[44]

Hugh Vernon White, former Secretary of the American Board, likewise opposed an embargo as late as March 1940.[45] It is clear that American missionaries in China were not able to win over the executives of mission boards to a program of stopping exports to Japan while continuing to give aid to China.

The Committee on East Asia of the Foreign Missions Conference became more and more perplexed by the problems facing it after September 1939. There was a very real sympathy with China, but this had to be reconciled with a conviction that the United States should not become involved. In September 1939 the Committee resolved that "every possible plan must be adopted to prevent the United States of America from becoming involved in war."[46] Another resolution stated that injury to missionaries or loss of property should not be made a cause for war.[47] But the Conference also called upon the citizens and business concerns of the United States and Canada "to renounce the profits made by warfare and to discontinue the sale of munitions and materials for the manufacture of the same, especially to those who invade the homelands of other

[43] A. L. Warnshuis, "The Way to Peace in East Asia," *The Christian Century*, January 3, 1940, pp. 11-12.

[44] Kenneth Scott Latourette, "A Church-Made War with Japan," *The Christian Century*, January 31, 1940.

[45] Hugh Vernon White to editor, *The Christian Century*, March 13, 1940, p. 356.

[46] Minutes of the meeting of the Committee on East Asia, September 19, 1939.

[47] *Ibid.*

peoples with armed force."[48] At its meeting on September 19 the Committee on East Asia prepared a statement for use in consultation with the Department of State. The Committee expressed its deep concern "because of the continued policy of the Japanese in bombing unarmed civilian populations in China." The bombing attacks on a number of Chinese cities, thought the Committee, could "hardly be explained except as a campaign of deliberate terrorization aimed at helpless victims,—the women and children, the sick, the young, and the very aged."[49] The Committee also expressed the view that bombings of mission stations did not appear accidental and that some officers in the Japanese army were opposed to the continued presence of foreign missionaries in China.[50]

The Committee on East Asia adhered to the goal that war must be avoided at all costs and they believed that an embargo against Japan would immeasurably increase the risk of war. On October 23, 1940, the Committee voted to recommend to the Federal Council of Churches that it send a delegation to see President Roosevelt and to confer with the Department of State. The deputation should be instructed to convey to the President that the Committee believed "that our Government while holding firmly to its present position, should not further increase its pressure nor at present assume the initiative in any further action."[51]

Those who may seek for some indication of pressure on the part of the organized representatives of foreign missions for a firmer course in dealing with Japan will find no evidence supporting such a thesis in the written records. At the close of 1940, on December 18, J. W. Decker, Chairman of the Committee, visited Washington and was briefed on the Far Eastern situation in the Department of State. He reported to the Committee two days later that the only change was increasing pressure on the government in Tokyo.

This pressure comes from domestic sources and from Germany too. Decision is being postponed by the government

---

48 *Ibid.*   49 *Ibid.*   50 *Ibid.*
51 *Ibid.*, October 23, 1940.

from day to day, in the hope of a more certain indication of the ultimate outcome in Europe. It can be said that water is piling up at the dam. It must get out, but how and with what results is the serious question. There is no evidence that Tokyo has abandoned its aims in East Asia.[52]

The chief item of discussion between the Committee Chairman and the officials of the Department of State concerned the withdrawal of missionaries from threatened zones. The government urged that everything be done to bring about their evacuation. There were similar meetings from time to time during 1941 between mission executives and government officials. In none of these meetings did the mission representatives urge stronger actions in dealing with Japan.

Although the missionaries in China failed to win over the interdenominational missionary organization to its point of view, there were Protestant leaders who viewed the peace movement as moral irresponsibility. One of the most influential was Dr. Walter Judd, who resigned from his missionary post in China in order to carry on a speaking campaign in the United States. He was determined to awaken the people at home to what he deemed the true nature of the crisis in Asia and to enlist the churches' support of a program of aid for China and an embargo against Japan. Judd was a convincing speaker who reached large audiences from coast to coast. Professor Reinhold Niebuhr and the President of Union Theological Seminary, Henry Pitt Van Dusen, vigorously campaigned for an embargo against Japan and needled the pacifist elements in the churches by accusing them of moral confusion in the face of a world crisis in which all Christian values were at stake.

Occasionally a church group or a denomination took a bold stand in favor of the United States using economic pressure to aid in the fight against the totalitarian nations. The New York Conference of Methodists condemned the neutrality act as early as April 1938 because it had contributed to the success of the dictators in Europe and to Japan's victories in China.[53]

[52] Minutes of the meeting of the executive committee of the Committee on East Asia, December 20, 1940.

[53] *New York Times*, April 17, 1938, p. 2.

In May 1939 the American Committee for Non-Participation in Japanese Aggression forwarded to Congress petitions carrying 156,231 signatures from seventeen states urging legislation to halt the stream of supplies to Japan.[54] A month later this Committee issued a statement drafted by Robert E. Speer and signed by sixty-nine clergymen calling for an embargo against Japan.[55] The General Assembly of the Presbyterian Church in the United States called on Congress in June 1939 to make it illegal to sell to Japan munitions and potential war materials.[56] In January 1940 thirty-two prominent clergy and lay leaders declared that it was a Christian duty to take sides against tyranny.[57] Nevertheless, American Protestantism as a whole backed away from assuming any responsibility to help halt totalitarianism, and voiced strong suspicions that President Roosevelt was plotting to involve the United States in war.

[54] *Ibid.*, May 7, 1939, p. 33.

In the hearings held by the Committee on Foreign Relations of the House of Representatives on revision of the neutrality legislation in the spring of 1939 two former missionaries testified, Dr. Walter Judd and Mrs. George A. Fitch. Both testified in favor of an embargo against Japan, and both made dramatic pleas for China. Mrs. Fitch's husband was still in China as a Y.M.C.A. secretary. She praised President Roosevelt for not applying the neutrality law. When Hamilton Fish of New York criticized the President for not applying the law, Mrs. Fitch remarked: ". . . but we were nevertheless, in China, extremely grateful to him that he did not find that a state of war existed, because it would have meant that China could not get the finished products, and Japan does not need the finished products as long as she can get the raw materials." She presented a petition in favor of an embargo with 40,000 signatures from California and stated that her organization also had 175,000 signatures in New York on the same petition. *American Neutrality Policy*, Hearings before the Committee on Foreign Affairs, House of Representatives, Seventy-Sixth Congress, 1st Session, April 11 to May 2, 1939, pp. 401-417.

Dr. Judd also spoke out against the sale of oil and scrap iron to Japan. He referred to these sales in the following plea: "That is the thing that hurt us Americans who live in China more than anything else. We almost to a man believe that Japan could never have started and she could not continue 3 months now, her military adventure in China without the indispensable assistance of the United States of America." He described his work as a doctor "removing these things from the bodies of Chinese men, women, and children. I never could go to sleep without wondering if my people back in America knew what they were doing." *Ibid.*, p. 337.

[55] *Ibid.*, June 18, 1939, p. 26.

[56] *Ibid.*, June 1, 1939, p. 20.

[57] *Ibid.*, January 22, 1940, p. 18.

Church opinion changed after 1939 but the transition was a response to the kaleidoscopic events that made clear the peril to national security. By February 1940 the American Institute of Public Opinion found that nearly 7 in every 10 favored shutting off the American export of war equipment and military supplies to Japan, "even if it may cause further troubled relations between the two countries." The poll also showed that Americans sympathized with China by a proportion of 37 to 1.

Many pacifist church leaders, opposed to war, continued to fight every measure taken by President Roosevelt and Congress to aid the democracies. The Ministers' No War Committee under the leadership of Harry Emerson Fosdick, aided by funds from America First, sent noninterventionist literature to 93,-000 Protestant ministers at the time the Lend-Lease bill was being debated in Congress.[58] Antiwar sentiments continued to be strong among the Methodists until the Japanese bombs fell on the American fleet at Pearl Harbor.[59]

The Japanese bombs that fell at Pearl Harbor reduced the peace movement in the churches to a negligible minority. Those who had been vocal now subordinated their views and accepted the fact of war. The editor of *The Christian Century*, a bitter antagonist against all interventionists, regretted that the American government had not pursued a different course, but he announced: "We stand with our country. We cannot do otherwise."[60]

Missionaries in Japanese-occupied parts of China were interned. Among them was John Leighton Stuart who later recalled his reactions to the disastrous news:

[58] Wayne S. Cole, *America First: The Battle Against Intervention, 1940-1941* (Madison: The University of Wisconsin Press, 1953), p. 48.

[59] Three conferences of the Methodist Church, the Illinois Conference, the Southern Indiana Conference and the Upper Iowa Conference, all passed antiwar resolutions in the autumn of 1941. "Methodists Firm in Peace Policy," *The Christian Century*, October 8, 1941, p. 1246.

The National Conference of the Methodist Youth Fellowship passed resolutions deploring "the warlike policy of the administration" and called for repeal of military conscription. *The Christian Century*, October 8, 1941, p. 1252.

[60] "An Unnecessary Necessity," ed., *The Christian Century*, December 17, 1941, pp. 1565-1566.

After my first discomfiture I began, however, to feel an unholy satisfaction over the dastardly Japanese attack on our navy. For years I had been sending highly confidential reports to our Yenching Trustees about the Japanese menace and the advisability of our doing something to stop this before too late. These were circulated among a carefully selected list of leaders. It was discouraging to observe how unheeded were all such warnings. It came over me that some such disaster as this was needed to arouse our people to action, and once that happened I was not seriously worried as to the ultimate result. The Japanese were woefully deficient in their understanding of the American temper. This was probably the most costly victory in all history when—as a Chinese adage has it—the clever failed because of their cleverness.[61]

[61] John Leighton Stuart, *Fifty Years in China* (New York: Random House, 1954), p. 138.

CHAPTER XVI

A BRIEF AND UNHAPPY RESPITE,
1941-1949

A NEW spurt of enthusiasm buoyed up the missionary movement at the close of World War II. The American people emerged from the holocaust having learned that their own destiny was tied up with the fate of humanity at large. By well-nigh unanimous vote the Senate approved entry into the United Nations.

The churches capitalized on the new world consciousness by launching a program for relief of the tragic refugees of war and for an expansion of foreign missions. Promotion campaigns flowed forth from denominational boards. The Student Volunteers emerged from the doldrums and two thousand students attended the Sixteenth Student Volunteer Convention at Lawrence, Kansas in 1951. Contributions to foreign missions mounted to the unprecedented figure of $56,567,292 in 1951, approximately twice what it had been in 1925. By 1950 the total number of Protestant foreign missionaries from the United States and Canada was 15,039, a significant gain over the earlier peak of 13,555 in 1925 and a very great increase over the 11,151 figure for 1936.[1]

The new enthusiasm never found one main channel; instead it dispersed itself in numerous denominational rivulets separated by the great theological divide between fundamentalism and something that was really undefinable but that the fundamentalists called modernism. The narrower fundamentalist streams rushed toward the great sea of heathenism with a zest that the liberals envied. Symptomatic of the suspicion the fundamentalists entertained for their rivals was their establishment of a separate organization for college students with an interest

[1] For recent statistics see R. Pierce Beaver, *The North American Churches and the World Mission* (New York: The National Council of the Churches of Christ in the U.S.A., 1952).

[274]

in becoming missionaries, the Student Foreign Missions Fellowship, which was associated with the Inter-Varsity Christian Fellowship. It attracted as many students to its convention in 1951 as did the more liberal Student Volunteers. The fundamentalists also set up a variety of new missionary societies. Though both the older denominational boards and the new societies had a common aim in seeking to win converts, the latter were determined to go after the heathen with a strictly defined program of direct evangelization. The older groups represented in the Foreign Missions Conference had a broader concept of the needs of the people in non-Christian countries. Both were to discover that they confronted difficult problems in China.

The war had sharply curtailed American missionary activities in China. Seven hundred and fifty-four American missionaries had heard the news of Pearl Harbor in the tremendous swarth of China occupied by Japan and within a few days all of them had been interned and later sent back to the United States.[2] Beyond the reaches of the Japanese, in Free China, hundreds of others helped carry on the new industrial cooperatives, the refugee universities and middle schools, relief work, and a program of evangelism. But inroads of Japanese troops in 1944 resulted in a great many evacuations and the total force of missionaries of all nationalities was reduced to 850.[3]

All was not idealism in Free China. In Chungking the picture of a democratic China, so skillfully communicated to the American people at home by Madame Chiang, seemed a cruel illusion. For while China's millions suffered and while American boys fought, the Kuomintang leaders profited in a foreign exchange racket. China was beset by inflation. To bolster the Chinese dollar vast American loans in gold were secured. Thanks to an artificially high fixed rate of exchange, those who ran China's national bank could buy the gold at a low price

[2] "Mission Societies Raise 20 Millions," *Christian Century*, January 28, 1942, p. 125.

[3] *Bulletin of the Committee on East Asia*, offices of the Foreign Missions Conference of North America, 156 Fifth Avenue, New York City, April 17, 1946.

with cheap Chinese dollars. The profits were deposited in American banks.

Equally shocking to Americans was the Kuomintang's callous disregard of the misery of the people. While famine and corruption reigned the Generalissimo wrote *China's Destiny*, a call to old-fashioned Confucian virtues, a book that, in the face of economic distress and corruption, caused many a missionary and other Westerner to writhe with anger.[4] The book, required reading for all schools and public servants, attributed all of China's troubles to Western imperialism. The two pictures of Kuomintang China survived the war and soon made China the central issue of one of the longest and most heated controversies in American history.

After VJ-day China was a scene of physical destruction and war weariness. What had not been destroyed in the lower Yangtze valley and along the coast, had deteriorated. Some cities such as Wuhan had lost a third of their population. There were towns and cities near Canton that had been entirely wiped out.[5]

The psychological effects of the war were almost worse than the physical. A deep schism had developed between Christian workers in the occupied areas and those in Free China. As Frank Cartwright put it, "Both had suffered tremendously but neither side could quite understand what the other had suffered." Chester Miao, long a native leader in Christian education, told about life in Shanghai: "Fear was burned into us: fear of the Japanese, of starvation, of imprisonment, of death." Hatred had flourished and "suspicion was almost like the air; you breathed it." It was present in the churches as well as out-

---

4 For one missionary's reactions see F. Olin Stockwell, *With God in Red China: The Story of Two Years in Communist Prisons* (New York: Harper and Brothers, 1953), pp. 28-32. Like many other observers, Stockwell put the blame on the Soong family rather than solely on Chiang. It was the Generalissimo's failure to break through the corrupt and reactionary group that surrounded him that caused him to lose the confidence of the people.

5 This paragraph and those immediately following are based in considerable part on a thirty-three page report to the East Asia Committee of the Foreign Missions Conference written by the Rev. Frank T. Cartwright after a six month trip through China at the close of the war. Missionary Research Library.

side. There had been a widespread ethical breakdown—"lying became an approved practice; deceit of the enemy was patriotic." There were so many deaths that "our estimate of the value of human life became lower than ever before." It would take years, he thought, to get back to healthy mental attitudes.

The Christian church was also a war fatality. The Rev. Frank Cartwright, who went to China shortly after VJ-day to get a firsthand report on the church, wrote that in most cases where church buildings had been destroyed or occupied by the enemy, the congregations had ceased to meet. A large percentage of the ministers had gone into business to exist and most of them did not return to their parishes. Few new leaders had been developed and Cartwright found only middle-aged or older people at conferences. Only here and there had there been a quickening of religious life. Some of the stronger congregations in the port cities survived the war and provided one of the few sources of encouragement.

The first task, as Frank Cartwright saw it, was to provide a series of retreats where pastors and laymen could gain a fresh inspiration. There were many such meetings where prominent American clergymen spoke during the next two years. The Forward Movement, initiated by the National Christian Council in December 1946, a broad program for expanding the churches' activities, represented another effort to renew sagging spirits, but political developments brought it to an end almost before it got underway.

In addition to the problems created by the war the mission boards had to take into account the difficulties inherited from the more distant past. Cartwright stressed the need for giving the Chinese control over the church. In spite of the transfer of authority by some denominations, the missionary continued to make the decisions. He also expressed regret over the multiplicity of Western denominations working in the larger cities. Neither of these failings, however, disturbed him as much as did the universal complaint among Chinese Christian leaders against the sense of racial superiority among missionaries. Some had told with bitterness of race prejudice revealed in some word or action. He had seen instances of "missionaries who quite patently were working for an 'inferior people.' " In one case a missionary was unwilling to have Chinese workers from rural churches come into her living room. In another case a missionary family, in planning for a new home, wanted a separate reception room for Chinese.[6] A prime consideration in the selection of missionary candidates, thought Cartwright, should be freedom from race consciousness. It took only a few instances to damage the entire cause; actually most missionaries had outgrown race prejudice.

In October 1946 more than 400 missionaries took off for East Asia on the *Marine Lynx*, which had been chartered by the Foreign Missions Conference. In San Francisco, amid the buoyant atmosphere of men and women eager to take up their tasks in their beloved China, Henry Luce spoke of the challenge ahead.

Missionary F. Olin Stockwell, head of the missionary group on board ship, wrote that "The hot and crowded quarters, with men in the center of the boat and women in the bow, sleeping and living in three-decker canvas bunks, soldier style, had been weathered with a fortitude and good cheer that augured well for the hard years before us. . . . Room was limited, but the recreation committee arranged for bridge tournaments in one part of the dining room and prayer meetings in another, to everyone's satisfaction."[7]

By 1948 there were 2,246 American and Canadian missionaries in China. Those engaged in evangelism and church work outnumbered all others. The educational staff ranked second. There was no departure of significance from traditional lines.[8]

. In the haste to get on with the work mission boards gave the funds at their disposal to institutions already in existence, evangelical work, schools, and hospitals. There was little left for innovation, and they lacked the will to deny the requests coming in from hard-pressed staffs. Consequently, advocates of new methods received little support. Creative men like

[6] *Ibid.*

[7] F. Olin Stockwell, *op. cit.*, pp. 14-15.

[8] *Bulletin of the China Committee*, March 19, 1948. This Committee was the successor of the former Committee on East Asia. The bulletin was made available to the author by the Missionary Research Library.

Frank Price, John Reisner, and Hugh Hubbard urged that missions be fitted into the crying needs of rural areas. Mission work through rural service unions seemed to hold considerable potentialities, but Reisner, after China was closed, testified: "The truth of the matter is, however, that so far as the American Mission Boards are concerned, there was not enough financial support to allow them to function in the way they should in order to be effective."[9] Though rural service unions made some progress, particularly in northern China, they constituted an almost insignificant aspect of the larger program.

A handful of imaginative missionaries courageously admitted that the rural churches lacked vitality because they were largely artificial appendages in the rural scene that had never been integrated into the peasants' lives. In a letter from Peking in 1947 John Reisner expressed deep concern "over this whole rural church situation in China." He had found no one who would disagree with a statement by Frank Price that the very most that could be hoped for after another ten years was "1000 self-supporting, vital, growing rural churches." He was prompted to ask:

> After over 100 years of evangelistic effort—a great deal of it concentrated in rural China—is that all we have to show for it? In what lasting direction has all our expenditure of lives and funds gone? Why is there so little permanent rootage?[10]

Reisner was not alone in his concern. A report by Dr. Irma Highbaugh to a committee of the National Christian Council on April 29, 1947, revealed a serious decline in the number of churches and chapels in the rural areas of Nanking and Peiping. Twenty-five years earlier there had been eighty recognized rural church pastors in the Nanking area; now there were only nineteen. A decline in the number of lay leaders added to the problem. Many of them had moved to the cities and those who remained were no longer able to provide the financial

[9] Letter from John Reisner to author, October 24, 1955.
[10] *Bulletin of the China Committee*, April 11, 1947.

support they had once given.[11] This long-term decline was not easy to reverse for, as Reisner noted, political chaos and inflation so absorbed the attention of the Chinese that they were unable to concentrate upon the much less pressing problem of the rural church.

In contrast to the decline of the rural churches, Christian schools were flooded by students eager for an education. In the fall semester of 1947 almost 11,000 registered in the colleges and ten times that many had to be turned away.[12] Approximately 10 per cent of all college students in the entire country were attending schools founded by missionaries.

The flight of these colleges to Free China early in the war had been dramatic. In the spring of 1946 faculty and students faced an almost equally difficult return trip of two thousand miles and more. Transportation was at a premium and hundreds made the trip on old-fashioned wooden junks, eating and sleeping on decks protected only by matting. Others made the trip in trucks, camping out at night.[13] On their arrival at their former campuses they found buildings in disrepair and, in many instances, their interiors destroyed. Scientific equipment and books had usually disappeared. Dr. C. J. Lin, President of Fukien Christian University at Foochow, described the damage in these words: "Our Foochow campus was occupied by the Japanese. Five frame buildings were torn down, and the roof of the Arts Hall was burned. The contents in all the remaining buildings disappeared, together with all the windows and doors, and in some cases, floors also."[14]

Inflation, already a serious problem at the end of the war, spiraled ever upward. By 1947 sky-rocketing prices deprived both faculty and students of the necessities of life. Students at Fukien Christian University paid 2,000,000 Chinese dollars for tuition alone for the spring semester of 1948 and total fees amounted to from 3,000,000 to 4,000,000 Chinese dollars per student.[15] Faculty salaries, in November 1947, had only

[11] *Ibid.*, May 29, 1947.
[12] *The China Colleges*, April 1948. This bulletin was published quarterly by the United Board for Christian Colleges in New York.
[13] *Ibid.*, October 1946.   [14] *Ibid.*, December 1945.
[15] *Ibid.*, April 1948.

15 per cent of their prewar purchasing power, and teachers found it necessary to sell family heirlooms, extra suits of clothing, stamp collections and anything else that could be exchanged for cash.[16] Students faced unprecedented hardships. At Yenching the students' menu consisted mostly of cornbread and cabbage, or bowls of millet cereal with a bit of salted vegetable. When 275 students of Yenching were given physical examinations, it was found that 103 had low blood pressure, 67 had trachoma, and 24 were suffering from tuberculosis.[17]

Middle schools also achieved great popularity in the early postwar years. In 1937 these schools had 53,000 students. The number rose to well over 74,000 for the school year 1946-1947. Many of these schools were located in the cities along the eastern seaboard. Almost half of them were in the three eastern provinces of Kiangsu, Fukien, and Kwantung and 71 of the 230 were in Shanghai, Foochow, Canton, Soochow, Nanking, and Peiping. The middle schools in these cities had 31,241 students.[18]

In the case of both the colleges and middle schools plans had been made for eliminating duplication of effort and strengthening the educational offering by concentrating the work in fewer institutions. The Planning Committee of the Associated Board of Christian Colleges in China strongly recommended unification in a report presented in May, 1946. The plan called for not over three or four centers of graduate study, five institutions to teach medicine, nursing, and public health, and one school in law, one in engineering, and one in commerce. The union of the University of Nanking and Ginling College was proposed and also a union of the three collegiate institutions in the Shanghai area.[19] Only the last of these was actually realized. One major obstacle to a more rational educational structure was the loyalty and pride of Chinese staffs and alumni in particular institutions. Also, the denominational mission boards had adequate funds after the war and they proceeded to sup-

[16] *Ibid.*

[17] *Ibid.*, March 1947.

[18] *Bulletin of China Committee*, January 13, 1948.

[19] Minutes of the American Board for China's Christian Colleges, May 13, 1946. Day Library of Missions, Yale Divinity School.

port the universities and middle schools as they were already set up.

The pitifully decadent state of the rural parish and the throng of 100,000 applicants for the 10,000 available places in the ¨Christian universities and colleges—plus the more than 70,000 in the middle schools—presents one of the most provocative contradictions in the history of Christian missions in China. The country parishes were often extremely conservative, their preachers devoid of a Christian theology with any intellectual content, and their activities for the most part confined to a sermon on Sunday devoted to childlike, and sometimes bizarre, expositions of Bible texts. The rural church failed to relate itself to the hard facts of Chinese rural life, to landlordism, tenancy, usurious rates on loans, and all the other evils besetting the Chinese peasants. In a majority of instances, the missionary and the Chinese pastor would have maintained that these problems lay outside their realm. Thereby they reduced Christianity to a soporific for a weary and hard-pressed people. In this art the faith healers and holiness groups were much more skilled. Their preachers knew how to lead their listeners through orgies of religious excitement. And having failed to face the challenge of a social order abounding in poverty and injustice, they left the door open to the Communists who were quick to recognize that China's society was bankrupt and who related the pressing problems of everyday life to the new divinity of dialetical materialism.

The educational institutions were quite a different matter—liberal, enlightened, relatively well equipped, and teaching the approved doctrines, economic and political, of Western middle-class society. Nothing elicited greater enthusiasm on the part of generous philanthropists at home, who supported the schools with some considerable degree of generosity. Supporters cited the fact that many leaders in professional fields and in government were graduates of these schools. They only worried about preserving their Christian emphasis. In 1948 they pointed with pride to the fact that some 3,000 college students had joined the church, but many of this number were students at government universities.

To the Chinese the Christian colleges were, in general, avenues to personal success. As graduates they became professional people, clerks in Western business concerns, and compradores. Certainly not more than 20 per cent manifested any interest in the religious program of the campus, and they soon came to look down on rural Christians as naïve and old-fashioned. Few of them brought from the campus a dynamic passion to solve the problems that beset China's millions. They became city dwellers with a taste for bourgeois comforts. So while schools were in one sense more successful than evangelical efforts—and much good was undoubtedly accomplished—they contributed little to the realization of two aims that were dear to the hearts of mission advocates. While there were exceptions, graduates of these schools did not become pious Christians and neither did they become zealous crusaders for a truly democratic society.[20]

Yet, though there was reason to be discouraged, all was not hopeless. In 1947 the Kiangsu-Anhwei Christian Rural Service Union was organized by seven missions and five institutions for the purpose of providing an adequate program in the rural churches of the Nanking area. In 1948 it conducted a school for twenty-four pastors, helping them to grasp the possibilities for service among the peasants. An institute for 132 farmers provided instruction in crop improvement, pest control, and introduction of improved seeds. The institute also conducted a nursery school, a clinic for the blind where some who had been without sight for fifteen years had their vision restored, an emergency medical clinic, hand-work classes, demonstration gardens, tree planting, literacy classes, and a primary school.[21] Dr. Fu-liang Chang, formerly Director of the Rural Department of the National Christian Council, expressed the ideals of the Rural Service Union in these words: "The Christian

[20] This point of view is best expressed by a former British missionary to China, David M. Paton, in his book *Christian Missions and the Judgment of God* (London: S. C. M. Press, 1953). See also "First Thoughts on the Debacle of Christian Missions in China," *International Review of Missions*, 1951, pp. 411-420.

[21] *Rural Missions*, Winter 1950. This bulletin was published quarterly by Agricultural Missions, Inc.

message to the Chinese farmer must include a full rice bowl, gainful work, healthful living, opportunities for education, security from fear, freedom for worship and sharing life's blessing with others."

Fu-liang Chang saw Christ championing the cause of the common people against exploiters and selfish rulers and was convinced that the Christian church in China must follow His example. He had faith that when "the Word is truly made flesh and incarnated in the lives of His disciples, humble folk will understand and gladly follow Him who is the Way, the Truth, and the Life."[22] To Margaret Barnes, Secretary of the North China Rural Service Union, this was a paramount truth and the opportunities revealed by his faith gave her an unlimited enthusiasm and a passionate desire to make every day count. In this she was not alone, and the new approach was beginning to make headway among missionary leaders at home.

In 1948 the National Christian Council established another new activity, the Committee on Christian Service in Industrial Relations. The Presbyterian Board of Missions appointed Henry D. Jones to take over this work. Jones worked first among Japanese prisoners-of-war, taking a real interest in their welfare; twenty-seven of them were converted. He went next to Chungking, where he found a number of Christian labor leaders. Jones asked if he might join them in a labor day rally on May 1, 1949; he was told that the government had called it off whereupon he arranged celebrations in the churches. He was also instrumental in setting up a training conference in industrial relations for theological students.[23]

As the triumph of the Communists approached, missionaries worked with great energy to get as much done as possible. Regional conferences were held in the hope of uniting the ranks of Christians and to help them face future trials.[24] The China Bible House set as its aim the sending of a three year's supply of Bibles to cities throughout the country. From November 1948 to May 25, 1949, it shipped 120 tons of Bibles, Testa-

---

[22] *Ibid.*, Winter 1949.

[23] *Bulletin of the China Committee*, December 1949.

[24] See Overseas Newsletter written by Victor E. W. Hayward, *Bulletin of the China Committee*, January 10, 1949.

ments, and portions of the Scripture; of this amount, 45 tons were flown to various areas.[25] A new program of mass education utilizing visual aids and tape recordings got underway. Under the auspices of the Chinese Christian Educational Association, Dr. S. Lautenschlager carried on an extensive program of evangelistic work in the schools. Chinese undertook student work on the campuses of twelve government universities. And missionaries, though discouraged by the severe slump in rural churches, took some satisfaction in the many active congregations in the cities. Tientsin had twenty-five churches and Peiping had fifteen, the majority of them self-supporting. An Easter service in Shanghai in 1947, addressed by Ambassador Leighton Stuart, had an estimated attendance of from 7,000 to 10,000.[26] Even as late as 1949 Sherwood Eddy, who had held his first meetings in China before World War I, was listened to by thousands.

No amount of zealous work could quite offset the handicaps imposed by a ruined economy and a raging civil war. Chinese and foreign Christians commented on the complete breakdown of the Confucian family system and the ancient faith in a moral order. Everywhere there was confusion, student rebellions, rice riots, and an ever declining standard of morals.

Strenuous efforts were made to reach the students at government universities through the Student Christian Movement, but its members were often drawn off into the broader political movement of the students. A Chinese leader described the student uprisings as revolts against physical hunger, and observed that "the torrential currents of the general student movement has somewhat swamped the S.C.M."[27]

And down to the bitter end there was division in the Christian ranks. There were scores of enterprises representing a union of several denominations, but in the closing years the schismatic fundamentalists went their own way or competed with older groups. On the campuses the fundamentalist Inter-Varsity Christian Fellowship seriously challenged the liberal Student Christian Movement. "Unfortunately," wrote a mem-

[25] *Bulletin of the China Committee,* May 25, 1949.
[26] *Ibid.,* May 28, 1947.   [27] *Ibid.,* December 22, 1947.

ber of the National Christian Council, "even when both sides endeavor to avoid conflict, which by no means always happens, it is still difficult to avoid a tension which almost inevitably creates a mutual opposition."[28] The Student Christian Movement charged the rival group with ignoring political and social issues and permitting itself to become a tool of the unscrupulous government. The Inter-Varsity Christian Fellowship considered the Student Volunteer Movement to be pro-Communist. The one stressed the social ideals of Christianity and the other emphasized personal salvation and a dogmatic adherence to a creed.

[28] *Ibid.*, July 22, 1948.

CHAPTER XVII

TOWARDS THE BAMBOO CURTAIN,

1941-1952

HISTORY is seldom as simple as partisan propagandists seek to make it, and the two sides in the China controversy have drawn a veil of partisanship over the struggle that is difficult to penetrate.

The United States became deeply involved in the internal struggle between the Kuomintang and the Communists as a result of the joint conflict of the United States and China against Japan. Differences in concept of proper strategy against the common foe set off a long and heated controversy between Chiang and the Kuomintang on the one side and General Joseph W. Stilwell and the Roosevelt administration on the other. "Vinegar Joe," an able and completely devoted officer, was convinced that the Chinese made good soldiers if given proper training and equipment, and he set about the creation of such an army. Secondly, he was intent on using it, along with other allied forces, to conquer Burma. This would reopen the famous supply route and make possible an effective campaign against the Japanese army in China.

Chiang and the leaders of the Kuomintang bitterly opposed Stilwell's strategy. They were deeply aware of the Red army in the north central provinces, an enemy that was using the war to consolidate its control over as large an area as possible. The Chinese Nationalists preferred keeping their forces intact rather than risking them in ambitious campaigns against the Japanese. They also resisted Stilwell's importunity to create a truly centralized army under a single effective command, out of fear that many of the generals would then desert, leaving the door open to a quick Communist victory after the war. Stilwell was not unsympathetic but he and others were convinced that only if the Kuomintang changed its course and asserted leadership would it be able to stand up against the Communists once the war was over.

In 1943 the long-standing strife between the Kuomintang and the Communists threatened to break out into a shooting civil war. The Communist army was growing with amazing speed, reaching possibly half a million men by the summer of 1943. Strong Nationalist troops were stationed south and west of the Communist center of concentration to block their path into the heart of China. Indeed, the executive committee of the Kuomintang at a meeting on September 13, 1943, would have decided on war had it not been for Chiang's opposition. In all probability he would not have taken this stand except for the urging of the American government.

The United States' major aim, and practically sole objective, was the defeat of Japan and an end to the war. An outbreak of civil war in China would have been a tremendous setback. To the members of the American Embassy in Chungking there seemed to be two ways that offered some slight possibility of avoiding a civil war. The first of these ways was to use every effort to promote a coalition government—a proposal that met with a cool response from leaders of the Kuomintang, who believed that the result would be a breakdown of effective government. Other Chinese, non-Communists outside of the Kuomintang, favored the proposal. The second way was to pressure the Kuomintang into broadening its base to include elements outside of the party and to push it into a program of economic and social reconstruction. Only then, urged many, both Americans and Chinese, could the Kuomintang overcome the popular appeal of the Communists.[1]

Missionaries were among those who pushed for democratization of the Kuomintang. Many of them could never fully concentrate their attention on mere military victory; they desired a richer and better life for the millions of Chinese than the Kuomintang appeared interested in giving. In the American Embassy were many sons of missionaries, some of whom

[1] The political story as told here is drawn largely from Herbert Feis, *The China Tangle* (Princeton: Princeton University Press, 1953) and Max Beloff, *Soviet Policy in the Far East, 1944-1951* (London: Oxford University Press, 1953).

played a prominent role, more especially John S. Service and John P. Davies. The stories of corruption and the lack of social concern in the Kuomintang disgusted them as it disgusted many missionaries. Some missionaries close to Chungking described the Kuomintang as "fascist," "corrupt," and "cynical."

An historian cannot cite documentary proof of corruption among many Kuomintang leaders, but the charges of it were widely accepted as true by many impartial observers. The most specific accusation was that high officials, whenever they knew a gold loan was forthcoming from the United States, would accumulate Chinese Nationalist currency and then, after the value of that currency had increased as a result of the loan, they would exchange it for American dollars at a tremendous profit The reputation of the Kuomintang likewise suffered as a result of the increasing influence of such reactionary groups as the CC and the Whampoa cliques.[2]

The outbreak of civil war was postponed until Japan had been defeated, in considerable part because of the exertions of the American government. A special mission under Patrick Hurley arrived in Chungking in October 1944, with the difficult assignment of promoting a coalition between the Kuomintang and the Communists. An endless series of conferences netted no gain, both sides insisting on conditions that would have placed the other at a great disadvantage in the future civil war, which both accepted as certain.

With the approach of the end of the war both Americans and Chinese Nationalist feared that the Soviet Union would take advantage of the situation to promote the Communist cause. Their fears were quieted by the repeated assurances of Stalin to American diplomatic representatives in Moscow and by the entry of Stalin into a treaty with Nationalist China in July 1945. How empty Soviet protestations were of real intent was soon to be seen.

History was made and the fate of China to a large degree was settled by the Soviet Union's entry into the Far Eastern war on August 9, six days before the final surrender of Japan.

[2] Theodore H. White and Analee Jacoby, *Thunder Out of China* (New York: William Sloane Associates, Inc., 1946), pp. 98-101.

Towards the Bamboo Curtain

Four Chinese Communist armies marched into the northern provinces of Chahar, Jehol, Liaoning, and Kirin and blocked the main roads before the Nationalists could transport their troops from the distant southwestern provinces. Seventy Russian divisions in Manchuria conveniently moved out as the Chinese Communists got ready to move in, thus enabling the latter to take over large amounts of Japanese munitions and military equipment. The United States helped transport Nationalist troops to Manchuria to accept the Japanese surrender, but by September 1945 it was clear that the Nationalists were in a precarious situation.

General Albert C. Wedemeyer, Stilwell's successor, warned that Chiang was short of able administrators and that many of his colleagues were corrupt. He had no hope that Chiang could hold northern China. Thus the one hope of saving Chiang, short of military intervention, seemed to rest in a truce. Such a truce would give the Nationalists an opportunity to initiate constructive reforms and to rally public support. It was a thankless mission fraught with difficulties, but the Truman administration decided to send General George Marshall to China to seek a truce. Marshall soon gained the respect of both parties and the unstinted praise and acclaim of numerous missionaries. The Rev. Frank Cartwright reported: "Ambassador George Marshall and his staff have accomplished a near-miracle. They have brought together high-ranking men representing Yenan and Chungking in long and painstaking conferences, seeking on the higher levels of leadership to evolve a workable program for a unified China." The Marshall mission eventually failed and civil war was resumed, blotting out the last chances of the Kuomintang to restore the economy, regain public faith, and face the Communists with a united front.[3]

[3] The author refers the interested student to the bulletins issued by the China Committee of the Foreign Missions Conference of North America. These were issued frequently and provide a rich source. For these years Rowland Cross served as editor. He was an arduous collector of letters and of reports from missionaries and from Chinese Christians. All shades of religious opinion from liberal to conservative were presented with the exception of the fundamentalists who refused to join the Foreign Missions

The tasks facing Chiang were enormous. Ninety per cent of China's railroad mileage had been destroyed, inflation was running riot, trade was at a standstill, considerable parts of many cities lay in ruins, and famine stalked the country. Chinese peasants were in a bitter mood and looking for relief from high rents and heavy taxes. The student class was angry and Kuomintang repression of dissident elements among both students and faculties only fanned the flames of hatred. Confronted with this situation the Kuomintang made efforts to rebuild railroads and to get the economy going once again, only to have the Communists destroy the lines as soon as they were rebuilt.

To Chiang there was but one way to meet the situation, and that was to defeat the Communists. He was a military man who saw only the military aspects of the problem. The necessity for political measures that would rally the people to his support seemed either unnecessary or probably impossible to take without undermining his support from the landlords.

Yet a military solution to the problem was never undertaken by a political leader under more unfavorable circumstances. He faced an extremely well-disciplined Communist army indoctrinated with propaganda and fanatical in its belief that it was fighting for a just cause. Chiang's patriotic appeals, on the other hand, were a call in the wilderness of war weariness. For thirty-five years the Chinese people had been the victims of internal and foreign war. They looked upon the new civil war as another stage in the age-old struggle of war lords. They simply lacked the will to fight. Consequently the Kuomintang was wholly unsuccessful in calling the nation to arms.

Secondly, the armies of the Kuomintang were a congeries of parts incapable of a unified effort. In Honan, testified one missionary, they were defeated simply because the generals would not help each other when attacked, enabling the Communists to pick them off one at a time.[4]

Conference and who never forwarded reports or letters. Except where some other source is cited the letters quoted are from the *Bulletin of the China Committee*, Missionary Research Library.

[4] Interview with the Rev. Erik Malm of the Swedish Mission to China and Japan, February 11, 1956.

Finally, the deterioration of conditions under the Kuomintang reached a stage where, as one missionary put it, the public came to the conclusion that any change, even a Communist triumph, could not make things any worse. Not all missionaries would have explained it this way. Much depended upon the area where they were stationed. In Honan, for instance, there was hostility toward the Communists and no deep dissatisfaction with the Kuomintang, but even in this province missionaries found there was no will to fight.

The only other alternative open to the Kuomintang would have been a drastic and revolutionary program capable of competing with Communist propaganda and a general renovation of the party and government to free it from the terrible incubus of a deeply ingrained reputation for corruption.

Missionaries, like the Chinese themselves, never had an opportunity to vote for or against the Kuomintang and no expert public opinion analyst made a scientific inquiry as to their views on major issues confronting China after the war. The historian, then, enters upon hazardous ground if he seeks to estimate missionary sentiment concerning the Nationalist government during this period. He can, however, safely determine various shades of opinion.

A considerable group of missionaries was violently anti-Communist and defended the Kuomintang and Chiang, finding no blemishes whatsoever. They cited Chiang's early morning Bible reading and prayer as evidence of his sincere piety and statesmanship. Criticism of the Kuomintang was usually explained as largely the insidious penetration of Communist propaganda.

Another group was equally anti-Communist but, in spite of friendship for some members of the Kuomintang, increasingly inclined toward restrained criticism of Chiang and especially of some leaders in the party.

A third group, and numerically very strong among missions associated with the National Council of Churches in the United States and the National Christian Council in China, was more forthright in its criticisms of the Kuomintang and disgusted with what they believed to be its ineptness and corruption.

A fourth group, represented especially by younger missionaries of the social gospel wing, dismissed the Kuomintang as hopelessly reactionary and corrupt. On occasion, at least, they somewhat righteously confessed to being "pink" and entertained the prospect of the triumph of China's Communists with considerable hope, in most cases because they had no real grasp of the far-flung revolution they confronted. Most other missionaries dismissed these liberals as naïve rather than as true Communists.

To this can be added the carefully considered opinion that most missionaries of the major Protestant denominations, excluding Lutherans, belonged to the second and third groups. They carried on an active and highly interesting correspondence with mission boards at home and their point of view became dominant in the China Committee of the Division of Foreign Missions of the National Council of Churches, by far the most powerful church body in the United States. They represented a spirit of adventure in idealism, concerned themselves more with ethics than creeds, conceived of Christianity as having a relevance for politics, and never had any illusion that morning devotions automatically were followed by twenty-four hours of statesmanship. They were possessed by a passion for humanity at large and for the Chinese in particular and they viewed the deterioration in Kuomintang China with anguish. They were not, in contrast to American diplomats and politicians, conditioned to the cold-war psychology whereby any opponent of Communism must necessarily be defended. With something of the spirit of prophets many of them saw through the tangle of selfish machinations and political ambitions rampant in their adopted land. Above all, they viewed the China scene against the background of their own progressive political outlook—an outlook they shared with the followers of Woodrow Wilson, with Harry Emerson Fosdick, Sherwood Eddy, and the virile tradition of what they would have called Christian humanism. A great many of them were associated with Chinese Christian educational institutions.

Frank Cartwright of the Methodist Board of Missions, who went to China in October 1945 to make a survey of conditions for the Division of Foreign Missions, found "widespread unrest and dissatisfaction." The difficulty, wrote Cartwright, was due to the lack of able and honest officials. People in liberated areas, he explained, "had looked for so long and with such intense fervor for the coming of peace and the taking over of the rule by Chungking officials in place of the puppet government" that they had built up high hopes for good government under "high-minded and worthy" officials. The reaction was serious when "many of these proved to be tragically similar to the ones appointed by Japan-controlled Nanking." Ronald Rees, serving with the National Christian Council at Shanghai, greatly troubled over the poor administration, found the most common explanation to be the shortage of first-class men.

This was a weakness that both the Generalissimo and Madame Chiang not only admitted but to which they ascribed most of their difficulties. Other missionaries went beyond this and placed the emphasis on corruption. Mrs. Henry Fenn of the American Board, one of the first missionaries to return to Peking after the war, listened to the stories of all types of people from all parts of China. They all without exception agreed as to the corruption of the Kuomintang and the government officials. Members of the North China Mission of the American Board were appalled by the gross corruption of the Kuomintang and when Congressman Walter Judd, Chiang's chief defender in the United States, visited their station they were determined to give him an accurate picture of the deterioration of the Kuomintang since he had left China in 1938. In the words of one of those present, they found Judd "a tense and emotional man" who did all the talking while the rest of them listened—he made no converts there but he, more than any other one man, built up a tremendous following for Chiang in the United States.

Hugh Hubbard, after long years in the Weihsien Internment Camp, got to Peking on the first plane to leave and joined in the great victory celebrations. He then shared in the gradual disillusionment "while nationalist officials took over and graft and squeeze started up on a vast scale."

One of the most prominent Baptist missionaries, J. W. Decker, Secretary of the International Missionary Council, had spent time in Chungking during the war. He warned that, after acknowledging the achievements of China in the face of defeat, "one must go on to the unpleasant fact that the present Kuomintang government is essentially a fascist government, and such a government cannot ultimately command the respect and support of the Chinese people." He reported that the "democratically minded intelligentsia is skeptical of these [democratic] professions, and does not believe that an admittedly corrupt Kuomintang can ever reform itself." He listed among the fascist characteristics of the Kuomintang its youth movement, its rigid regimentation of curriculums of schools and colleges, its political censorship, and its "Gestapo-like methods of repression."[5]

A Methodist clergyman, who had left his church in Denver to work with UNRRA in China, in October 1946 estimated that seven million faced starvation and expressed fear that "only a small part of the supplies shipped to China will go to the people who need them and that the larger part will be used to enhance political positions and to enrich the more fortunate." There was, he said, no political freedom in China.[6]

Among the more cautious missionary observers was Frank Price, a Southern Presbyterian whose long Chinese robe and fine Chinese accent were so familiar in the environs of Nanking, a personal friend of Chiang and also a man who wished the Kuomintang well. In May 1947, after the temporary reorganization of the Nationalist government and the formation of a coalition including representatives of the Young China party and the Democratic Socialist party, his hopes for the future rose. He thought the liberals had won a strong position in the new government and praised General Marshall for

[5] J. W. Decker, "China's Unity at Stake," *The Christian Century*, August 8, 1945, pp. 905-907.

[6] Edgar M. Wahlberg, "Politics and Hunger in China," *The Christian Century*, October 9, 1946, pp. 1209-1210.

strengthening the liberal and the democratic forces outside the Communist party. Price saw in the liberals the only hope of averting complete catastrophe and only questioned whether they had enough power and influence to effect much needed political reforms, to prevent a serious collapse of the economy, and to inspire new ideas. Price found the very influential book *Thunder Out of China* far from objective and he regretted the portrayal of Chiang as a sinister master of a reactionary plot and the placing of every move of the Kuomintang in the worst possible light. Nevertheless he, too, found in the realities of the regime much to criticize.[7]

By the fall of 1947 the very liberals in whom Price had placed so much confidence had been outlawed and their leaders had fled to Hongkong. By 1948 a great many missionaries agreed with Robert Root, a journalist in China, who wrote that a Communist victory was inevitable and attributed this contingency to the fact that feudal lords generated the power behind Chiang. Root observed that perverted Confucian principles of family loyalty had become supports for a web of patronage and graft that enriched the ruling class while neither philosophy nor religion had produced in the regime an effective concern for society.[8]

The tragedy moved towards its culmination by the fall of 1948. The thoughtful and fair-minded Frank Price no longer had any hope and as he viewed the drawing down of the Communist curtain he tried to analyze the reasons for the catastrophe. The primary factor was the failure of the people to rally to the support of the Kuomintang. This was not because of any enthusiasm for Communism, he said, but because they "are utterly weary of war and hungry for peace, food and economic recovery at almost any price." "Moreover," said Price, "they see the government defending not only China's national freedom but also favored families, special classes and privileges, vested financial interests, speculators and profiteers, useless

[7] Frank W. Price, "China's Liberals Get Their Chance," *The Christian Century*, May 14, 1947, pp. 622-624.

[8] Robert Root, "If China Goes Communist," *The Christian Century*, October 27, 1948, pp. 1140-1142.

officials and bureaucrats." He observed that China's millions were asking why they should "sacrifice themselves further for a government that is unwilling or unable to carry out its repeated promises of reform?"[9]

Olin Stockwell, Methodist missionary at Chengtu, saw the old regime collapse and then spent two years in a Communist prison. This tall, angular, and almost Lincolnesque character combined a rollicking humor with a penchant for perceiving the weak spots in everyone's armor. He accepted people about him at their true worth, loved them, and still managed to laugh at himself after two years in solitary confinement. The YMCA, he said, could quite properly have changed its title to fit its political point of view without changing its initials. He was amused by the naïveté of some young missionaries who thought they would be able to work with the Communists but who, when they later found that they had to choose between Marxian dialectic and Christian love, discovered how fully committed they were to the latter, whereupon they scurried off to the nearest consul for a passport. Stockwell had no illusions about the Communists but their utter devotion and zeal struck a kindred spirit in him and he never underestimated them.

But of the postwar Kuomintang, Stockwell had nothing good to say. He described how the politicians and bankers had conducted "a legalized racket" whereby they got American gold in exchange for cheap Chinese paper currency. He described the government as "a family-archy." The heart of the tragedy was in Chiang's compromises with the war lords during his rise to power for these were the men who, when the war opened up opportunities for graft, plunged the whole regime into disrepute. He told of the inflation that was the necessary result of bankers "who were more concerned about making millions than in putting China on her feet," and he could cite as his authority T. G. Ho, financial adviser to the Central Bank of China. Nor did he spare the Soong family—they had been

[9] Frank W. Price, "Bitter Dilemma in China," *The Christian Century*, December 15, 1948, p. 1365.

faced with a choice between private profit and public good, and they had chosen the former.[10]

Missionaries at work amid the deteriorating scenes of civil war and the breakdown of the economy saw their last faint hopes glimmer away in the late summer and fall of 1948. In August the government made one last effort to halt the inflation, which had proceeded to the point where it took six million dollars in Chinese currency to get one dollar in gold. Chiang made a patriotic appeal to the people to exchange their gold and foreign currency as well as their old Chinese currency for new Chinese dollars. Foreign observers were surprised by the success of the appeal. Gold and foreign currency were exchanged for the new Chinese national currency beyond the fondest expectations.

But hope gave way to angry frustration when the new currency soon became worthless, leaving those who had exchanged sound currency for the new without any resources. Ugly rumors soon circulated that the leaders had quickly tapped the government's supply of gold and sound foreign currency, converting cheap Chinese currency for American dollars. Whether this happened cannot be determined. Certainly there were other factors contributing to the decline of the new currency. The shortage of goods, the closing down of shops by merchants who refused to exchange their goods at the prices fixed by the government, and the overissue of the new currency were sufficient to wreck the attempt at currency reform. Whatever the causes, the result, as Victor E. W. Hayward of the National Christian Council observed, was that such confidence in the government "as had been at least potentially present was irretrievably lost." E. Plummer Mills, veteran missionary, considered the abortive currency reform the greatest single factor in the final collapse of the Kuomintang.[11]

The constant downhill slide of the Nationalists since the war led both missionaries and Chinese Christians to comment on the possibility of greater American aid. The prevailing attitude

[10] F. Olin Stockwell, *With God in Red China* (New York: Harper and Brothers, 1953), pp. 26-31, 43-46.
[11] Interview with E. Plummer Mills, April 28, 1954.

among missionaries in the coastal region of China was expressed in a report from Ronald D. Rees in March 1947, namely, that many were of the opinion, "even among men most friendly to America," that too much pressure from abroad would be a kind of interference in China's internal affairs. Frank W. Price strongly opposed intervention by the United States. It would, he said, embitter the Chinese and it should be avoided even if noninterference meant the triumph of Communism.[12]

Fourteen Chinese Christians, who set forth a program for liberalizing the government to General Wedemeyer in September 1947, also said that they wanted financial aid from the United States for reconstruction and rehabilitation but not for military purposes. When a Communist victory seemed almost certain in January 1949, Victor Hayward ventured the opinion that "the amount of American aid which would be required at this late stage to maintain the Government would be colossal, while the amount of protest which would rise from vast numbers who are not themselves Communists but would oppose large-scale military aid in the circumstances might of itself deal a death blow to the Government." The opposition to intervention on the part of missionaries was based on their conviction that the Chinese could only interpret such a step as an endorsement of the hapless regime and an effort to impose on them permanently the sufferings that this government had done nothing to relieve. Like their Chinese colleagues they believed that the solution lay not in foreign intervention or in a war against the Communists, but rather in thoroughgoing reform.

During the postwar years Chinese Christians, especially the leaders in Christian universities and in the National Christian Council, protested more vigorously than did the missionaries against the Kuomintang. In the summer of 1946 a group of them called for peace, civil rights, and reform, and reminded the Generalissimo that all human beings were God's children and entitled to freedom of thought and speech and the "privilege of religious faith, worship and propaganda." Laws that

[12] Frank W. Price, "Bitter Dilemma in China," *The Christian Century*, December 15, 1948, p. 1367.

infringed on these rights should be repealed, they said, and "subversive means of threat and terrorism" should be halted. They boldly declared:

> There is no denying the fact that there is corruption, rottenness and inefficiency in the present government. Especially has this been revealed after V-J Day in the liberated areas where the liberated people, who were longing for a good government, have been disappointed and have turned from pessimism, and from a positive attitude to one of passiveness. We are confronted with the rapid rising costs of living, the interruption of transportation, the monopoly of official capital, and the paralysis of industry and commerce, so that the whole economic structure and the peoples' livelihood are thrown into hopeless confusion.

Again in the summer of 1947 a group of Christian leaders made an appeal to the Nationalist government. The civil war was still raging and everywhere the people faced disaster—"refugees, pitiful in their misery, are one sign of this." Rice riots, rowdyism, bitterness among the farmers who reaped but little profit, labor disputes that had their source in the inflation, and student revolts, said the Christians, all "retell the dismal tale " Only an end to the civil war could bring recovery. The Kuomintang and the Communists were both blamed by the people and, said these leaders, rightfully so.

> Look at the facts. In Government areas: corruption, inflation, administrative inefficiency, inequitable taxation, unjust conscription, and most recently, on the verge of what has been called the period of constitutionalism, a dangerous repression of civil liberties. In Communist areas: needless destructiveness, trials that are often a mockery of justice . . . , forced levies on both grain and manpower, widespread economic deterioration, hard and fast regimentation of community life, and a suppression of fundamental liberties which is the antithesis of democracy. It is no wonder that the people, when they look at conditions in both areas, Government and Communist, feel

that both parties are responsible for the nation's unhappy state and for the continuance of the war.

In July 1947 five Christian leaders associated with the National Christian Council went to Nanking and interviewed several government leaders including Madame Chiang. They reported back to the group in Shanghai that the situation was very critical. It was decided to seek an interview with Chiang and a conference of fifteen Chinese and three foreigners conferred on what should be said.

The interview took place on Saturday, July 12. The Chinese leaders first met with Madame Chiang for a two-hour session that opened with a short period of devotion. The Christians outlined their ideas. If Communism was to be avoided, military measures were not enough. These could only succeed if the confidence of the people in the government was restored by a program of thoroughgoing reform, protection of human freedom and rights, and a dramatic demonstration that the government was anxious to establish an order that would give the people a better livelihood. Madame Chiang was polite and friendly. She said that she, too, had an appreciation of the hardships of the people. However, the Communists must be defeated and the first duty of Christians was to support the government in this fight. Christ had not appeased Satan. Christians should blame those on whom blame for the war properly lay. It was true that the government faced severe difficulties but this was due to the lack of well-trained officials in the middle and lower ranks.

The Christian leaders, in a brief session after the interview, disagreed with two of Madame Chiang's arguments. She was wrong in asserting that the government came from the people —they felt strongly that there was a gap between the people and the government. Secondly, they felt that fighting by itself was no solution.

Much the same ideas were presented to President Chiang in a meeting with him. Chiang admitted some of the difficulties but attributed them wholly to the lack of good people and good organization. He criticized the Protestant group for not taking a clear stand as the Catholics had done in support of national mobilization. Hugh Hubbard reported that members of the Christian delegation "were scolded like school boys and dismissed." In another discussion after this interview, the Christian leaders agreed that both President and Madame Chiang "seemed to underestimate the strength and ability of the people to take part in a democratic form of government." Able administrators could be secured, they thought, if they would take the people at large into their confidence.

Missionary opposition to the Kuomintang was by no means tantamount to support of the Communists. Time and again missionaries spoke of the latter as thoroughgoing Marxists. Long experience with Communist guerrilla governments during the war had banished the illusion that they were democratic reformers. Only a very small minority of younger American missionaries welcomed the prospect of a complete Communist triumph. At a church guest house in Hong Kong in 1949 a group of them told a Swedish colleague, "We are 'pinks' you know," and talked excitedly of returning to their posts on the mainland and carrying on Christian work. The Swede, who had seen the Communists at work in Honan, thought these men naïve idealists, rather than Communists, who simply reflected traditional missionary optimism and a lack of understanding of the real aims of the Communists in China.[13]

The great majority of missionaries were strongly anti-Communist. The young Presbyterian missionary Wallace G. Merwin, who had spent ten years before the war in Hopei, questioned the journalists who, in 1945, were writing that the Communists were democratic. In his experience with them, he had seen "little evidence of democracy in their regime." He testified: "That regime, in the areas where I saw it and heard of it, had all the earmarks of a totalitarian order. No criticism was tolerated. The slightest open expression of dissatisfaction was met with imprisonment or even death."[14] Merwin thought the Communists killed far more Chinese than Japanese and re-

[13] Interview with the Rev. Erik Malm, February 11, 1956.
[14] Wallace C. Merwin, "The Chinese Communists," *The Christian Century*, March 21, 1945, pp. 366-367.

ported that they buried traitors alive and "anyone was a traitor who came out of a town occupied by the Japanese, or with Japanese-sponsored puppet money on his person." J. W. Decker, who once described the Kuomintang as fascist and gave the Communists credit for economic reforms, thought that Communist Yenan was not one whit less repressive than Chunking.[15]

In 1948 missionary leaders eagerly scanned reports from Communist areas to determine what could be expected. There was conflicting evidence ranging from the reports of missionaries who had found the Communists friendly and cooperative to the contrary statements of those who had found it impossible to continue their work. John Reisner wrote home after a meeting in Peking that it had been brought out "there was not a single communist territory known where church work had not been interfered with." Victor Hayward, reflecting opinion in the National Christian Council, thought that missionaries might be permitted to continue their work in the early stages of Communist rule, but that later all except those rendering social service or technical assistance would be excluded.

Yet, when the Communists first took over northern China, especially after the spring of 1948, they were in many cases so fair-minded and their troops so well-disciplined that a few missionaries began to take hope. Leaders of the party assured the missionaries that the new regime would guarantee freedom of religion and even expressed regret that so many missionaries had left their posts. The innumerable instances of persecution in Communist areas were attributed to mistakes of local officials. And to this assurance was added the fact that there was a definite lessening of Communist interference with the Christians.

A veteran of twenty-eight years with the Free Methodists wrote after the Communists had moved into the territory where he was stationed that he had met with only friendly cooperation. They had assured him that he was free to preach the

15 J. W. Decker, "China's Unity at Stake," *The Christian Century*, August 8, 1945, p. 906.

gospel in the country or anywhere he chose, and that there had been no interference with the middle school or the Bible school. He had met several Christian Communists who had at one time been his students. Not long before, a Chinese evangelist had conducted a week's revival meetings and "many seekers were at the altar." This was in a town where the Communists had been in control for two years. "We are here," he wrote, "and until we are actually driven out I personally feel we should stay."

Among favorable reports was one from the Kiangsu-Anhwei Christian Rural Service Union in Anhwei early in 1949. The writer told of the excellent behavior of the soldiers—"not one person was molested, nor an article taken forcibly by the newcomers." The military officers had assured the missionaries that there would be freedom of religion and high officials of the party who had been in the vicinity explained "that when and if Nanking and other territory is occupied, the same generous treatment will be accorded mission institutions and their personnel." Three weeks of experience with the Communist soldiers (almost all friendly country boys) so impressed the writer that he had nothing but praise to give them.

> They have a democratic outlook, generally dominated by a very definite purpose to raise the standard of living of farmers and working classses. They express little bitterness and have no desire to destroy anything except the government against which they fight. It would be regrettable indeed if political or economic groups are permitted to manoeuvre Christian people and Christian countries into a position of opposition to these masses of people who so justifiedly are struggling for something better for their country.

In conclusion he observed that the same desperate needs that the Communists were trying to meet "have from the beginning been the concern of the Rural Service Union."

Letters from another missionary in Communist-controlled territory spoke of the most friendly cooperation and related that churches had been little affected by the change. At evangelistic services held on the Chinese New Year's Day, the churches were thronged and some Communist officials attended.

Perhaps, after all, the Communists had been misjudged. At least the experience of the first few weeks and months were not what had been expected. When the Communists occupied Shanghai, both missionaries and members of the foreign business community were favorably impressed. Soldiers, who had always been unruly and brutal in China, now behaved admirably. The new officials were honest and manifested a passionate interest in the welfare of the people. In an overseas news letter, Victor Hayward of the National Christian Council was cautious about the future, but in reviewing the causes of the Nationalist downfall he observed that in the light of the complete failure of the Nationalists "China could not in fact afford, . . . , *not* to go through the throes of a Communist revolution." The liberals, he thought, had failed to offer a practicable third alternative.

In September 1949 a missionary in Shanghai weighed the good and the bad. The excellent organization and discipline of the Communists, their sacrificial public spirit, their attacks on graft and corruption, their professed concern for the common people, and their "tremendous dynamic drive" impressed him, but he regretted other aspects of the new regime. It restricted civil liberties, was a dictatorship and used police state methods, employed thought control, regimented education, put forth anti-American propaganda, stirred up bitter hatred toward those who disagreed, and gave all news in the press and over the radio a Russian slant.

The Communists proclaimed freedom of religion but missionaries soon learned what the Communists meant by "freedom." The hopeful beginnings in the Rural Service Union in Anhwei were reversed within a few months and everywhere the Communists moved in and took over useful social services quite as readily as they did other missionary enterprises. Some missionaries faced the Peoples Courts, charged with being the "agents of foreign capitalism," and accused of strange crimes against the state, of spying, and of concealing arms. Not infrequently missionaries were put in jail without any explanation. Those who had been enthusiastic about the new regime and convinced that Christianity dedicated to a social purpose could live under the new government found themselves open to the same charges. It was one thing to do "good" as a Christian and another to be oriented in the faith of the Marxian dialectic. Only the latter could be accepted. The group of young missionary idealists who were making every effort to adjust to the new day learned that they were hated as enemies of the "people."

The Communists distinguished at first between foreign missionaries and native Christians. The missionaries were squeezed out on the ground that they were foreigners. At the same time the Communists professed friendship for native Christians who were willing to subordinate their religious activities to the new proletarian state.

By the close of 1948 a majority of American missionaries were leaving. Some Chinese Christians thought their action precipitate—they should face the new order; there would continue to be a need for Christian witness. Not until early 1949 did Chinese Christians come to the conclusion, thanks to Communist pressure, that the church should be freed of all "imperialist" connections and the missionaries should leave so that the church could be purified.

At first Chinese Christians bade the missionaries farewell wistfully and faced the future with uncertainty. In the autumn of 1949, after the triumph of the Communists, the Chinese Christians sent a message to mission boards that revealed a deep agony of soul. The Communists, said this message, "have a deep seated feeling that the Chinese church has been intimately related to imperialism and capitalism." It was true, admitted these Christians, that the church had benefited by the unequal treaties, that Western forms of service and Western denominationalism had been introduced and that missionaries had retained administrative control in many cases. These things gave a certain semblance of truth to the Communist charge. However, asserted these Chinese Christians:

We do realize and so wish to assert that missionary work

in China never had any direct relationship to governmental policies; mission funds have always been contributed by the rank and file of common ordinary Christians and church members; missionaries have been sent here for no other purpose than to preach the Christian gospel of love, and to serve the needs of the Chinese people. The central Christian motivation will not and can never be questioned, but these other social implications can very easily give rise to misunderstanding and accusation.

The message spoke of the problem to be faced—"Just how the Christian gospel can be witnessed to in a clime that is, by virtue of its ideology, fundamentally materialistic and atheistic presents a challenge stronger than ever before." The new political regime, they rightly saw, would demand that all of life be made a service to what the party considered to be the good of society.

In the closing days of the Kuomintang regime L. H. Lee, a Chinese Christian layman, wrote an article entitled: "Why the Goodwill Failed." His criticisms of missionaries and of the United States were temperate and worthy of consideration. Concerning the well-intentioned missionaries, he wrote:

Throughout the missionary movement, however, there has never been a clearly defined theory, practice or experiment by and for Chinese Christians as to what a better and more abundant life, the brotherhood of man or the Kingdom of God would mean in China. To, by and for the Chinese the Christian message was one of personal salvation. There was no clearly defined socio-personal preaching that one could be saved only in relation to the society in which he lives. The result has been that the Christian convert in China might become a better parent or child but not a new man of the world as St. Paul exemplified, nor a new citizen of his community. Without new citizens there can be no new China. Accordingly Christianity has so far failed.

It was not enough to tell a Chinese to love God and follow Jesus. He must be taught "how to act upon Christian principles in the problems that confront a Christian every day, in this common, mundane world."

The government of the United States had been friendly toward China. Lee extolled its defense of China's territorial and administrative integrity. But American officials had failed to put forth any constructive national ideals that the Chinese could follow. American teachers had likewise rendered invaluable service but very few "have ever attempted to inspire or develop a creative leadership for the building of a new China and for the work of a revolutionary China." Americans had been generous in providing relief, but relief was not enough.

Now a new day had dawned and the ineffective but friendly relations with the United States had been replaced by the leadership of Russia. Whereas Americans sought somewhat indifferently to apply American ideas in China, the Russians had adapted their system to meet conditions in China. Consequently, Communism had become the guiding principle not only in China but in Southeast Asia. "Freedom shall exist of, by and for it. Through re-education all ideas to the contrary will eventually die out." Russia had never been indifferent; she had cancelled the unequal treaties, and insisted on the abolition of colonialism everywhere—in short, she had shrewdly played the game to win the confidence of the masses. Communism, possessed of confidence and tremendous drive, was setting out to rally the propertyless of the whole world to its banner. She was already looking forward to victory in Southeast Asia and the Middle East.

Good will was not enough. The American missionary movement and the official Far Eastern policy of the American government had failed because they did not offer solutions to the problems faced by a society in the process of disintegration and economic collapse. The Communists had triumphed because no one else had really seriously worked at a solution of the economic and social problems faced by a nation in despair, and in a mood of desperation the Chinese were ready and willing to try Communism. The Chinese laymen posed the question as to whether the United States would meet the same problem elsewhere with a more positive approach. A missionary of the socialized Christianity wing might have summed up the failure

[308]

as due to sins of omission rather than commission, and he would have meant much the same thing.

Many Chinese Christians joined in the new proletarian Hosannas with gusto. The most ardent leader was Dr. Y. T. Wu, an American-educated Christian leader. In the summer of 1949 he was entertained in Peiping and, along with four other Protestants and two Buddhists, was asked to serve on a commission to advise the new government on religious matters. The leaders of the new government explained that freedom of religion was a permanent party principle and they believed oppression of religion would be a mistake. And why not, said Wu, in view of the fact that Marxists looked upon religion as the product of an unhealthy social system and they believed, therefore, that in the course of time it would disappear anyway. In a speech before the National Christian Council he welcomed the revolution. For the first time, he said, "the rulers are now the people." The New Democracy, according to him, differed from the democracy of the old bourgeoisie, under which the common people had nominal political equality, but were actually under capitalistic domination, and were not free economically. In the discussion following the meeting of the NCC, Wu said that "since Communism is practicing what Christianity merely professes, Christians have no right to stress the points on which they differ from Communists, until they are similarly practicing their beliefs."

Wu was by no means alone. T. C. Chao, Dean of the School of Religion at Yenching University, one of the six presidents of the World Council of Churches, and a man who had won great respect among foreign missionaries, although disclaiming he was a Communist, wrote: "To be brief, we are glad to see the destruction of feudalism in China. Dynasty after dynasty, the masses of our nation have endured exploitation like dumb driven cattle." He regretted that groups of poor Christians were "still unconsciously too much bourgeois in outlook and sentiments." "They need," he said, "to be thoroughly shaken to realize that a new day has dawned and that a change of ways, of life and communication, is necessary." Chao was later relieved of his post as Dean at Yenching, but as late as

1955 he praised the new regime in an interview with an American Quaker.

In the winter of 1950 the NCC sent a message to the Christians of China that revealed how quickly a reorientation had taken place.

> Brothers and Sisters in Christ: Our country has already entered upon a new era in its history, and as Christians we should give praise and glory to God for that awakening of the social conscience which we see spreading under the New Democracy.

In 1950 the Christians issued a manifesto calling for the rooting out of foreign influences and all support of a "capitalist" and "imperialist" character and full participation in the political life of the new regime. By the end of 1951 it was estimated that 277,000 Christians had signed this document. A missionary still in China in 1951 spoke of the leaders who were supporting Communism as believing in it and said that as Christians they felt they had a contribution to make.[16]

Marcus Cheng, a theological conservative and evangelist, was close to the Communist leadership and rejoiced in the new order. He professed to find Christianity and Communism wholly compatible and denounced the United States for its imperialism. In January 1952 he wrote an article for *Tien Feng*, a church publication endorsed by the government, in which he said:

> From the heart I can sincerely say, I fervently love Communism and accept the teachings of the Communist Party and the teaching of Mao Tse-tung, which is the science that society must accept, just as I accept astronomy and the fact that the earth is round, at the same time as I accept statements in the Bible that the sun rises in the east and sets in the west.[17]

Cheng closed his article with the story of his three-year-old

[16] "Inside Communist China," by a Missionary, *The Christian Century*, August 23, 1950.

[17] Edward G. Nelson, "Christianity in China," *The Covenant Weekly*, April 8, 1955.

grandson, who on seeing a picture of former president Harry Truman shouted, "Truman, the American Devil: I will strike him." The grandfather was moved to tears: "My eyes had seen what I had been looking for for many years, a three year old lad who knew how to love his country and fight against American imperialism."[18]

Chinese Christians were permitted freedom to preach—provided they took the "positive" approach as defined by the party. Their preaching was more than countered by a powerful anti-Christian propaganda sponsored by the government. Christian middle schools gave courses in Marxism. The universities of a Christian background were taken over by the government.

Amid the feverish climate of opinion, the parades, the popular "anti-movements" against corruption, the small group meetings where eager party followers confessed their past shortcomings and gained guidance from the more experienced adherents, amid the fanatical crusade of youth in behalf of the new order, it would have been difficult to remain a critic. To do so was to invite retribution and to suffer because one was still smitten with the disease of the reactionary bourgeoisie. Yet, there were unquestionably people who were troubled. Some Christians—the number is uncertain—refused to go along. The first of these groups were older conservatives who simply remained silent and drew a line between politics and Christianity. A few took issue with the Communists and suffered persecution at the hands of their aroused neighbors.

A young Christian attended a Communist Political School in 1949 and found it a Marxian crucible where basic tenets of Christianity were tested. Religion was explained to him as the invention of supernatural explanations to satisfy the primitive mind. The upper classes had perpetuated these primitive beliefs so that the oppressed might have another-worldly escape from their miseries. Jesus had failed because he had not understood the laws of social development. He had "tried to leap directly from a slave society to the Kingdom of God." "Naturally this revolution was dialectically unsound and so did not

[18] *Ibid.*

[311]

work." The question had been asked, "Can a Christian believe in the New Democracy?" The answer: "Yes, a Christian can believe in the New Democracy, *but he cannot be an official worker in the party or the government.* If a Christian is to enter into the building of the New Democracy he must recognize certain facts about the social effects of Christianity—e.g., that it has been used in the past by exploiting classes to control the exploited; that it has prevented the solution of this-worldly problems by other-worldly promises." The young student asked if it was not good that Christians believed in love. The Communist answered that love could only function when classes had been removed. It was of no avail to tell a tiger to repent— he must be eliminated as a menace. There was a question about Christian rural service—it, too, was an evil for it confused class distinctions. The party leader said: "It blurs the fundamental issues by preaching love, forgiveness, and hence, reducing the farmers' will to resist the landlord and accomplish the revolution."

Here, indeed, was a revolution. If some Chinese Christians did not recognize that it clashed directly with Christianity, the Communists did.

Missionaries who remained in China after 1948 felt useless. Word from a mission station in November 1949 sadly noted:

At first some preachers were hindered from continuing their work by fear and a sense of uncertainty, so church activities were spasmodic. Then efforts to revive the church work met a condition when Christians and people in general were too occupied with political rallies and work to overcome the slump in business, loss through inflation, and heavy taxation to have any time for church services, and even personal devotions.[19]

Most missionaries, in the words of F. Olin Stockwell, "found that they were an embarrassment to any church they might be helping, and quietly turned their work over to others."[20] A

19 *Our Covenant, 1950: An Illustrated Annual of the Evangelical Mission Covenant Church of America,* ed. by G. F. Hedstrand (Chicago: Covenant Press, 1950), pp. 59-60.
20 F. Olin Stockwell, *op. cit.,* p. 61.

social point of view proved to be no protection. The YMCA, known for its crusading activities in China, and various social service units found themselves quietly driven into bankruptcy by taxes. Even the Friends Service Unit, which had rendered medical and other aid to both Communist and Kuomintang forces, was immobilized.[21] Christian institutions, hospitals and schools, were usually the first victims, for all "good" was now a monopoly of the Marxists, who had notions as to how these institutions would better serve the common people if in Communist hands.

The few remaining missionaries discovered that the New Democracy was driven by a furious dynamic akin to the spirit of Calvin's Geneva, where those guilty of sin had been dealt with as enemies of the Lord. The "sin" of the missionaries was that they were symbols of that evil world of imperialism and capitalism—whether they were sympathetic or even critical of those institutions did not matter. Moreover, in the New Democracy anything short of an affirmation of faith in the Marxian dialectic was "sin." He who was not for it must be against it, and opposition, even silence, was stamped out with a righteous indignation worthy of New England's Puritan fathers. A hundred years earlier missionaries had damned moral goodness and denounced Confucianism in particular as a dangerous counterfeit of Christianity. The Communists knew the "counterfeits" even better, and anything except the new gospel of salvation was a "counterfeit." Less than seventy years earlier a Southern Presbyterian had said that what Chinese heathenism required was a series of protracted revival meetings where the hopeful cases could be won over. China now had its protracted "revival" meeting—mass political meetings, parades, small group discussions where doubters could confess their troubles and be helped to see the light. In all these the sinners received the "grace" to repent of their bourgeois transgressions and were given the power to follow the true way. The reorientation of the individual was no less than that required of the first Christian converts. And like the latter, who had been cherished as "babes in Christ," the Communist converts would

---

[21] *Ibid.,* p. 62.

have to be watched over, disciplined, reprimanded, and nurtured. The dominant psychology of both "religions" called for a precipitous act of faith. Those hardened beyond redemption would suffer the sword, under the earlier Christians in a future world, under the Communists in the present.

Missionaries who remained in China went to prison. The charges against them were usually vague. Solitary confinement was the general rule. On occasion they would be called forth to discuss their transgressions and to be enlightened in the ways of Marxian dialectic. Without exception they adhered to their Christian faith. Their Christianity had generally become more tolerant and their dogmatism concerning a literal creed more mellow than those of their nineteenth-century predecessors. In most cases they understood only too well that the whirlwind that threatened to destroy them was the inevitable product of a society that had become callous and, on occasion, corrupt and decadent. Therefore, they did not condemn their persecutors. They often, like F. Olin Stockwell, abhorred the war party at home, advocated China's admission to the United Nations, and refused to play the popular role of martyr before their home audience. Perhaps they could become missionaries at home, where the very real dangers of the frightening new foreign faith aroused a crippling fear that threatened for a time to destroy the very values to which they had given their all.

The books, articles, and eyewitness accounts coming out of China after the victory of the Communists had two sides, one was a story of constructive achievement, the other a tragic tale of persecution. The dynamic was the vision of a new and strong China built on the Russian model. Everywhere there were new roads, improved train services, amazing progress in mass hygiene, definite advances in the elimination of the pestilential diseases that had long cursed the country, the rooting out of corruption, an extension of education to the masses, but the most significant change was to be seen in a wild enthusiasm to get on with the construction of a new society. Every individual had a role to play giving his life a new meaning and direction.

The Chinese masses joined the patriotic parade in part because it was hazardous for anyone to remain on the sidelines, but many thoughtful observers concluded that the dynamic energy of the new political movement was less a product of threats of punishment than it was the result of the successful indoctrination of the masses with Communist ideals. Factory workers, village peasants, hospital staffs, school and university faculties, church congregations, clergy, and every other economic and social group attended classes in political affairs, where all bent their energies to gaining an understanding of Communist ideals. All of China became a network of confessional meetings where one subjected himself to self-criticism and group criticism. The ideal was the negation of selfish ambition and the dedication of oneself to society.

The Christian church survived only because it lent itself to indoctrination in the new ideals. In all communities there was a Three Self Reform Committee that sponsored political meetings of clergy and laity. In Shanghai in 1952 there were classes for the study of the Common Platform every Thursday evening. Pastors and church leaders signed up—362 of them. At Changsha there were sixteen such political study groups for church members. At Nanking in 1952, 188 Christians met every afternoon for two weeks to study how the church could conform to the government demand to increase production and decrease waste. Those in attendance examined themselves to find bourgeois virtues inherited from the days of the missionaries. Those who could not immerse themselves in the new ideology were helped by the others. If they still retained their old point of view, they were called before public accusation meetings where all their neighbors poured forth charges against them. Thirty such meetings were held in the churches of Changsha during the first six months of 1951. Often such accusation meetings were followed by government trials and in turn by a sentence to forced labor.

Tien Feng, the government-controlled Christian periodical, abounded in stories of accusation meetings. An evangelist, Tung Ling-ku, was indiscreet enough to say that Russia was as imperialistic as the United States, that the Chinese press gave only one side of the Korean war, that the People's government was the devil, and that the church was following the evil example of Esau in selling its birthright for a mess of "red" bean soup. When called upon to confess his "sins," he refused to do so, whereupon he was arrested and then taken before the church, where he met with rough treatment. Finally, he faced a government trial.

Offenses were usually less bold and consisted only of failure to admit that one had been guilty of trivial transgressions. The real crime was never what one did or said but the failure to go along.

The seeking out of recalcitrants was referred to as "Tiger Hunting." A returning missionary in 1952 told the gruesome tale of the way in which all who failed to become positive and outspoken champions of the new order were dealt with:

> There is no such thing as trial before impartial juries. No lawyers to plead, no witnesses permitted on behalf of the accused. The police arrest, frame the charges, find accusers and tell them what to say or read. The accused kneels in silence and listens to the accusations. Then the crowd is asked "Is he guilty?" Anyone failing to shout assent is in danger of being considered reactionary.

Punishment was seldom meted out by the state itself. The People's Courts were infinitely more effective and had the advantage of giving all those in attendance a sense of participation.

Most Christian leaders appear to have had the grace to adjust themselves to the new order. Helen Djong, well-known Dean and professor of education at Ginling College, experienced a conversion as early as 1951 as she was finishing a required course of study at the High Political Institute. In her confession she admitted to having been poisoned by American imperialist thinking. All her life, she said, she had been so completely under American influence that she hardly knew there was such a thing as the country of China. Her confession closed: "I have determined to ally myself with the People, I want to stand on the People's platform, use the sharp instruments of criticism and self-criticism to go still farther in my struggle against slave education, I want to cast out all 'love, praise, and fear America' thinking, and by study, analysis and criticism to cure my former sickness. From now on I will be a new person, for it is only through a sincere change of myself that I can be really liberated and fully serve the People."

A confession of similar sort was made by Dean Chin Tzu-chung, of the School of Agriculture, University of Nanking. Among other evil acts had been a desire to study in America so that he might get a larger salary. He had been wholly corrupted by capitalist thinking. A national reform committee sent out teams to instruct the churches in how to cleanse themselves and everywhere Christians made confessions, but there were also some who refused or who failed to make satisfactory confessions. These were expelled from their positions and, at least in some cases, sent to labor camps.

The Christian church in China was clearly subordinating itself to the revolution, but reports indicated that most churches were holding services, attendance was good, and in some places the number of members was on the increase. A missionary of the English Presbyterian Church who left China in September 1953 had deep fears for the future of the church, but she was likewise tremendously impressed by sermons she listened to and the high spiritual tone of the services.[22]

A group of Friends who visited China in October 1955 gave mildly encouraging reports of church life.[23] Yet, the future seemed uncertain not only because of the restrictions on the churches but even more because of the heavy anti-Christian emphasis in schools and in government propaganda. The young and vigorous new religion of Communism and feeble Christianity, enjoying the support of less than one per cent of the people, existed side by side. The one was a rising order with the force of the state and a furious fanaticism on its side. The other existed only by the tolerance of the more powerful, and it was tolerated only insofar as it was willing to serve its master, the new proletarian dictatorship.

[22] E. Margaret Kiesaw, *China: The Challenge* (London: The Presbyterian Church of England, 1954), p. 21.
[23] Gerald Bailey, "Out of Red China," *The Christian Century*, November 30, 1955, pp. 1393-1395.

[317]

The English Presbyterian missionary who lived under the new regime for four years, in commenting on the official proclamation of freedom of religious belief, summed up the situation in these words:

> Freedom of religious belief does not mean, however, that Christians are free to base their whole life and thought on the teachings of Jesus Christ. That honour is reserved for Marx alone, as he is interpreted by Stalin and Mao. Nor does it mean that the Christian is free to decide what is true and right by the light of the scriptures and the Holy Spirit. Truth and right are decided by the Communist party according to what is expedient, and what is right today will not necessarily be right tomorrow. . . . When one thinks of religious freedom in China, one should also remember the Marxist view that religion is only the opiate of the masses groaning under capitalism. In the ideal environment provided by the Communist state, it will gradually wither away. In China it is also encouraged to wither, especially in young people and professional people, by keeping them very busy, by reserving the best jobs for Communist party members and sympathizers, and making it very hard for them to decide between their patriotic and religious duties. It is so much easier for them to give up the struggle and swim with the tide.[24]

Whether the Christianity nurtured by 120 years of missionary effort in China will survive this hostile environment remains to be seen.

[24] E. Margeret Kiesaw, *op. cit.*, pp. 16-17.

CHAPTER XVIII

"UNTO THE CHINESE FOOLISHNESS"

It is a striking paradox that many of those who sought to carry Protestant Christianity to the Chinese failed to observe the caution uttered by one of their own preceptors. When Saint Paul spoke the celebrated words "unto the Greeks foolishness," he noted with remarkable prescience (as well as hindsight) that the innovators of a new doctrine must not ignore the attitudes and spiritual values of those whom they sought to change. However noble Christianity might be, it could not hope to persuade those who saw in it a body of precepts unrelated to their own needs and aspirations. And it is in large part the failure of many missionaries to have fixed Saint Paul's warning firmly in their minds that accounts for the failure of the movement to win China to Christianity.

Over thousands of years China's millions of people had risen to great heights in art, philosophy, and in solving the problem of living together in crowded conditions and amid poverty. The Chinese had learned the hard lesson of living with dignity and in a noble spirit in a society that promised limited material rewards. The idea of personal success was subordinated to the welfare of the group, the family, and clan. Disaster might overtake them physically but never spiritually. The misfortunes of life were faced with equanimity and even humor.

Christianity had been highly relevant to the experience of Western man in answering his need for peace of soul in a society that was at once individualistic and productive of tensions between his ideals and actual behavior. The individual's failure to achieve the ideal gave rise to what the orthodox Christian called a sense of sin. Such was not the case in China. Confucian society created no inner struggle between the ideal and the actual, and consequently the Chinese had no sense

[319]

of what the Christian termed "sin" or of the love of God versus the love of self.

To be sure, the old order crumbled under the impact of the West, and the Chinese were faced with the necessity of change. China had to reorganize itself if it were to withstand the external pressures of modern imperialism. There was still another reason why it had to change. It was wholly lacking in the advantages of Western science, especially technology and medicine.

After 1890 faith in the Confucian order was being questioned, and the Chinese were absorbed in the problem of Westernization. In the early stages of their search for a new orientation, a few Chinese included an examination of Christianity, and missionaries won more converts than in any other period. However, the primary aim of the politically conscious Chinese was to find a way to create a powerful state capable of defending itself against Western intrusion. This goal Christianity was not designed to meet, and consequently the mood that favored a hearing for Christianity had largely passed by the close of World War I.

In the decade of the twenties the economic problem came to the fore, and the Chinese had no time to consider ideas that were not relevant to the improvement of living standards and the formation of a central government strong enough to exercise sovereign powers. The social gospel wing of missionaries tried desperately to make Christianity relevant to the problems of hunger, disease, floods, famine, illiteracy, and the deplorable working conditions of factory labor. The great majority of missionaries did not go along; they side-stepped political and economic issues and sought to convince the Chinese that their problems were spiritual. Neither group of missionaries had any significant success.

Because the Christian church in China met no generally recognized needs, it remained largely an esoteric enterprise without roots in the Chinese soil. Only a very small group accepted Christianity and a still smaller number grasped the full meaning hidden in the Christian dogma. Thus, the dogma became not a vehicle of grace as intended by the missionary but too often merely served as a chariot for old feelings and traditional attitudes.

Another barrier to success was the paternalistic attitude of many of the missionaries and especially the sense of racial superiority among a few of them. As we have seen, it was a frequent source of irritation and sometimes of disgust. It must be said again, however, that missionaries were not as guilty of arrogance as other groups of Westerners in China.

Judged in broader terms, it is not only the missionary who failed but American society and the American government. This failure is not a product of ill intention or of an exploiting capitalism. American diplomacy was on the whole laden with good intentions. It is ironic indeed that today the United States should face the new China and receive all the blame for Chinese miseries of the past, miseries inherent in the process of converting a semifeudal and agrarian society into a modern, powerful, and semi-industrial state. The United States finds itself the scapegoat not because of what it did but because of what it failed to do.

America did not offer the Chinese something that impressed them as an immediate and effective solution to what they felt were their real needs. Few Americans ever fully grasped the appalling demand for political and economic change in China; and when they did understand to some degree they could only offer solutions in terms of their own experience with capitalism and democracy. We were the prisoners of our own experience, an experience different from that of China. It is doubtful that we could have offered China a solution to her economic problems. Economic planning and a considerable degree of state enterprise were called for and few Americans had faith in such an approach.

Why were the Russians able to export their institutions when we failed? Were these importations from the Soviet Union not also essentially alien to the Chinese? The Soviet ideology was certainly wholly foreign to traditional Confucian society but it was presented in terms of meeting the needs that the Chinese themselves felt. Reluctance to accept what was

[321]

alien was thus overcome. If Christianity had been first and foremost an economic and political doctrine rather than a religion emphasizing the spiritual, it might have overcome the handicap of being foreign. Of course no missionary, true to his faith, could place the primary emphasis on the material.

Why did not Americans devise methods for convincing the Chinese of what Americans assumed to be a need for Christian values, democracy, and Western institutions? Apart from our traditional moralism and legalism, the answer lies in the fact that Americans, while good-willed, were conditioned to the ethos of democracy and thus were reluctant to intervene in the same bold way in which the Soviet Union trained young Chinese for important roles in the revolution. At best the Americans were altruistic and willing to help, but they never made a careful analysis of the struggle within China. A second reason why the United States played the role of a mere casual observer in the years between the two great wars was that the American people were not convinced that the China problem was also their problem, a vital stake in the great struggle to determine which of two ways of life would prevail in the world at large. The Communists entered the struggle cognizant of the great stakes and worked accordingly.

The alertness of the Soviet Union to the real meaning of the revolution in China led it to cancel the hated "unequal treaties" as early as 1920, thereby freeing itself from Chinese charges of imperialism while placing the onus of "capitalist imperialism" on the West. The liberal missionaries of the West, who favored treaty revision, were never able to throw off this yoke, for Western governments prized the commerce of China and knew that this commerce would suffer if the treaties were not continued. At any rate, we preserved our treaty rights for the time being but only at a tremendous loss in the end. The Soviet Union sacrificed the petty advantages of commerce in order to win the larger battle.

The missionary caught glimpses of these facts, now so readily discernible through the wonderful telescopic qualities of hindsight. Their brief insights, however, were obscured by the very nature of the inner drive that brought them to China. One must say it with caution and with qualification, but China was to many a missionary something of a monastery where he could attain more fully his religious aspiration to be Christ-like. Denial to oneself of the material advantages of the West, an escape from the absorbing and demanding competition of making a living in order to be free to live a religious life, an opportunity to live ascetically, these were the advantages offered to a missionary in China. At the same time, in spite of his ideals, the missionary remained a human being, and this inner drive never completely mastered him to the degree of extinguishing his other ambitions and interests. Therefore, he often became involved in the secular aims of the people to whom he had come to minister. Many missionaries became immersed in translating Christian ideals into practical efforts to bring to China the advantages of Western education, medicine, and even political democracy.

What influence did the missionary have on our government's policy toward China? In the years prior to 1890, missionaries often occupied strategic posts and even wrote some of the treaties that regulated American-Chinese relations. The missionary point of view in those years was one of impatience and disgust with Chinese recalcitrance in the face of demands to become as other nations were.

After the Boxer Revolt the missionaries, generally speaking, encouraged by Chinese attempts at reform, became defenders of China and sought to gain the cooperation of the American government in Chinese attempts to build a strong nation. In most crises they failed. American officials were generally sympathetic to Chinese aspirations but sympathy is scarcely the determining factor in foreign policy. American Far Eastern policy was the product of a whole set of considerations. Economic interests were always important. There were also the relations with Japan and Europe to be considered, for what the United States did in China would affect those relations.

In 1912, when the question of recognizing the Chinese Republic came up, the missionaries' hope for quick recognition was frustrated by the down-to-earth considerations occupying the minds of the Taft administration. Again in 1915, all of

"Unto the Chinese Foolishness"

Wilson's and Bryan's zeal for righteousness and sympathy for China was defeated by the hard facts of international politics, and the missionaries had no appreciable influence. Once again in the 1920's the liberal group of missionaries did their best to have the United States revise the "unequal" treaties but their attempts came to almost nothing. They championed China's cause anew in the 1930's, and this time the government eventually pursued a policy in accord with their wishes. However, the evidence indicates that it was not the missionaries who were responsible for the policy as much as the force of events, which left the Roosevelt administration with little choice. Missionaries played only a minor role in influencing day-to-day decisions on China.

Yet, while the missionaries were unsuccessful as a pressure group seeking to influence the Department of State, especially after 1900, they and the Christianity they represented had great influence in the larger context of general approach. China was treated as a moral problem, a country to be encouraged to adopt Christian values, technology, popular education, and constitutionalism. It is not necessary to question the desirability for China of these institutions, but it is worthwhile to note that China's highly decentralized and semifeudal society was far removed from such Western patterns.

Americans were also legalistic in their foreign policy. George Kennan has pointed to the unrealistic nature of the traditional Open Door policy. The United States stood for a fiction when it made China's territorial and administrative integrity and independence the keystone of its Far Eastern policy. China had no real administrative integrity in the Western sense and the boundaries within which the successive central governments exercised effective jurisdiction shifted every few years. Moreover, the treaty rights so staunchly defended by the United States were inconsistent with the Open Door policy.

Surveying the China scene today, the efforts of the Protestant missionary movement resulted in apparent failure, and yet the missionaries unquestionably left a mark. Whatever their shortcomings and inner motivations, in hospitals, schools, and chapels they stood forth as men who believed in the sacredness of human personality. For one hundred years men of good will dedicated their lives to giving to the Chinese an understanding of the Christian view of life and of Christian values. While only a very small percentage of Chinese came to understand them, it would be rash indeed to conclude that the values they endeavored to impart have been forgotten.

The missionary movement is not dead. Africa is the new land of missionary opportunity—an area radically different from China where there was already a highly advanced society. Nevertheless there is even now apparent a rise of nationalism on that continent that forebodes trouble. Perhaps someday the missionaries will be booted out. In the light of the China experience we may never be lured into such nationalistic illusions as to believe that we can shape the future of Africa. If so, we may be disillusioned by whatever develops there.

The experience of China's missionaries in educational, medical, and agricultural work shows that intense nationalism is capable of stirring up quite as much resentment against humanitarian enterprises controlled by foreigners as against the evangelical efforts of a foreign religion. The present technical assistance program of the United States faces the necessity of freeing itself from suspicions of imperialistic aims, for its potentialities as a contribution to the building of free societies will otherwise be nullified. Whether the American people will be willing to refrain from seeking to link the program to political indoctrination or to grant it sufficient funds remains to be seen. The missionary experience suggests that for maximum effect technical assistance may have to be carried out through the United Nations if it is to avoid charges of imperialism. If Americans are intent on gaining credit for their contributions, youthful nationalists in underdeveloped countries can be expected to be resentful.

After the experience of the 1920's, mission boards were very much aware of the necessity of sending men who could adjust themselves to working with the Chinese as equals and who would be willing to permit the Chinese to exercise authority. As a nation we stand in need of learning the same lessons of humility and cooperation. It is relatively easy to cooperate with peoples who happen to pursue a policy in accord with our own interests, but we need to learn to work with them when they pursue their own interests, which may conflict with our point of view as to what is "good" for them. Many of us in the United States have yet to learn that American society itself is pluralistic and that differences of color, religion, and political beliefs must be tolerated.

It is infinitely more difficult to learn that we cannot Christianize the world *after our own image* and that even when we try, as we did in China, the product of conversion is still foreign to us. The convert inevitably reflects the cultural level of the society of which he is a member. Religion is only one phase of culture and will inevitably reflect the education and total experience of the individual. In China, in the 1930's, many a liberal was shocked to discover that he had helped produce Chinese fundamentalists akin to his religious enemies at home. The democracy we export may similarly lead to disillusionment. Religious, political, or any other form of missionary work is a highly complex task that we ought to enter upon with caution. Self-confidence is no substitute for wisdom.

Index

Index

Index

Oberlin College, 58, 59
Ohio Wesleyan University, 59
Olney, Richard, Secretary of State, 40
Opium War, 4
Open Door Notes of 1899, 135
O'Shea, Right Rev. J. A., complaints against Kuomintang and Communists, 244

Parker, Dr. Peter, works in the United States for opening of diplomatic relations, 5; his hospital at Canton, 7; negotiations with Chinese in 1854, 8; Commissioner to China and his aggressive program, 9-10
Peffer, Nathaniel, 163; evaluation of Laymen's Inquiry, 172
Pierson, A. T., 58, 60
Pitkin, Horace, 3; family's claim for indemnity after his death in Boxer Revolt, 50, 61, 88
Porter, Lucius, early advocacy of Chinese control, 104, 155; and the social gospel, 215-216
Presbyterians, 103; Presbyterian Church, North, leads in number of missionaries in 1890, 13; Ministerial Association of Chicago, urges punishment of Chinese engaged in attacks on missionaries, 40; Board of Missions, revises policy on indemnities, 127-128; schools, 217
Price, Frank W., 234; survey of rural churches, 239; establishment of China Information Service, 260; urges new approach in rural areas, 279; observations on rule of Kuomintang after World War II, 295-297; opposes intervention by United States, 299
Price, P. F., comments on failings of converts, 29
Princeton Foreign Missionary Society, 59

racial prejudice, Chinese pastor charges missionaries with, 35

racial superiority, 100; missionaries charged with, 277-278
Rawlinson, Frank, support of treaty revision, 202; support of Chinese control of church, 204-205, 236
Rea, George Bronson, 198
Reed, William B., 10, 11
Reformed Church, urges Department of State to protect missionaries, 40
reform movement of 1898, influence of missionaries in, 44-45
Reid, Gilbert, role in reform movement of 1898, 44, 107, 111
Reinsch, Paul, 142-143, 145
Reisner, John H., 230, 234; disappointment over failures in rural areas, 279; critical of Communists, 303
revival meetings, prior to Boxer Revolt, 25, 87-88
Revolution of 1912, 99, 136-137
Richard, Timothy, role in reform movement of 1898, 44
Riggs, Charles H., 231-232
Robbins, Raymond, 65
Roberts, Issachar J., instruction of leader of Taipings, 8
Rockhill, Minister, W. W., minimizes danger of Boxers, 46, 126, 128-130, 134-135
Roosevelt, Theodore, 67, 79, 85, 133
Root, Elihu, Secretary of State, 129, 133
Root, Robert, explains why Communists won, 296
Roots, Bishop, 130
Root-Takahira agreement, 136
Ross, Edward Alsworth, 75
rural churches, decline of, 279-280; weakness of, 282
rural missions, missionary difficulties in, 226-230; new experiments, 234-239
rural pastors, problems among, 227
Russell, Bertrand, 99
Russia, 138

Sankey, Ira, 53
Schieche, Mrs. Emil, 193
Scott, Charles E., 132

[333]

Index

Index

[335]